In the Wake of the Poetic

Contemporary Issues in The Middle East
Mehran Kamrava and Carol Fadda-Conrey, *Series Advisers*

Director's Choice

Our Director's Choice program is an opportunity to highlight a book from our list that deserves special attention. This work celebrates the emergence of a vibrant Palestinian cultural scene of visual artists, filmmakers, performance artists, and poets. It highlights the vital importance of artistic expression to communicate and transform experiences of dislocation and shifting identities.

Alice Randel Pfeiffer
Director, Syracuse University Press

IN THE WAKE
OF THE POETIC

PALESTINIAN ARTISTS AFTER DARWISH

NAJAT RAHMAN

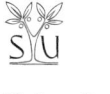

Syracuse University Press

∞ The paper used in this publication meets the minimum requirements
of the American National Standard for Information Sciences—Permanence
of Paper for Printed Library Materials, ANSI Z39.48-1992.

For a listing of books published and distributed by Syracuse University Press,
visit www.SyracuseUniversityPress.syr.edu.

ISBN: 978-0-8156-3408-9 (cloth)   978-0-8156-5341-7 (e-book)

Library of Congress Cataloging-in-Publication Data
Rahman, Najat.
In the wake of the poetic : Palestinian artists after Darwish /
Najat Rahman. — First edition.
pages cm — (Contemporary issues in the Middle East)
Includes bibliographical references and index.
ISBN 978-0-8156-3408-9 (cloth : alk. paper) — ISBN 978-0-8156-5341-7 (e-book)
1. Darwish, Mahmud—Criticism and interpretation.
2. Darwish, Mahmud—Appreciation. 3. Arts, Palestinian. I. Title.
PJ7820.A7Z8265 2015
892.7'16—dc23   2015022659

Manufactured in the United States of America

To the memory of Mahmoud Darwish, the poet,
To the writers and scholars of his generation,
And to the artists after him and in his wake,
who create in the face of devastation,
restoring beauty and meaning,
profoundly touching our lives

And to all those
whose lives have had to contend
in no small part with history
and with loss

Contents

Illustrations

Acknowledgments

I would like to express my deep and infinite gratitude to Deanna McCay at Syracuse University Press for her strong support of this book, for her tremendously generous and careful guidance with the process of publication. I also warmly thank the team at Syracuse University Press and its director, Alice Randel Pfeiffer, who honored this book as her "Director's Choice" for fall 2015. Special thanks to Brendan C. Missett for seeing the project through to its publication with Kay Steinmetz, to Mary Petrusewicz for her meticulous editing work, to Fred Wellner for his beautiful work on the cover, and to Lisa Kuerbis, Jessica LeTourneur Bax, and Cathy Goddard for their critical support of the book. I am indebted to the anonymous reviewers and readers of the manuscript, whose exceedingly careful and insightful reading offered me valuable feedback that guided me to improve it.

The generous support of the European Institutes for Advanced Study (EURIAS), in the form of research fellowship, and of the Mediterranean Institute for Advanced Research (IMéRA) at the University of Aix-Marseille granted me a year of residency that allowed me the needed time and the stimulating environment to complete this book. Thanks to Richard Jacquemond, who was my scientific referent in Marseille, Nicolas Morales, Kenneth Brown, and Thierry Fabre for the helpful links that facilitated my work. I also thank the residents at IMéRA for the many intellectual exchanges and camaraderie, especially William Kornblum, Malik Nejmi, Mike Osborne, and Daniele Santoro.

I am grateful to Jean-Pierre Marquis and Simon Harel at the Université de Montréal for supporting my research in granting me an essential sabbatical that allowed me to make use of the EURIAS grant and to complete this project in a timely manner.

Earlier grants from Canada's Social Science and Humanities Research Council (SSHRC) and Fonds du Québec sur la société et la culture (FQRSC), respectively, have enabled me to pursue work on humor and multilingualism in Middle Eastern cultural production, which are also features of this book.

The following institutions have invited me at various stages of this research: Fondation Maison des sciences de l'homme in Paris, Université Aix-Marseille, Centre d'études internationales à l'Université de Montréal (CÉRIUM) and the Department of English Studies at the Université de Montréal, the Islamic Institute at McGill University, Najah University, Birzeit University, Dar al-Kalima in Bethlehem, the University of Wisconsin–Madison, New York University, The New School, and Johns Hopkins University in collaboration with Paris XIII and CRASC in Oran, Algeria. Special thanks to Dr. Yahya Jaber.

The artists in this volume have been very generous in sharing their work: Suheir Hammad, Ghassan Zaqtan, Rashid Masharawi, Elia Suleiman, Mona Hatoum, Sharif Waked, Steve Sabella, Till Roeskens, Rehab Nazzal, Tamer Naffar and his group DAM. I am especially indebted to Eman Haram, whose beautiful image of an ancient olive tree was also offered for the cover of the book. The dialogue with Eman has been substantial and meaningful. Her artistic and intellectual visions have profoundly touched me. Liana Badr has offered generously her time, her works, and her thoughts in my visits to Ramallah in the last two years.

Livia Monnet has been an exemplary mentor and colleague, and I am indeed indebted to her. She has been an intellectual inspiration and a most stimulating interlocutor to me throughout this project and since the beginning of my career at the Université de Montréal. Special thanks also to Norma Rantisi and Wilson Jacob, who have been tremendously supportive. And to Philippe Despoix for his early interest in my work. I thank my colleagues in Montreal for the intellectual camaraderie, especially Khalid Medani, Setrag Manoukian, Christine Tappolet, Christian Nadeau, Amaryll Chanady, and Jean-Claude Guedon.

I would like to acknowledge Mary Layoun and Prospero Saiz for their mentorship and for supporting my work on Darwish, but also Luis

Madureira. The work of Judith Butler and Hamid Naficy have especially accompanied me in my reflections. I acknowledge the many interlocutors of Darwish's writing who enrich my work, especially Ibrahim Muhawi, Jeff Sacks, and Muhammed Siddiq.

Special thanks to Michelle Woodward, whose research help has been most invaluable at the last stages of this project, and to Mélanie Deit for all her help throughout the years and beyond the call of duty.

Warm thanks to my students and research assistants who contributed to this book through their insights, ideas, diligent research, enthusiasm, and good humor: Rym Khene, Luis Fernando Franco Mendez, Sothea Chhum, Rim Bejaoui, Imen Oueslati, Noémie Crépeau, Charles De Bock, Tassia Trifiatis, and Nizar Ghazzawi.

To my unwavering siblings: Adeeb, Fardouse, Nadia. This book is dedicated also to my nieces and nephews. You passionately inspire me. And to Farha, my grandmother, born before the British mandate and under the Ottoman rule in Palestine, alive and lives, always, in little Kuza, near Nablus. And to Hamdallah and Khadra.

And to Mary, who accompanied my work throughout this last academic journey. And to M., whose warm welcome in the early mornings at a café in the old port kept me on track.

In The Wake of the Poetic

Mahmoud Darwish and Emergent Palestinian Arts
An Introduction

One finds Mahmoud Darwish's verses, as if set apart, in "A Player of Dice," a poem that deals with the unexpected turns of identity and of life. In it, he returns to an organic image that recalls the links of the self to the land and connects these verses to his earlier poems:

> O green land, how I love you green
>
> . . . .
>
> Plant me with care . . . in a handful of air[1]

A wistful awareness, however, remains of how this rootedness hovers in a "handful of air." Nonetheless, the poet gestures to his poetic endeavor, to the relation of the poet to that remaining place, to the opening and germinating possibility of life and of poetry.

Although the voice of Mahmoud Darwish (1941–2008), one of the most celebrated and important poets in contemporary times,[2] resonated (almost solely) on the international scene, especially from the late 1980s onward, his passing away on August 9, 2008, after a prolific life in poetry spanning forty years, seems to have linked with the increasing proliferation of Palestinian poets and artists, internationally recognized, who engage with Darwish's poetry. These artists, local and diasporic, are inevitably the inheritors of a long and vibrant tradition of Arabic poetry.

This book explores contemporary Palestinian artistic practices since the Oslo Accords and how these artists rearticulate the political in their

1

aesthetic in the absence of a true politics. I argue that this art in dispersion, diasporic or fragmented between the Palestinian territories and Israel and across continents, constitutes practices of "dissensus."[3] I follow Jacques Rancière's theorization of "dissensus" (2010) as a new way of redefining the political in the arts, where art interrupts dominant and consensual forms of power and of identity. The political is henceforth the dissensual, issuing from rupture and dissent, constituted by a unity of experience articulated around a common cluster of topoi, as I will discuss further: dispersion, loss, dispossession, and belonging, all of which constitute a struggle against effacement. None of these topoi have a fixed form, and they are anchoring points for various artistic visions. The aesthetic strategies used are extremely varied, whereas humor and irony are recurrent. Works of mourning, desire, and ambiguity, they are also deterritorializing and aim at the production of new, empowering forms of (collective) subjectivity. These artists envision and practice postidentitarian, postnational political art. They locate questions of identity elsewhere (in poetry, in various art forms, in transnational networks, in new forms of belonging) and reframe the political. They refuse to adhere to predetermined notions of aesthetics and politics, but they all claim a common historical legacy: historic Palestine, "national poets" such as Darwish, the Nakba of 1948, Beirut 1982.[4] These four anchoring points and modalities are the basis of a new belonging. They define Palestinian nationhood in Palestinian art. One of these four terms is highlighted in each chapter of this book, although all four terms are interconnected.

In addition to centering on and acknowledging the accomplishment of emerging Palestinian artists in the various domains of poetry, cinema, visual art, performance art, and music, the book is also meant as a tribute to the late poet Mahmoud Darwish, whose prolific poetry has now been translated widely and has attained a vibrant critical engagement in English, French, and other languages besides Arabic. Darwish has not only achieved stunning world recognition but has also visibly engaged younger Palestinian artists (although he clearly engages other Arab and international artists as well) in performance art, visual art, spoken-word poetry, and music, in North America, in Europe, and in the Middle East. Honoring the artists that have proliferated in the last two decades seems appropriate now in paying tribute to his legacy. Focusing specifically on Palestinian artists in this book, I argue that these artists continue the legacy of Darwish without being derivative. Although their work is indebted to Darwish and to poetry to varying extents, it cannot simply be located there. Darwish is a crucial reference for many of these artists but not for all; nonetheless, poetry remains a vital part of this art, and especially Darwish's poetry, and so a productive dialogue with his legacy and that of his generation ensues. The engagement with Darwish's poetry is an important reading (among other possible ones) when considering emerging Palestinian art. *In the Wake of the Poetic: Palestinian Artists after Darwish* has as one of its principal threads, then, the engagement of this new aesthetic with the late poetry of Darwish, whose readings often drew crowds in the thousands in the Arab world. Some of these artists are more established, like Mona Hatoum, and others have just emerged recently, like Emily Jacir, Steve Sabella, and Sharif Waked, but have received impressive international recognition for their work. This interdisciplinary analysis of the aesthetics and politics of Palestinian cultural production in the last two decades—in light of its significant presence on the international scene and following on the heels of the immense influence of Mahmoud Darwish's poetry that has dominated Palestinian culture for decades—argues that the 1990s heralded a new period of creativity in the wake of the Oslo Accords and "as a result of the decentralization of the Palestinian political scene."[5]

Through a selection of works that provide an overview of Palestinian art post-Oslo, I hope to examine, then, the practice of Palestinian cultural production in film, visual art, and lyrical expression. This book is a critical examination of the works of several key artists such as Suheir Hammad, Liana Badr, Ghassan Zaqtan, Rashid Masharawi, Elia Suleiman, Hany Abu-Assad, Mona Hatoum, Emily Jacir, Eman Haram, Rehab Nazzal, Till Roeskens, Sharif Waked, and Tamer Nafar.

The increasing visibility and recognition of these writers on the international scene is testimony to the innovations of the young poets and artists and is crucial to the dissemination of an artistic experience that has historically remained on the margins. To name only a few examples, Emily Jacir's artwork received the prestigious Hugo Boss Prize in 2008,

Sharif Waked's art has been exhibited in museums such as the Tate Modern and the Guggenheim, Elia Suleiman's film *Divine Intervention* was awarded the Cannes Jury Prize (2002), Hany Abu-Assad's film *Paradise Now* won a Golden Globe Award (2006) and was nominated for an Academy Award for Best Foreign Film. Poets such as Suheir Hammad (Tony Award in 2003 for the HBO show *Russell Simmons Presents Def Poetry Jam* and an American Book Award in 2009) have heralded a new generation of lyric artists in music groups such as DAM, Ramallah Underground, and Checkpoint.

Their art also introduces new modes of belonging in poetic, cinematic, artistic, and musical form. These Palestinian writers and artists, who live between many countries and languages, resist a fixed identity while expressing a desire for home and for belonging.[6] Their art has incorporated aspects of global culture to affirm its belonging against collective dispossession and has addressed itself to international audiences. Identity is revealed in their works as plural and dynamic. I explore, then, how the diasporic and the transnational transform notions of the "national," of "home," and of "belonging." For their aesthetic expresses profound experiences of displacement, fragmentation, belonging, and transformation. Whereas each artist interrogates identity in his or her own manner, it is the negotiation of the personal and the collective, the historic and the aesthetic, that they seem to share.[7] Neither the artists nor their works can be considered as *representative* of an identity, but neither can their works exist entirely outside of the particular and the historical.

These hybrid works, wherein different art media are combined to create innovative forms, demand an approach that explores the boundaries between poetry and other modes of artistic creativity (particularly film, video, performance art, and music). The visible evocation of Darwish's poetry by artists from spoken-word poets such as Hammad to hip-hop artists such as DAM, and by visual artists such as Jacir, has necessitated an approach that addresses poetry's relation to other arts and the transformation not only of what is "national" through this transnational and diasporic art—for, as Judith Butler writes, the diasporic may "inform/disrupt ideas of the national" art—but also the transformation of the distinct boundaries of emerging art forms, whereby the poetry of Suheir Hammad beckons that of Darwish in a language composed of Arabic and English, in written poems also performed as slam poetry.[8] The emerging innovative artworks call for an approach that is multilingual and intermedial, a "new comparative literature," as Emily Apter has proposed in *The Translation Zone*.[9] The demands of the project are both innovative and challenging not only because one is working across different media but rather because each work already seems to be multimedial and therefore demands a new approach. If the innovative artworks themselves have opened new paths of analysis, it is essential henceforth to systematically account for this considerable body of work. These cultural works may transform our understanding of the tools of analysis that we use to study them.

The innovative wave of experimentation that has emerged post-Oslo in the Palestinian context in its conceptualization of the national through the diasporic and the transnational, and in its theorizing of the multilingual in relation to the intermedial that the diasporic has also spawned, draws on and offers new intellectual approaches—to transnationalism, diaspora, hybridity, belonging, aesthetics, and politics.

This comparative analysis of the role and impact of recent Palestinian cultural forms, local and transnational, theorizes and contextualizes a predominant cultural phenomenon in different artistic forms that is for the most part yet to be analyzed. Notwithstanding the long tradition of Arabic poetry and its impact on the other arts, there are very few studies devoted to this lineage and imbrication, in Arabic or in English. The exceptions include a recent special issue, edited by Haim Bresheeth and Haifa Hammami, devoted to Palestine/Israel that treats poetry, film, and art: *Third Text* 20, nos. 3–4 (2006). The illuminating study is invested in showing the span of this cultural production from the 1940s onward, with the exception of a few essays that turn toward the period from the 1990s onward. Moreover, the articles tend to focus on specific media rather than the interaction of media. Another promising special issue devoted to Palestine is *Horizons Maghrébins: Le droit à la mémoire*, no. 57 (2007), which treats novels, poetry, and theater. Again, the articles and translated selections do not reflect developments in the last two decades but focus instead on the early writings of such authors as Ghassan Kanafani and Mahmoud Darwish. The articles in this issue constitute only one-quarter of the material presented. *Afterimage* dedicates an issue to art and activism in 2006, in which Ariela Zoulay's "Cartography of Resistance" appears, and in which she reviews Ganit Ankori's book *Palestinian Art* (2006) and infers a linkage between Palestinian visual culture, poetry, and Gilles Deleuze and Felix Guattari's concept of "minor literature." One has to add the rich edition *Palestine, Israel, and the Politics of Popular Culture*, edited by Rebecca Stein and Ted Swedenburg, which discusses cinema, music, comics, the Internet, etc. (2005). My project builds on it by including a reflection on the intermedial dimensions of these arts and accounting for other forms such as the visual and performative arts as well as spoken-word poetry. Walter Armburst's collection *Mass Mediations: New Approaches to Popular Culture in the Middle East and Beyond* (2006), on the other hand, does address the question of media in arguing for the impact of mass media on popular culture in the Middle East. It does so in an expansive fashion, focusing on Egypt, Syria, Iran, etc., without delving into poetry. My project remains distinctly separate from it.

Several recent publications attest to the growing interest in the work of the major visual artists. Among recent contributions by scholars are the groundbreaking books by Kamal Boullata (*Palestinian Art: 1850–2005*, 2008) and Ganit Ankori (*Palestinian Art*, 2006). In fact, they are the only substantial studies on Palestinian visual art in English. An older study exists with the same title: *Palestinian Art* by Ulf Thomas Moberg (1998). In Arabic, one also notes the overall contributions by Kamal Boullata that constitute the basis for his work in English and the basis for any critical work done on Palestinian art. The linkage of Palestinian visual art with Arabic literature is made by Boullata and Ankori. Yet this artistic experience, especially in relation to poetry, remains to be theorized. As Kamal Boullata has indicated in *Palestinian Art*, no history of Arab art exists. The same could be said of Palestinian (and Arab) cinema, although since 2010 we are seeing more studies emerging, for instance, Hamid Dabashi's *Dreams of a Nation* (2006).[10] The lack of more major works on Palestinian art has to do as well with the relatively marginal status of the visual arts in Arab culture, as Boullata argues. It is the poetic word that has been privileged above all, historically. Ankori's work goes beyond exposing the general, underlying affinity between word and image and connects specific paintings (e.g., the work of Ismail Shammout and Asad Azi) and conceptual/video/performance pieces (e.g., the work of Mona Hatoum and Khalil Rabah) with particular poems, especially those of Darwish, and with literary texts. Moreover, broader notions relating to hybridity and fragmentation are theorized in relationship to art, film, and literature. Although grounded in these scholarly works, my book explores in a substantial manner the relation of poetry to the other arts. It examines new works of art and new genres (spoken word and hip-hop) that have not been discussed by my predecessors. And it engages new theoretical perspectives (theories pertaining to transnationalism, the multilingual and the intermedial, the aesthetic and the political, as well as humor—irony, the absurd—as an aesthetic category).

Recently, one also notes the appearance of a few books on Palestinian cinema: *Palestinian Cinema: Landscape, Trauma, and Memory* by Nurith Gertz and George Khleifi (2008), as well as *Dreams of a Nation*, edited by Hamid Dabashi (2006). Gertz and Khleifi present a substantial study of Palestinian cinema; Dabashi includes accounts by the filmmakers. Dabashi argues for an emancipatory aesthetic in Palestinian cinema, whereas Gertz and Khleifi see film as somewhat arrested by its own ironic techniques and trauma. No studies have delved into visual art and film in relation to poetry in the Palestinian context (and even in the larger Arabic context), with the exception of Hashim al-Nahas, *Al-insān al-miṣrī ʿalā al-shāsha* (1986; The Egyptian on the screen).[11]

In the course of forty years, only a few substantial works have been devoted to Arab cinema in English: those of Roy Armes, *Postcolonial Images: Studies in North African Film* (2005) and *Arab Filmmakers of the Middle East: A Dictionary* (2010); Terri Ginsberg and Chris Lippard, *Historical Dictionary of Middle Eastern Cinema* (2010); Lina Khatib, *Filming the Modern Middle East: Politics in the Cinemas of Hollywood and the Arab World* (2006); and Viola Shafik, *Arab Cinema: History and Cultural Identity* (1998). Books on Arab cinema exist in Arabic (notably by George Sadoul, *Cinema in the Arab Countries*, 1966). More works exist on Arab art, most notably by Nada Shabout, *Modern Arab Art: Formation of Arab Aesthetics* (2007).

Although Palestinian poetry has received critical attention in English—see for instance Sacks (2014), Mattawa (2014), Alshaer (forthcoming,

2015), Parmenter (1994), Ghassoub and Sinclair-Webb (2000), Jayyusi (1992), Nassar and Rahman (2008)—very little criticism addresses itself to the most recent literary trends. Suheir Hammad's spoken-word poetry constitutes one important element of my book, as she engages directly the poetry of Darwish and extends poetry into a space of performance, multilingualism, and diaspora. Zoe Anglesey's work (1999), as well as that of Alix Olson (2007), are the very few books on spoken-word poetry.

The essays of Helga Souri-Tawil (2010) and Joseph Massad (2005) are notable exceptions to the apparent lack of scholarship on contemporary Palestinian music. Books have recently appeared by David McDonald (2013), Sunaina Maira (2013), Moslih Kanaaneh et al. (2013), Benjamin Brinner (2009), and Dalia Cohen and Ruth Katz (2006). The popular emergence of Palestinian rappers in the last ten years, including DAM and MWR, has mostly been addressed by Maira's work. Whereas Massad situates rap in a tradition of revolutionary Arab political songs since the 1950s, groups such as DAM have claimed inspiration from a tradition of poetry, from Darwish to Samih al-Qasim and others. As Souri-Tawil has indicated, "Rap has become a tool for sharing news of social and political realities as well as a vehicle for political critique and mobilization."[12] Critics intriguingly consider it as "a poetics of displacement and protest,"[13] as Darwish's poetry has sometimes been characterized.

My book also draws on the substantial body of theories and philosophies generated by these dynamic cultural forms, including theories of aesthetics and politics (mainly Rancière 2010, but also Deleuze and Guattari 1975). It builds on Jacques Rancière's *Dissensus* (2010), which examines the relationship of aesthetics and politics and moves beyond a collapse of aesthetics into politics or a negation of this relationship. It also draws on performance theory and belonging (Dickinson 2010; Schechner 1988; Bell 1999), on theories of diaspora, especially in the Palestinian context (Hall 1990; Rogoff 2000; Ahmed 2003; Rabinowitz 2000; Araeen, Cubitt, and Sardar 2002; Braziel and Mannur 2003; Mercer 2008; Campt 2008), on transnationalism (Appadurai 2001; Baubock and Faist 2010; Radhakrishnan 1996), and on globalization and the impact of new technologies on culture (McLuhan 1966; Méchoulan 2003; Oosterling 2003). Helena Lindholm Schulz's *The Palestinian Diaspora: Formation of Identities and Politics of Homeland* (2003) is of particular significance to my book: her informative and insightful contribution, anchored in the social sciences, argues for a constant longing for a lost homeland in the diasporic ethos; my engagement with the cultural works shows how this diasporic belonging opens into a future.

From the textual reinscription of home in lyric and narrative through a revision of heritage—*Literary Disinheritance: The Writing of Home in the Works of Mahmoud Darwish and Assia Djebar* (2008) and *Mahmoud Darwish, Exile's Poet: Critical Essays* (2008)—and the linguistic inscription of difference in multilingual literature (*littératures sans patrie*, or literature without country, research supported by Québec's Funds for Research on Society and Culture), this book builds on my previous publications and considers another significant dimension of the articulation of home, which is that of the medium. It turns to a generation of young Arab poets and artists who create through their medium and through combining together different art forms, languages, and identities. They create new possibilities for the dissemination of their work. In extending my analysis beyond poetry and novels, which are more substantially commented on, this book allows for new readings. It addresses a vibrant new cultural phenomenon that is essential to understanding the new emerging cultural realities: how poetry, especially diasporic poetry, and art "employ mass culture and media, and how they are in turn pluralized and hyphenized by this use."[14] The new artworks constitute "a cultural expression marked by unique cadences and rhythms, by hybrid images and languages," and yet it affirms a belonging without the *identitarian* conditions of belonging in which art engages with traditional local forms as well as with transnational ones.[15] The crucial role of women artists such as Suheir Hammad, Liana Badr, Mona Hatoum, Emily Jacir, Eman Haram, Rehab Nazzal, will be emphasized.

Aesthetics: An Art of Relation

The term "art," broadly conceived in this book, is a relational aesthetic: in the face of loss, it appeals to a shared condition. Reconsidered as a relation, art is in relation to loss, to other arts, to other voices, to the past. This art is an art of the present, however, for it intervenes in the present while it reinscribes a historical loss. It creates an internal difference and transforms, as it is itself in transformation. It ruptures frameworks of consensus, representation, and understanding and calls forth new poetic and political subjects. It is a process, not an object. It challenges us to go beyond existing categories of interpretation and aesthetics and beyond distinctions of object and method.

This art is an "aesthetic of loss" and an "aesthetic of listening."[16] It is an aesthetic of loss because it argues that contemporary Palestinian art is founded on loss (loss ensuing from the destruction of history and of traditions). These artists, whether local, transnational, or diasporic, claim a common historical legacy (that of historic Palestine, "national poets" such as Darwish, and the Nakba of 1948).

It is an aesthetic of listening because it compels us to listen to muffled voices, collective voices rendered as "mere noise." "Dissensual" speech has often been transformed into private noise, rendered incomprehensible, denied the status of public discourse, and therefore excluded from political space:[17] it takes on the predicament of being "loud and muted," in the words of the poet Suheir Hammad.[18] The late Edward Said, likewise, described a movement of "regenerative" struggle, a new lyrical and intense language that "wants to transform [language] from a force for identity statement into a transgressive, disruptive . . . mode."[19]

Although the aesthetic strategies are extremely varied, this art tends to respond to loss in two striking ways: humor (dark humor, irony, the absurd) and mourning, both of which I argue open into politics, "in the face of the death of the political project," where the term "politics" will signify an undeniable "attachment to a life of freedom" and to a future, as I will discuss further.[20]

Politics: Is Art a Refuge for Politics?

For Darwish, all poetry is preoccupied with a future and is in this sense political, as he indicated in many of his interviews. Poetry can change only the poet (and the reader, not history, as he once thought), so that the nature of the possible transformation for Darwish is henceforth aesthetic, which nonetheless has implications for the individual's humanity: "Its role is to resist that which is an obstacle to the reader's humanity, to his being. Its role is to deepen the idea of beauty in human beings, which leads to the idea of peace: peace between the individual and himself . . . between the individual and his environment, between the individual and his nature."[21]

In latter works like *Ka-zahr al-lawz aw ab'ad* (2005; *Almond Blossoms and Beyond*, 2009) and *Ḥīrat al-'ā'id* (2009; The hesitation of the returned), or in *Fī Ḥaḍrat al- ghiyāb* (2006; *The Presence of Absence*),[22] Darwish seems to return to his earlier vision of poetry as a bearer of change. Ultimately these positions may not be so irreconcilable, since the change that poetry enables may be imperceptible, but it endures. It does not necessarily change reality through its message but through its act, through the affirmation of its voice.

Palestinian art has long been politically charged. Although one cannot altogether deny its political dimension in the name of its aesthetic value, one cannot continue to consider it simply as an oppositional art with a message, or an art of resistance. Rancière's conception of "dissensus" will be particularly relevant to highlighting art as a potential site of politics, exposing how art disrupts dominant frameworks of consensus predicated on classification and hierarchies of power and identity. For him, dissensus is more than dissent and is connected to a vision of democracy as true politics. For politics today has been reduced to a regime of policing. To what extent, then, can the artistic practices to be discussed be conceived as constituting provisional acts of dissensus, acts that rupture frameworks of consensus? If very little, if any, politics exist today in the world, where policing now substitutes for true, democratic politics, as Rancière contends, is art then "a space of refuge for dissensual practice . . ."? Is art the displaced space for politics?[23] What is the relation between art and politics? If politics is "a struggle to have *one's voice heard* and *oneself recognized* as a legitimate partner in debate," and if speech is the ground for all historical instances of politics, can art, in a large sense, then become a space for politics in the absence of politics elsewhere?[24] Are Palestinian artists reconfiguring what is meant by art? Are they reconfiguring art as (true) politics? And if art is politics, is it no longer art? These questions are not, of course, limited to Palestinian artists. In defining the term "politics," to quote Rancière, as "the cluster of perceptions and practices that shape this common world . . . a way of framing, among sensory data, a specific sphere of experience . . . *a partition of the sensible, of the visible and the sayable*" (152; emphasis added), the aim will not be to argue for art as the place for politics but to show how dissensus produces an internal difference in a society through "the intervention in the visible and the sayable" (37). Art and politics, as forms of dissensus, can possibly disrupt dominant forms of power and of identity in "reorienting general perceptual space and disrupting forms of belonging" (15). Palestinian artistic production allows us to assess the extent to which artistic practice can be understood as an act of political subjectivity, a process of subjectivation that exposes politics as a disruption of what can be seen, heard, and said, that is, as a reconfiguration of the sensible. Rancière signals that these forms, which include film and other visual arts, may create new "political subjectivation" (151); however, they remain fundamentally aesthetic and provisional, since artistic intention may not yield what is intended or quite guarantee the result. Art, therefore, cannot be simply collapsed into politics, nor can it be completely separated from it. This possibility for new communal life nonetheless is the opening into politics.

Palestinian cultural works, which present different voices, counter the erasure not only of history but also of the condition of the political that Palestinian art frames. In a geography that is also shrinking, increasingly there is no place for the Palestinian.

These artworks propose that art is life. More than that, they propose an art of death, since the art itself evokes the death of politics. The art image of Mona Hatoum's installation *Negotiating Table* (1983) is emblematic in this sense. It reveals a breathing corpse shrouded on the surface of a wooden table, possibly tortured, and absent figures missing on the opposing empty chairs while speeches by state heads can be heard about peace; in the absence of interlocutors, it announces art as preoccupied with death in its violent contemporary forms. Humor also emanates from and signals a certain kind of death.

In this context, what if we were to willingly read Hegel's famous proclamation "art is a thing of the past" not as an eclipsing of art as it has existed in Europe, so that all art is subject to the history and demarcations of Western aesthetics, but rather as art that enacts a tension with the past? What is taking place today in Palestinian art is the reinscription of a historical loss and an art that makes a claim on the present. As Rancière also argues, loss promises a "new form of individual and community life" through an art that could be available to everyone. With the aesthetic, "this knot between *poiesis* (a way of doing) and *aisthesis* (a horizon of affect) is undone . . . the loss brings . . . a promise of a new form of individual and community life." This possibility for new communal life is the opening into politics. And the art that engages loss also holds a promise, in that it is democratic (16). For it potentially addresses itself to anyone.[25] The promise of "political accomplishment" can never altogether be fulfilled, however, and aesthetics remains distinct from politics (133).

As a call for a new approach to literature and art, one that is cognizant of new cultural and historical realities, Emily Apter, in *The Translation Zone* (2005), argues for a new comparative literature that is "attuned to the problems of translation, the multiplication of media forms, historical realities and acts of dispossession, and the unequal relations of power that cross the globe and become imparted in cultural forms." This new comparative literature is one that brings together the multilingual and the intermedial as dissensual practices that can be found in recent Palestinian artworks, for instance. Apter conceives of translation as a "medium," "intermedial technology," and "fulcrum" for comparative literature. Translation is, more important, "an act of disruption," "a means to repositioning the subject in the world and in history," "a way of denaturalizing citizens."[26] Translation is a crossing from the poetic to the political, bridging the intermedial and the multilingual and enacting a transformation in subjectivity. Implying the possibility of continuous transformation rather than identity, this conception of translation is akin to Palestinian art, which is "a work of transformation" and akin to diasporic identities that undergo continuous change. Apter's theoretical contribution is important in showing how this often diasporic art has the possibility to create new subjects and new communities, to create passages out of impasses, like translation. Although in the first chapter I read the poetry of Hammad in relation to the art of translation, I believe translation can be related to other parts of my book, including how the artworks I discuss translate what has been rendered illegible into the visible and the sayable. Apter is also calling for the acknowledgment of new developments in practices that are multilingual and intermedial.

In the Wake of the Poetic, in its exploration of the aesthetics and politics of Palestinian art, investigates such questions as: How are various influences negotiated in the search for form? How does one conceptualize this nexus between national, transnational, and diasporic culture? To what extent does this Palestinian cultural production offer alternative forms of communal and gendered identity? How does the medium, and an intermedial analysis, supplement existing approaches and allow us to rethink belonging without mitigating its reason or its power?

As I focus on Palestinian cultural production, situated as it is between the local and diasporic, and constituting a certain transnational art, my approach is necessarily comparative: I compare the work of artists from diverse linguistic and cultural contexts who employ different media. It is also intermedial, exploring the links and passages within and between different poetic and art media in order to theorize and contextualize such a development in Palestinian culture. This approach is reflected in my choice of texts, which incorporate poetry, film, music, performance art, and visual art in order to examine interesting developments. In addition to analyzing recurrent themes, I examine artistic techniques, structures, and their linguistic strategies. I pay special attention to the medium itself and its formal elements, noting its interaction with other media and the use of fragmentary narration and radically subjective perspectives. If realism, in its sociopolitical commitment, was considered an expression of national culture, as Viola Shafik indicates, then how do we read the complication of this realism in recent Palestinian poetry, films, and artwork where the ironic, the absurd, and the imaginary intrude?[27]

My approach is also intertextual, closely reading across poetic texts, and contextual, examining the emergence and proliferation of different cultural forms, taking into account the transnational nature of these works and raising questions about their conditions of production and reception: Who supported these projects? Where were they published and distributed? What challenges did the artworks encounter? How were they received by the critical community and public institutions? What discernable cultural impact have they had? The most salient aspects of the works relate to the incorporation of the absurd, the ironic, the mythic, the temporal, and the spatial, and in the figuring of "home," where belonging is "expropriated of all identity, so as to appropriate belonging itself."[28]

In poetry, I examine Suheir Hammad's *Breaking Poems* (2008), Liana Badr's *Zanābiq al-ḍaw'* (Lilies of light, 1998), and Ghassan Zaqtan's *Ka-ṭayr min al-qashsh ya-tbaʻunī* (*Like a Straw Bird It Follows Me, and Other Poems*, 2008). I consider the following films: Rashid Mashrawi's *Laila's Birthday* (2008), Elia Suleiman's *Divine Intervention* (2002), and Hany Abu-Assad's *Paradise Now* (2005). I focus on the following art works: Emily Jacir's *Where We Come From* (2003) and other works, Eman Haram's *Involuntary Memory* (2006) and subsequent art, Mona Hatoum's selected art, Till Roeskens's collaborative art with the Palestinians in the Aida refugee camp, Rehab Nazzal's videography, and Sharif Waked's more recent videographies *Chic Point* (2003) and *To Be Continued* (2009). Finally, I explore the proliferation of youth music groups that have taken the form of hip-hop, such as DAM, MWR, Ramallah Underground, Checkpoint, etc., analyzing particularly DAM's lyrics and performances.

If this aesthetic corpus can be defined, it is by its diversity, whereby diaspora and rupture, which began in 1948, become points of inscription. As Edward Said has noted in *After the Last Sky*, it is impossible to compose a single narrative of the Palestinian experience.[29] This diversity also manifests itself in the choice as well as the use of the medium, in the creation of a new language in the poetic text (spoken word, slam poetry, rap lyrics), or in the visual work of art (photography, art installation, video, personal performance, film). Not only is the medium preoccupied with memory, and a certain poetic memory, but the art itself becomes a "defiant memory," to use Said's term, that articulates a "logic of irreconcilables" and is "unwilling to let go of the past" while being marked by change.[30] It is an art that reflects the dispersion: "an image of absence, without narration, marks incomplete lives, and yet it creates links with others; private and reserved images are created as a private archive countering the disappearance of the more public ones."[31] Loss and the need for memory transcend the particularities of identity without eclipsing them.

Said points to the role cultural discourses and institutions play in giving durability to Palestinian identity in exposing power and questioning authority.[32] He sees the Khalil al Sakakini Cultural Center in Ramallah, where Darwish had his office, as a symbol of national and intellectual life.[33]

Artistic evocations of Mahmoud Darwish are everywhere, in paintings, photography, popular art, music, cinema, dance, and mass culture generally.[34] During the Tunisian revolts and other Arab uprisings, verses of Darwish were circulated in virtual forums and public spaces. One can find his words in graffiti and on walls. His lyrics are evoked both in experiences of the struggle for freedom and in experiences of collective dispossession.

Darwish attracted audiences to his poetry readings by the thousands in Beirut, Damascus, Cairo, Tunis, and elsewhere, which would be unthinkable for poets today. From his simple lyric poems learned by heart to his late experimentations, long and complex, Darwish's readers remained enraptured. His individual experience of dispossession echoes a collective pain. Ghassan Zaqtan writes of the difference that separates his generation from Darwish and the impact that has had on their poetry. The demands of readers on Darwish to carry a political image of Palestinian is one that Zaqtan feels, yet he acknowledges that there is more freedom for his generation: "He didn't sever himself from this image, but developed it. This transformation and development lifted the burden [from] . . . myself. . . . Our generation is 'freer' than that of Darwish. . . . Perhaps because we were born amongst losses. . . . When the dream shattered we were able to take small fragments from it, and this has granted us greater freedom."[35]

Darwish's audience seemed to recognize in his abundant poems that words could still be meaningful among such continued devastation of the historical present. He transformed dispossession and aspiration to an epic, historicizing it poetically. In writing poetry prolifically, innovating and surprising his readers each time, there was a certain "steadfastness in the face of the death of the political project," an undeniable "attachment to a life of freedom."[36] In a tribute to the visual artist Ismail Shammut, he wrote that the painter has become the portrait,[37] and perhaps Darwish has become an infinite poem. Reading Darwish, his audience celebrates the power of the creative endeavor to overcome and "the dead who do not die."[38]

His individual experience of dispossession echoes a collective pain, one that continues daily. He writes in *Ḥīrat al-ʿāʾid* (The hesitation of the returned, 2009), a collection of articles: "When I began writing, . . . I was seeking to express, not dreaming of changing anything except for myself. But my individual case, the great uprooting from place, was the story of an entire people. So, the people found in my individual voice their individual and collective voices."[39]

In his death, as in his life, there was no true return. Birwa, the village of his birth, was obliterated in 1948. At the age of six Darwish experienced his first exile in Lebanon. His family returned after a year, a return considered "infiltration" by the newly created state of Israel, where he will henceforth be classified as "present-absent." He writes in *Ḥīrat al-ʿāʾid*: "I was six when I left to the unknown, when a modern army became victorious over a childhood. . . . An entire people was being wrenched from its . . . present to weld it into an oncoming future . . . we will be one thing, without distinction . . . : Refugees" (39).

And so the absence he experienced as a child will characterize the historical present for much of his poetry. The "return" was a lasting encounter with absence: "We did not find any trace of us or anything to indicate our previous world. The Israeli bulldozers have remade the place so that it suggested that our presence was part of the Roman ruins, not allowed for us to visit" (41).

Later he would be imprisoned many times for his poetry and his life would be an exile already commenced from the "interior." Conscious of poetry's possibility and power, he wrote: "Poetry was not an innocent game, as long as it suggested a being that exists who was not supposed to exist" (45). In 2000, when Yossi Sorid, the Israeli minister of education, wanted to include Darwish's poems in the school programs, a veritable political crisis was unleashed in Israel. The prime minister at the time, Ehud Barak, declared that the country was not ready for the poems of Darwish. The Palestinian writer and critic Ghassan Kanafani, in presenting to the Arab world in 1966 the young poets of the interior—Mahmoud Darwish, Samih al-Qasim, Tawfiq Zayyad—called them "poets of resistance," and Darwish progressively became for his readers a "national poet," a designation he resisted without renouncing the complex relation between poetry and history. Darwish returned to Ramallah in 1996, but exile remained at the heart of his poetry.

Mahmoud Darwish's unique place in Arabic poetry, beginning with the rise of modernist tendencies in the second half of the twentieth century up to the present day, can be attributed to his innovation and popularization of poetry as well as to his renewal of a familiar heritage of poetry: "He wrote genuinely popular poetry, at a time when Arabic poetry and its readership were both in decline; he preserved the spirit and values of poetry, while renewing and refining them, as no other writer was able to do."[40] Darwish is a lyric poet with a capacity for ceaseless innovation, whose poetry embodies a humanizing and cosmic vision of the self in a historical context wrought with catastrophic events. His emergence as a poet coincided with the call for modernization of Arabic poetry. Two generations of modern Arabic poets emerged around two literary journals: *Al-Shi'r* was founded by poets such as Adonis who were more interested in translations and experimentation with language, whereas *Adab* attracted Darwish and other Palestinian poets concerned with the movement of history and with innovations in meter. Darwish took a stance that did not reject a tradition of Arabic poetry in the name of blind experimentations with language and prose poetry; rather, his experimentations worked through a rich inheritance of Arabic meters, guarding the musicality: "Darwish has had a profound influence on generations of readers and poets throughout the Arab world . . . he is credited with reviving Arabic lyrical poetry, taking it beyond, as the critic Hassan Khader puts it, 'immediate political concerns into more metaphysical subjects.'"[41]

Darwish's work is seminal in modern Arabic poetry and is often considered in that context, and he is also without question one of the world's most important contemporary poets. Darwish has been recognized internationally and was the recipient of many prestigious international literary awards.[42] A prolific poet, he produced over thirty collected works and has been translated into more than thirty-five languages. Having been influential in transforming the poetic landscape of Arabic poetry in the twentieth century, Darwish's poetry has now become known in North America.

For a long time, anyone interested in modern Arabic poetry would have had difficulty finding substantial translations or critical studies in English on the general subject, let alone any that focus on Darwish specifically. Translations of Darwish's work into English have especially proliferated since 2000.[43] Critical studies are also thriving in English at the time of this writing.[44]

Edward Said has written in *After the Last Sky*: "Our need for new consciousness emerges in literature."[45] And indeed, Said believed that all forms of artistic production, from film to theater to music to the visual arts, have contributed to this new consciousness that allows for the rethinking of selves out of dispersion and fragmentation, out of this opposition of the self and the collective. Said stated in an interview with David Barsamian that all Palestinian art forms have consolidated Palestinian identity and made it endure in its struggle against erasure. Said acknowledges a "distinctly Palestinian discourse" that fights for Palestinian critical and political identity whenever it is threatened.[46]

This new consciousness "remains enigmatic enough to be preoccupied . . . by a thinking of 'the future.'"[47] The poetry of Darwish, from his early lyrics to late experimentations, has heralded a future, creating out of loss, inscribing an experience against fear and despair, reasserting freedom in the face of its antithesis. Darwish, and his generation of poets and writers from Ghassan Kanafani to Emil Habiby to Samih al-Qasim, has reclaimed a space from which to speak in the absence of other narratives. He writes in *Fī ḥaḍrat al-ghiyāb*: "Who will narrate our story, we . . . the banished from place and from myth."[48] He establishes poetry not only as a space of survival but also of freedom, and of possibility, and of future. The possibility of poetry opening onto a future can be noted in Darwish's conception of poetry as relation (to language, to nature, to place, to beings, to self), as affirmation, and as transformation.

In a context in which words are used to bolster a project of historical violence (of continued dispossession, occupation, denial of the right of return, and negation of those remaining), it is this path of poetry, which restores to words meaningfulness and beauty in a vision for the future, and in which the impossible can be envisioned, that gives such hope and force to his poetry.[49]

It is not surprising, then, that poetry should still flourish, with beings inhabited by history, by a collectivity, by loss, by promise.

Belonging

To trace the path of Darwish's poetry, which so poignantly expresses a loss of home, to artworks (poetry, lyric, performance, visual art, film) that often evoke this poetry directly and yet can be said to be "at home and in the world" demands a thinking of "belonging without the conditions of belonging," as Giorgio Agamben has argued.[50] Darwish's writing and this kind of art (which is significantly diasporic) testify, in the face of loss, to a belonging that persists against disappearance and fragmentation. But it is a belonging reconstituted by "dislocations felt by displaced subjects towards disrupted histories and to shifting and transient national identities"[51] and in which identities are "reproducing themselves anew, through transformations and difference."[52]

This kind of art reinscribes the notion of "belonging" and is oriented toward solidarity and the quest for future. These new forms of belonging are hybrid expressions of hope and of politics. Belonging is detached (but not altogether) from the national, and is tied to a transnational entity that encompasses the refugee, the diaspora, and is not limited solely to the national territory. Belonging and dispersion can be brought together as a critique of nationalism but also as the reminder of national claims. In a dynamic relation between the diasporic and the local, belonging and nonbelonging are simultaneous in the "home space" and elsewhere. For artists often traverse both configurations. Although these artists may be considered "local" or "exilic" or "transnational," they can be situated in relation to a collective condition of dispersion, fragmentation, and displacement, whether internal or external. The diasporic can also mean "nonbelonging" even in the home space. The Palestinian condition is diasporic because of a continuous experience of dispersion. Belonging is henceforth also inscribed in poetic statement, in artistic practice.

What these artists after Darwish show, and what Darwish's poetry already reveals, are the possibilities of rethinking belonging, the relation to the other, the vision of the self and of the collective.

Loss

In this kind of artwork as well as in Darwish's writing, events are inscribed as defining and enduring experiences of loss that return with subsequent losses, but it is a loss not only of place or of self but also a severance of relation and of "the means of your belonging to the world," as Darwish indicates in *Journal of Ordinary Grief* (translated 2010).[53] His writings gather that which has been torn asunder, whereby the losses unfold a personal history that echoes a collective grief. The vision of history remains intimate and enfolded in writing, where the self is constituted by history. Although homeland is a topography of loss in Darwish's early poetry, it is consciously assumed as a search and a struggle, a "proof that I refuse to get lost in my loss," despite the burdens and the limits of all claims to a homeland: "You will not find freedom outside these chains, and you will not find ease or relief from the burden outside this pain."[54] Poetry, on the other hand, is this abundant, creative, and mysterious force, born from this loss but not defined by it. Artists follow this poetic posture of Darwish regarding loss.

Judith Butler, in *Precarious Life: The Powers of Mourning and Violence*, argues that mourning, which necessitates an acceptance of a transformation in loss, may open onto politics: "It is not that mourning is the goal of politics, but . . . without the capacity to mourn, we lose that keener sense of life we need in order to oppose violence."[55] Butler argues that grief is not simply a private state; rather, it provides a sense of *political community*: "If my fate is not originally or finally separable from yours, then the 'we' is traversed by a relationality that we cannot easily argue against" (22–23). The experience of loss and mourning is one that could inspire solidarity and justice. Addressing those of us *"beside ourselves,* whether in . . . passion, or emotional grief, or political rage," she addresses those "undone" by loss: what is lost is not simply a place or an other, but something in that place or that other that cannot be altogether known; something of the self is lost as well, for the self is constituted by its attachment and relation to an other (24). In the experience of dispossession, a certain relation to the self and to place, to things, a certain tie whose nature remains enigmatic, is lost (22).

As Rancière has argued, loss proffers a promise of new forms of subjectivities and forms of communities.

Dispersion

Contemporary Palestinian art is an art that reflects dispersion. As Butler has argued in *Parting Ways,* "dispersion is a condition of possibility for thinking justice," and therefore for envisioning a different kind of future (5). For Palestine is already diasporic (*al-shatāt al-filasṭīnī*) as a result of the Nakba of 1948 when almost eight hundred thousand Palestinians fled their homes, and the subsequent forced migration of the Naksa of 1967 most notably. Today there are over ten million Palestinians living outside of historical Palestine, by some estimates, although it is difficult to determine the exact number. Seeing dispersion's political possibilities, Butler argues, "might be useful for finding a way to think about cohabitation, binationalism, and a critique of state violence" (15).

Intriguingly, Butler conceives of dispersion's ethical and political horizons as a condition "where no one religion or nationality may claim sovereignty over another, where, in fact, sovereignty itself will be dispersed" (5). Dispersion, that of the self as well, grounds a different politics, for it implies relationality founded on difference, heterogeneity, and multiplicity. Butler joins Said in conceiving of the diasporic in a context of "affirming difference or plurality as a condition of its own existence" (215). But her conception of "relationality" is at the heart of an ethical project that presupposes a political project that is founded in reconceiving the individual subject: "The kind of relationality at stake is one that 'interrupts' or challenges the unitary character of the subject, its self-sameness . . . something happens to the 'subject' that dislocates it from the center of the world; some demand from elsewhere lays claim to me . . . even divides me from within, and only through this fissuring of who I am do I stand a chance of relating to another" (6).

In the prose poem "A House Fallen," Darwish speaks of everyday dispersion that amounts to a dispossession where the severing of relation is that of being and home:

> In one minute, a lifetime of a house ends. . . . A mass grave for primal matter prepared for meaning. . . . A house murdered is the severing of things from their relations and from their names. . . . Every being suffers . . . the memory . . . of a scent, of an image. . . . And slain too is the memory of things: stone, wood, glass . . . scatter like remains of beings. Cotton, silk, linen . . . torn like words unsaid. . . . Dishes, spoons, toys . . . all break like their owners . . . dried tomatoes and okra, rice, and lentils, crushed just like the household. Rental contract, marriage certificate, birth certificate . . . torn apart like the hearts of their bearers. Pictures, toothbrushes, combs . . . swept off like family secrets, displayed in the open and in ruins. All these things are a memory of a people emptied of things . . . everything ends in one minute. Our things die like us, but they are not buried with us![56]

Dispossession

What Palestinian art reveals is a condition of dispossession, but as Butler so poignantly argues, dispossession is the predicament of those who endured loss of home, of loved ones, of place, of land, of "the very condition of belonging to the world," as Darwish has written in the *Journal of Ordinary Grief*. Elsewhere Butler writes that dispossession is the predicament of those who have lost "citizenship, property, and a broader belonging to the world." For her, it is both "what happens when populations . . . become subject to military violence" and "a term that marks the limits of self-sufficiency and that establishes us as relational and interdependent beings."[57]

She recuperates dispossession as "responsiveness," a possibility for resistance and a necessary condition for justice and for solidarity, in the ability of the self to *respond* to the other, to be decentered, and to be carried away to an elsewhere, to form an alternate collectivity:

> The predicament of being moved by what one sees, feels, and comes to know is always one in which one finds oneself transported elsewhere, into another scene . . . in which one is not the center. And this form of dispossession is constituted as a form of responsiveness that gives rise to action and resistance, to appearing together with others, in an effort to demand the end of injustice. And so we take up the question of *how to become dispossessed of the sovereign self and enter into forms of collectivity that oppose forms of dispossession that systematically jettison populations from modes of collective belonging and justice.*[58]

This is a fruitful understanding of dispossession that wrestles it from a "logic of possession, a hallmark of capitalism, liberalism, and humanism," where dispossession describes resistance, opposition, and a response to "disenfranchisement associated with unjust dispossession of land, economic and political power, and basic conditions for living."[59]

Butler grounds ethics in relationality and not primarily in the subject or its actions. Ethics is privileged as a "relational practice" that responds to the other, an "ec-static relationality," "a way of being dispossessed from sovereignty and nation in response to the claims made by those one does not fully know. . . . From this conception of the ethical relation follows a reconceptualization of both social bonds and political obligations that takes us beyond nationalism."[60]

What the artists after Darwish reveal through their art is both aspects of this dispossession, the decentered, diasporic subject who actively allies itself in active struggle with others, who enters in relations with others against those violently enforced. Art becomes an intervention, whether willed or not, in calling into question practices of power that lead to collective conditions of dispossession as well as the struggles of resistance against it. What they affirm is a belonging against collective dispossession, one that can no longer pretend to be grounded in identity but one founded on solidarity and on struggle with all dispossessed. If practices of state dispossession have been grounded in identity, then the art itself finds new ways of resisting the logic and the historical reality that ensues from it.

As the work of Suheir Hammad shows, an effect of continued dispossession is dispersion, which faces such violence with poetry, with a belonging that remains open, barely able to be articulated but a horizon to be sung. In engaging the poetry of Darwish, she creates her own unique expression, from Arabic to an English inhabited by the Arabic, from lyrical verses to spoken-word performances. Dispersion proves innovative and already at work in any creative endeavor. Likewise, the poetry of Liana Badr and Ghassan Zaqtan speak to this experience of dispersion in the first chapter of this book. In the second chapter, loss is highlighted. Loss establishes a relation to another's poetry, to other people who have endured loss. Across the dispersion in geography, forms, media, experiences, and languages, there are commonalities. The three filmmakers discussed all present life under occupation, and yet the visual language of all three is highlighted as part of an aesthetic project that innovates while it dissects a collective experience of daily loss.

Palestinian art, in chapter 3, like the voice of Darwish, has dispersed internationally and has found a public forum that political voices have not. The extraordinary accomplishments of artists such as Mona Hatoum, Sharif Waked, and Emily Jacir present us with a prolific production that is rich with experimentation and preoccupied with the experience of dispossession, whether of the homeland or of the domestic home or of the body. The openness of Palestinian art to new forms of being together, of belonging, of resisting have appealed to many others who are in solidarity or who simply have taken notice of its force, innovation, and vitality. It challenges the rigid distinctions of local and diasporic and has ensuing implications beyond aesthetic considerations. It creates new ways of belonging in its struggle against effacement.

In music, the fourth chapter, the hip-hop Palestinian bands, whether from Gaza or "from 1948" or from Ramallah, have incorporated this political American form in its origins to address youth grievances and to protest the dispossession of their youth in their homes, and have claimed it as their own. Inspired by the great poets of Samih al-Qasim, Tawfiq al-Zayyad, and Mahmoud Darwish, they created an expression of struggle and of survival, both ruined in its traditional forms and vibrant. The proliferation of such musical groups in the Palestinian territories and in the diaspora, as in Palestinian bands in the United States, speak to a common grievance and a common resistance to an experience of dispossession that continues to inflict its damage.

Palestinian art in its broad meaning may be a space of refuge for politics in a seemingly depoliticized age, as Jacques Rancière has argued in *Dissensus*. It is a living example of the artificial opposition between politics and aesthetics and shows their complex relationship, whereby art gains greater force given the historical impasses before it.

In "Colonization of the Imagination" Steve Sabella argues, following Fanon, Césaire, and others, that colonization is also that of the imagination and of the mind and not just of the physical forms of body and place, which "subjects people to a severe mental and physical paralysis that restricts development and obliterates all notions of personal freedom." For Sabella, exile becomes one of the ways of attempting to counter colonization and regain freedom, to "re-conquer my imagination, until I reached my states of Euphoria (2010) and Beyond Euphoria (2011)."[61] It is in this sense that Palestinian visual art, and other forms of art, have been critically important, politically as well as aesthetically. It becomes incumbent to wrench language, whether poetic or visual, from the hegemony of a tired language about Palestine.

Palestinian visual artists like Tayseer Barakat, Tayseer Batniji, Raeda Saadeh, Larissa Sansour, and Steve Sabella are among the artists who are reclaiming imagination and creating against an occupation that has been physically brutal and corrosive, locally and globally, and hegemonic in discourse and images. In this sense, the rural portraits of Tayseer Barakat are no longer the nostalgic landscapes of the past nor the deformed ones of the present, deformed by an occupation that inflicts violence not only on the people themselves but also on nature, on trees, and on space. The natural and humble beauty of the villages is also violated by this continuous occupation. Barakat's images, however, recall this beauty and this violence at the same time.

Raeda Saadeh's "Conquering Space" alludes to this violation directly, in portraying the subject as physically constrained. Here, the visual imaginary becomes a way to liberate from the occupation that confines one's space and movement, specifically in calling this "conquest of space" into question and doing so through humor, so that one's subjectivity escapes from the constraining and imposed paradigm of occupation. In the image of the installation, a woman stands outside a house with an open entryway; as if undecided about going in or leaving, one foot stands next to a suitcase and another is stuck in a block of cement. The image calls attention not only to physical constraints on movement but also to the inability to fully claim a home and forge new roots elsewhere in exile.

In Steve Sabella's haunting work *In Exile*, images recurrently depict a somber but meticulously constructed exile. Each image seems to repeat and proliferate images of houses or apartments, as if they are settlements or homes artificially constructed and imposed. The images are imbued with the dark colors blue and gray, brown and black, as we see in the image *In Exile 1*. In *In Exile 2* spaces are surrounded with barbed wired. As Sabella once proclaimed, "I stitch my wounds with barbed wire." The "reconstitution" of self is paradoxically one of violent suturing that has not been able to rid reality of barbed wires, at home or in exile, but remains liberatory. With light emanating from the inside of these interiors at night, the images are not without a sense of hope. Despite the dark gray, blue, and black, the flitter of interior light suggests movement nonetheless, perhaps a breakthrough from all limitations.

Mona Hatoum's *Turbulence* recalls the marbles of childhood, an insouciance of play and connection to a place that has since turned to transience, disconnection, and disarray, shared with so many others, a collection of instances of beings and nonbeings. One more loss, one more devastation, and everything the image suggests is asunder again. When

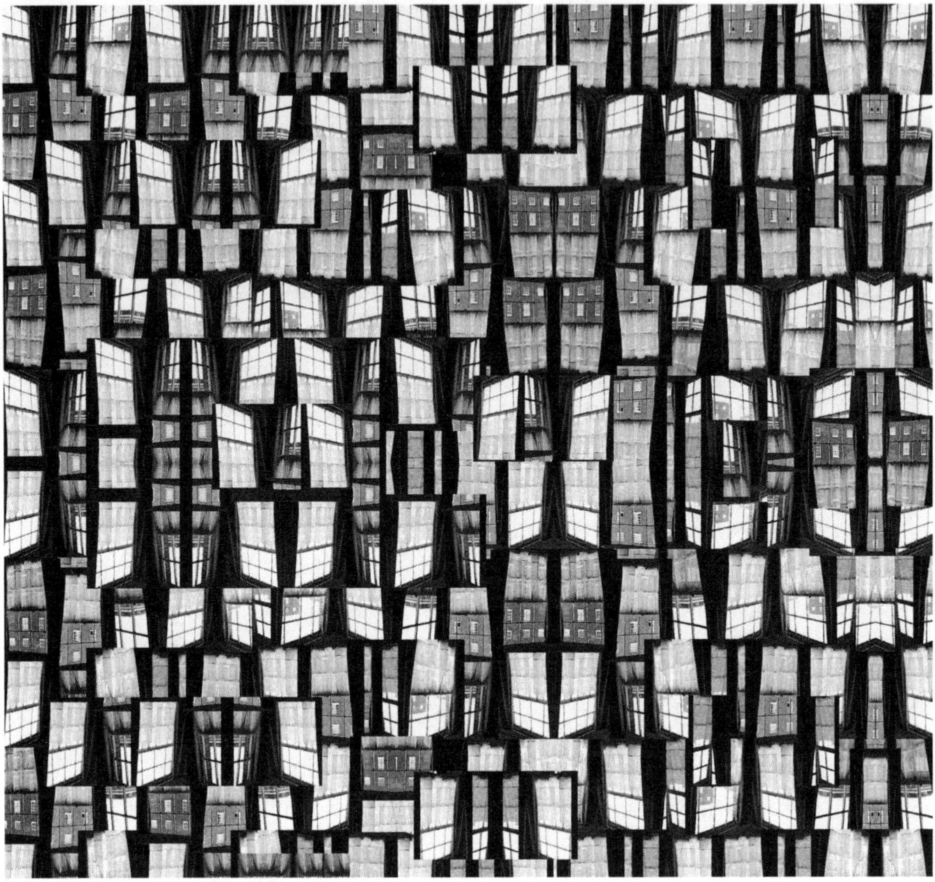

1. Steve Sabella, *In Exile 1*, from series *In Exile*, 2008, series of five works, lambda prints on aluminum, 136 x 125 cm each. Ellen Auerbach Prize 2008 of the Academy of Arts in Berlin, Germany. Reproduced with permission from Steve Sabella.

Palestinians meet today in the diaspora, it is as if they constitute such a collection.

Tayseer Batniji's series of destroyed houses in Gaza just after the Israeli attack "Cast Lead" (the end of 2008 to the start of 2009), pictured and displayed like ads in a real estate agency, emphasize the toll of dispossession. The image, however, is not without subversive irony. It confronts the viewer with the reality of what it is to lose a home, which is unfathomable, in a visual language, a cultural practice, and an economic exchange that

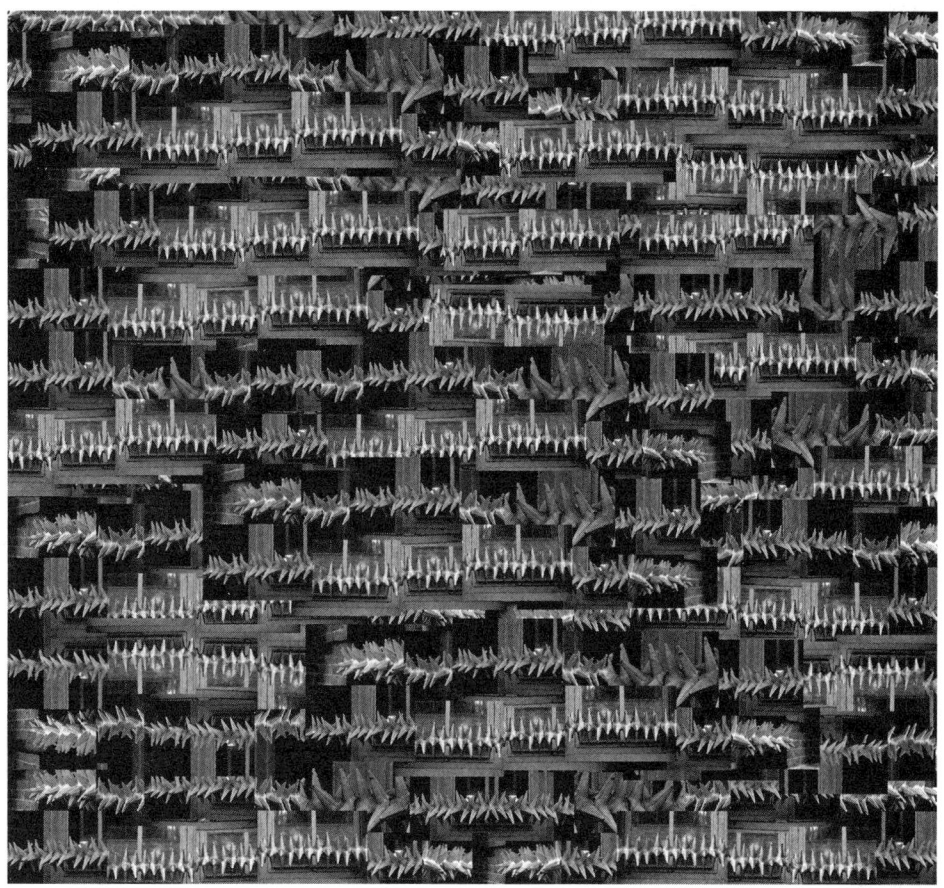

2. Steve Sabella, *In Exile 2*, from series *In Exile*, 2008, series of five works, lambda prints on aluminum, 136 x 125 cm each. Ellen Auerbach Prize 2008 of the Academy of Arts in Berlin, Germany. Reproduced with permission from Steve Sabella.

are familiar. It showcases what has been irrecoverably lost, with no insurance, no exchange, no going back. It recalls Darwish's poem "A Murdered House," in *Athar al-farāsha* (The butterfly effect). I translated the poem's title here as "fallen," since these homes are demolished, but the term mitigates the violence of the original.

This is an art of dissent that crosses over political impasses and renders what has been muted and excluded legible and public. Art and politics interrupt the framing of perceptual space, creating difference and

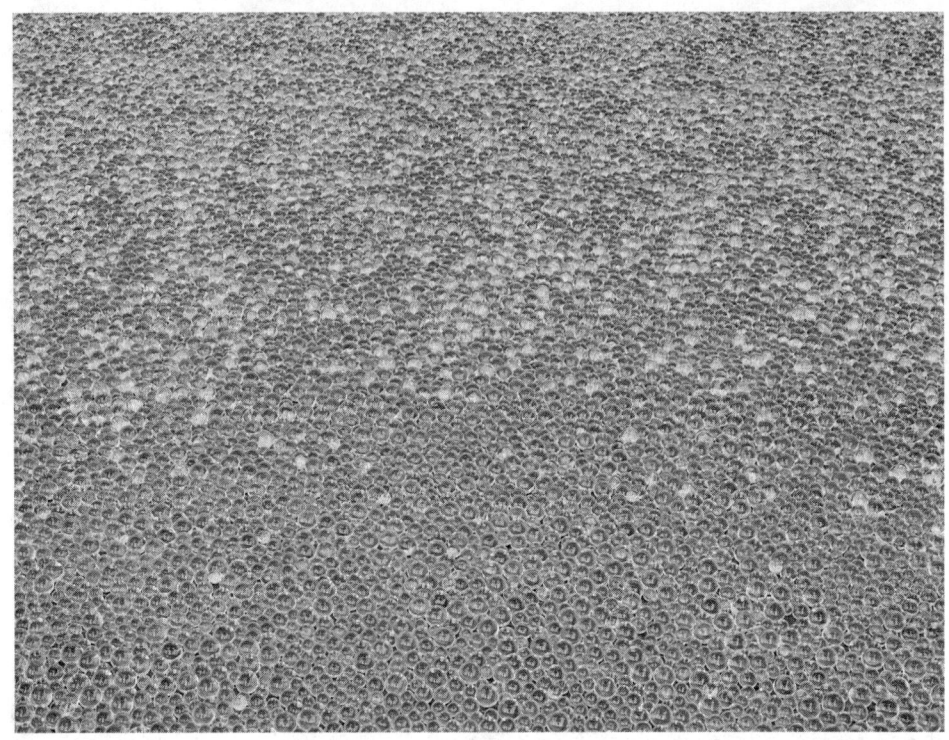

3. Mona Hatoum, *Turbulence* (detail), 2012, Clear glass marbles 1%₁₆ x 157½ x 157½ in. (4 x 400 x 400 cm) © Mona Hatoum. Photo: def image. Courtesy Galerie Max Heztler, Berlin/Paris, and White Cube.

challenging consensual forms of power, where art allows the subject to appear and where politics allows excluded speech to emerge. This art compels a response and calls for reflection on the act of interpretation at a time of devastation. It is an act of intervention in the present, a critical act of listening and of dissension.

1

Language's Passage from Mahmoud Darwish to Suheir Hammad, Liana Badr, and Ghassan Zaqtan

In the summer of 2000, I met a group of young Palestinian poets in Ramallah, Palestine. I presented my work on Mahmoud Darwish and they read some of their poems and discussed their relation to Darwish as a towering poetic figure. Darwish had returned to Palestine only a few years earlier, in 1996, and he was at the height of his poetic career. These young poets were charting their own paths. Notable among them were Mahmoud Abu Hashhash and Abdulrahman al Shaikh. Abdulrahman al Shaikh has been interested in Darwish and has lectured on his work since Darwish's death in 2008, and one notes flourishes of Darwish's poetry in Abu Hashhash's collection *Istibāha,* which came out in 2006.[1] What these poets reveal is that their relation to Darwish has not been solely one of influence as it has been one of intersection in poetry, precisely because the poetic and historical experiences have been shared, both the common Arabic poetic heritage and the historical dispossession and dispersion. It is precisely this dispersion that is highlighted in this chapter, whether in the experience of exilic journey, subjective fragmentation, or breaks of poetry—knowledge of which is shared by all Palestinian poets. This chapter highlights the passage of Darwish's poetry into a gendered experience and into a new generation of poetic forms where the "shattering of the dream," as Ghassan Zaqtan put it, has allowed for greater poetic freedom.

In Suheir Hammad's engagement with Darwish's poetry, in that passage from a poetry deemed "national" to one that is "diasporic," it can be argued that the diasporic offers alternative forms of communal and gendered identity in Hammad's foregrounding of women's experience and incorporations of peoples beyond national confines. Yet what Hammad's poems reveal about Darwish's poetry is that the national was born of an experience of dispersion, dispossession, and erasure, where the boundaries of time extend from the mythic to the quotidian and those of place extend from the house's threshold of sage to its many paths. Hammad grew up in Brooklyn and was influenced by the hip-hop scene. Born to parents from Lyd who were made refugees by the 1948 dispossession of Palestinians, Hammad's poetry joins that of poets who live in Palestine, those having returned after numerous experiences of exile and displacement or those having stayed and experienced fragmentation and internal displacement. These poets reveal how the national is already characterized by an experience of dispersion and displacement, whether internal or external. Hammad's poems as well as those of Liana Badr and Ghassan Zaqtan open Darwish's poetry for new readings.

In analyzing Hammad's work, one has to also address how poetry impacts new forms of performance art. Darwish's popular poems, even the long poems, like spoken-word poetry, managed to appeal to a stunningly wide popular audience and were performed musically (whether by Michel Kheleifeh and other artists or by Darwish's own recital accompanied by the Trio Joubran). This testifies to poetry's ability to renew and transform and proliferate into other art forms. Hammad's spoken-word poetry reminds us that the poet creates original works so that poems will not merely be experienced through the linguistic meaning of words.

The poetry addressed here allows us to consider how to cast this poetry after Darwish. Is the poetry one of "dissensus"? Does the poetry after Darwish break with or constitute "resistance poetry"? Palestinian cultural production, especially that of the poets of the late sixties and early seventies, was dubbed "resistance poetry" by the late Palestinian writer and critic Ghassan Kanafani, speaking of those "inside" the boundaries of 1948 Palestine. The term was applied to Darwish well into his career when he was still being associated with, and requested to recite, such early poems as "Identity Card."

Darwish's later poetry shows how the conception of the "political" changed. Henceforth, it would be a poetry preoccupied with *rethinking the future, subjectivity, and the self's relations to others.* Poets like Hammad, Badr, and Zaqtan highlight how the political is also what ruptures existing relations and existing narratives. Their poetry allows for certain displacements that open to the possibility of a new political and poetic subject.

Suheir Hammad's poetry presents poetic creation as a significant act of translation and subject reformation. Her collection *Breaking Poems* (2008), which pays tribute to the poetry of the late Mahmoud Darwish, engages it in many instances through *translation* of some of his verses.[2] Hammad translates poetically, marking a passage between her innovative work and that of Darwish.[3] In her translations the passage is not from one language into another (from Arabic to English) but rather within a poetic language that inhabits and is inhabited by both languages, an English constituted by Arabic, where poetry and translation are not separate processes or activities. Translation is further evoked in the poems as a problem and a possibility for reflection.

She translates from such poems in Darwish's collection *Limātha tarakta al-ḥiṣāna waḥīdan? (Why Did You Leave the Horse Alone?)* as "A Rhythm for Muʻallaqāt . . . ," when the poetic voice proclaims:

I am my language

. . . .

This language of mine pendants from stars[4] encircling the
embraces of the beloved: migrated
They took the place and migrated
They took time and migrated

. . . .

They took the words and the fallen heart migrated with them

. . . .[5]

These verses of Darwish are rendered in Hammad's poem "Break (Me)" as:

ana my language always broken . . .
   . . . wa
i miss my people.[6]

A rendering of Darwish's verse "I am my language," Hammad's words continue a poetry interrupted with the death of Darwish in 2008, the same year as the publication of her poetry collection *Breaking Poems*. She inscribes herself in a tradition of Arabic poetry as an "interruption" or "departure," all implied in the term "breaking," and a continuation of a *heritage* of poetry, in the spirit of Darwish's poetry, which announces itself as simultaneously continuing a long tradition of Arabic poetry and constituting a singular voice from within it in a certain departure. This poetic departure is due to the experience of the diasporic in which the poet finds herself and which then imposes a certain multilingualism and a certain hybridity on the self already announced in the "ana" and "I" of Arabic and English, respectively. For her poetry to be written in a hybrid language is to perform a poetic departure that estranges the language from its familiar uses, calling attention to displacements enacted within the poet and within geographical dispersions. Her poetry points to a reality of hybrid multilingualism that she claims for its poetic possibilities and destabilizing effects on the national, monolithic claims of identity. This poetic translation, which recalls the loss, the breaks, and the migrations, becomes common experience and allows for an affirmation of belonging for the "I" or "they."[7] For the taking of the homeland, as noted in the introduction, has meant for Darwish the taking away of the very "means of . . . belonging to the world."[8] In this way, the struggle itself, as well as the poetic quest, constitutes this belonging: "And," Darwish writes, "the homeland is this struggle."[9]

Although Hammad's poetry can be situated within spoken-word poetry and can claim other poetic traditions (for instance, the African American poetry of June Jordan with its deliberative and distinctive use of Black English, the Arab American poetry of Noemi Shihab Nye with its accent on the ethnic experience, the unconventional Beat poetry, or the slam poetry composed specifically for a performance),[10] in this work she claims Arabic poetry, and specifically Darwish's poetry, as her poetic heritage. Such a claim is grounded in a complex and ironic way in the verse "I am my language," for Darwish's language is distinctly Arabic whereas Hammad's is an English language born out of Arabic. For both poets, however, "I am my language" is a verse that gestures to a common poetic language that unifies a poetic legacy but that, nonetheless, divides the self from itself and from its "people." Many languages gather the sense of "self"; in Arabic and English this sense is expressed as "ana" and "I," respectively. The self can no longer adhere to an imposed logic of monolingualism but reflects the reality of dispersion. In the verses of both poets, the "people" is evoked only in its dispersion, diaspora, and migration: Darwish's line "they took the place and migrated" and Hammad's "I miss my people." The collective "they" in the verses is always already distant from the self and absent to it. For what does it mean to speak of a people? Is the "people" a translation? A dissension? This idea of "belonging to a people" is constituted by a lyrical continuation and its breaks, by the act of affirmation of a belonging.

The sense of "belonging" is painfully predicated on "brokenness": one that reveals poetic language as fundamentally a break, a caesura, a cut, an interruption, built on the experience of historical fragmentation. The poetry of Darwish and Hammad thus joins a belonging that is predicated on solidarity rather than on strict identity. For the term *intimā'* in Arabic, like the English term "belonging" or the French *appartenance*, refers us back to this divide of being apart and its counter desire of connectivity and attachment, a longing also to fully *become* that can only be realized in relatedness to others and to oneself, to be self-possessed. The word *appartenir* suggests an attachment in its Latin origin *adpertinere*, which is rendered as *se rattacher à*. In its modern significations, the word suggests first of all ownership, belonging as possession: "appartenir à quelqu'un" (to belong to someone). Only in its fourth sense does it mean to be part of something ("faire partie de quelque chose"). The word *appartenance*, however, suggests belonging to a collectivity ("le fait pour un individu d'appartenir à *une collectivité*"). Likewise, in English, to belong is "to relate to; to be the property or rightful possession of; to be connected . . . , to form a part of . . . something."[11]

Hammad evokes a certain attachment that cannot be simply disowned or completely known, and in this case it is assumed out of an expansive sense of collectivity. It is a "be-longing," where fulfillment of being is anchored in this longing and where longing is inextricable from being. In *Drops of This Story*, Hammad writes: "I write of longing for a land I have yet to feel under my feet." This belonging is, most important, expressed and enacted through writing. She continues: "This story travels with me. . . . This wetness was with me in Jordan wetting my cheeks, as I sat on a mountaintop where my uncle used to sit to get a good view of Palestine over the sea. This is the story I was born to write."[12]

In a poem that insists on the rhythm and multiple meanings of the word "break," it is the reader who has to insert the caesura (the break) in the poem, since the breaks are visually unmarked, and so the reader becomes part of this poetic endeavor and this collective "translation," part of the notion of "my people." Moreover, the word "break" in the title is what structurally ties Hammad's poems together, each poem distinguished only by the words in parenthesis that vary and that are like walls that separate.

The word "break," which is also part of the vocabulary of hip-hop youth culture, has many meanings: among them, it can refer to "a short solo or instrumental passage in jazz or popular music"[13] or to the act of separating into pieces. It can also suggest a wound or a fracture, for something to become inoperative. It can even signal birth or rebirth, as in "to break water." Alternatively, it suggests a certain violence, as in "to open forcibly" or to crush the emotional resistance of someone, as well as departures and surpassing, as in "break through," "break clean," and "break of dawn." And it also means "to interrupt" and recalls such interruptions as the natural course of the history of languages, cultures, and identities.

The words in Arabic for "self" (*ana*) and for "continuation" (*wa*) create a break in the English poems, create another rhythm, an "off beat." Since the poems are written in English and introduce Arabic words, cadences, and rhythms, these rhythms interrupt the flow of the English verses and "break" the continuity of the English words. The English expressed is no longer monolingual.

Darwish's identification of language with an Arabic poetic heritage is more specifically a desire to link language with continuous beings. Darwish writes: "This language of mine is pendants from stars encircling the embraces of the beloved: migrated."[14] The Arabic word for pendants or necklaces, *qalā'id*, can also mean exquisite poems, thus tying language specifically to poetic language. Here the belonging is specifically to a people, but through poetry.

Hammad creates a new poetic language through a process of translation. Carolyn Forché describes the new language this way: it "introduces English to an Arabic vernacular that startles into being an altogether new language, bridging the archipelago of a Palestine under siege to the diaspora and beyond . . . a music . . . that Mahmoud Darwish should have lived to see."[15] It is a poetry that links experiences, cities, languages, and peoples defined by dispersion, exile, and wars. Poetry is a matter of survival, as Carolyn Forché writes on the cover of Hammad's *Breaking Poems*, "written for a people who have endured the winds of hurricanes and invasions."

In *Breaking Poems*, then, poetry itself is conceived of as translation, of the unspeakable passage into a new poetic language, of another's poetry into a continuation of poetry. A break—also an instrumental *passage* in music—recalls poetry's affinity with translation. Hammad's poems propose that *breaking* is the very possibility of language and of poetry. It is the cross between creativity and wounding history. There is also a break between the poet and the poem. For Maurice Blanchot, the caesura mitigates the excess of desire (and longing) in the poem, so it can become itself a poem; meter is, after all, measure in rhythm, in sound.[16] In the poems where Arabic words are constitutive of the English formed by Hammad, Arabic's rhythms link the breaks between the lines. Thus untranslatability is the very thing that allows the poem to come into being, not as an essential difference between languages but as a tie that complicates the point where one language begins and another ends. Arabic left mostly untranslated in Hammad's work emerges as infinitely translatable, as it flows in the very rhythms that announce unspeakable breaks. In a syntax that fractures, the Arabic connector *wa* continues one language into another, forming one poetic language. Hammad's poems are at the limits of a monolingual reading. Hammad reconfigures the limits of language, where one begins and another ends. She reconceives the encounter of languages so that the relation between them is no longer one of "original and target, or native and foreign," nor one of "language as a border war," in the words of Emily Apter, but between the monolingual and the multilingual, the national and the diasporic.[17] Language is henceforth at the limits of readability. The added index at the end of Hammad's collection of poems, which provides English definitions for the Arabic words, assists the non-Arabic reader only to decipher that limit of language. The reader is cognizant of the need to know both languages in order to read. More important than mere legibility, however, the poem issues forth music. Key to this reconceptualization of translation has been Walter Benjamin, who, in "The Task of the Translator," "moved away from a 'fidelity to the original' model . . . toward one in which 'everything is translatable and in perpetual state of in-translation,'" as Apter indicates.[18] Unlike Benjamin, however, who sets apart the figure of the poet from that of the translator, Hammad bridges poetry and translation. Benjamin sees the translator's relation to the poet as derivative, owing to translation's linguistic predicament of following a source language from which it translates.[19] The poet is seen as the one who creates original works, so that poems are not merely experienced through the linguistic meaning of words. Such a conception echoes today, where poetry is defined by its force, intensity, and vitality. Hammad, however, sees in the poet the translator who renders what cannot be said across a chasm,

> translating waves into language bas missing
> what i had wanted to say.[20]

Darwish likewise conceives of the poetic voice as emerging from a long lineage of poets but which is able then to create a unique individual voice in this chain of poets, as we see in his poem "Crypts, Andalusia, Desert."[21]

Broken idioms. Hammad introduces a "minor" language into another: not a literary Arabic and not a standard English. For those who do not speak it altogether fluently, or who have lost their fluency in it, the Arabic idiom, Palestinian, an almost rural dialect, is "broken"—an expression in both English and Arabic—and constitutes and is constituted by the English of Brooklyn youth, of "blacks." She fractures syntax and vocabulary and breaks language to renew it. Poetic violence issues forth a poetic rebirth: "brooklyn broken english wa exiled arabs sampled," she writes;

> we rhyme of rivers
> swim in vernacular.[22]

Hammad's poems reconstruct, show the fractures (breaks) already there in any language. The break emerges as the natural rhythm of language, and of poetry, a link of history and of poetry, already there in Darwish, an innovative poetic that speaks more forcefully to new realities. It is a poetic language that ties and cuts and flows in the face of the fragmentation of "selves," the dispersion of "peoples," and the shrinking of "geography," as Darwish has also shown. Poetry emerges as a gathering of languages, of bodies, of voices, of sounds, as it was in Darwish's poems where the long poems gather across time and place different voices, peoples, and sounds. Hammad writes: "ana gathering selves into new" (35). The diasporic poet through her voice gathers fragmented selves into new possible collective identities.

The poet is figured throughout as Isis, who gathers the loss, remembers the body that has been torn apart, restores to life with a work of mourning necessary for creation and proper remembrance.[23] As an Isis whose quest is to search for her beloved, the poet resurrects, stitches, and reconstitutes what has been violently torn asunder. A break is also damage rendered inoperative. The poem gestures to mourning as a going beyond, a "break (clear)," but more directly to rebirth, a "break (water)" (43–44). She writes:

> break into language insurgent
> . . . .
> hagar springs isis remembers mary reaps. (39)

A coming into language is a coming into life. The poem is also a surpassing: in "break (through)," "break (clean)", "a retrieval from the very heart of loss," as the writer Chris Abani points out.[24] And as the scholar Wail Hassan reminds us in his preface to Abdelfattah Kilito's *Thou Shalt*

Not Speak My Language, there are at least two words for "translation" in Arabic. In addition to the usual understanding of translation as "transfer" or *naql,* another word, *tarjama,* can mean "biography" and "life"; and *tarjama* can be associated with the "condemned word" and death, as in *rajama,* but also with the possibility of survival.[25]

As translation, the poem "Break (Clear)" carries forth violence and transforms it, for the poem is also a dissension in a body broken by violence. The poem finds its vitality in the broken body—a break can also be of someone. It comes to life from a fracturing of history, of the self, of language, "lived in one fractured body/a relic of war."[26] As in this verse, Hammad's poetry translates itself. It is a metapoetic that reflects on itself. She places the word "here" in parentheses in this poem as if to protect this fragile geography. The poem is affirmation of itself in the face of any denial (43). Poetry becomes the fragile passage as it was in Darwish, the opening of a "here," a departure from violence.

Translation as passage is a poetic demand in Hammad's work, and yet it is resisted. The poem will not fully give. Unlike Darwish's poetry, Hammad's is gendered. Women and their bodies are at the heart of this poetic endeavor, often likening women to poems she writes (45). In this, she places women at the creative center of her poetics. The poem in "Break (Water)" is a body that experiences breaks and (re)births (39). She writes in "Break":

> i am looking for my body
> in translation. (11)

Although translation is critical to any knowledge and to any creation of form, it also risks irrecoverable loss. Translating Darwish in the poem "Break (Naher el Bared)," where "refugees rewind exile," she writes: "poem is my body my language my country" (49).

Through her poetic translation, Hammad's spoken-word poetry—multilingual, performative, and diasporic—helps us rethink ideas of the "national" and of "belonging."[27] Her language is performed in a fringe form, reflecting what Deleuze and Guattari called "minor literature."[28] It reflects what Stuart Hall has described in "Cultural Identity and

Diaspora" as diasporic identities "that are constantly producing and reproducing themselves anew, through transformations and difference."[29] This
diasporic art proposes a persistent belonging despite the fragmentations
and dislocations of the subject. It is a belonging born out of these historical ruptures and "shifting and transient national identities."[30]

Hammad and other diasporic artists are reconfiguring what is meant
by their art and how they use translation as a way of framing specific
experience, as an "intervention in the visible and the sayable" to shape a
common experience.[31] Their art disrupts dominant forms of belonging,
creating internal difference, and possibly creating a new "subjectivation,"
however provisional that may be.[32]

Between the impossibility of translation and its necessity is an intervention against monolingualism in a plurilingual world. Such an intervention would also examine multilingual practices and the "development
of new languages."[33] In her conclusion, Apter imagines a translation that
"heralds a condition of linguistic postnationalism and denaturalizes
monolingualisation (showing it to be an artificial arrest of language transit and exchange)." In effect, Apter's conception destabilizes the national
links between language, people, and state, creating a condition of "linguistic non-identity."[34] Hammad, on the other hand, seems to rework the
national through the diasporic, charting out a claim of belonging in an
open space of the "here" poem, incorporating peoples who have suffered,
whether through "hurricanes" or "invasions," forging a new language
from the continuation of one language into another, creating passages
out of obstacles. Rather than postnationalism, Hammad shows the necessity of thinking the nation through the diasporic. Her poetry allows us to
rethink belonging without mitigating its reason or its power. It points to
ways in which the diasporic may offer alternative forms of belonging.

Hammad also gestures to the intermedial. Spoken-word poetry or
slam poetry can be situated between poetry and such musical forms as
hip-hop, as we will see in chapter 4.

In bringing together the *intermedial* and the *multilingual* as dissensual practices, Emily Apter establishes translation as a fulcrum for a new
comparative literature, where translation is "a significant medium of subject re-formation and . . . change." Translation is important for conceiving

of a subject differently. She writes: "Cast as an act of love, as an act of disruption . . . translation becomes a means to repositioning the subject in the world and in history, a means of rendering self-knowledge foreign to itself; a way of denaturalizing citizens."[35] It is a dissensual practice, "where the relation between sense and sense continue to be questioned and re-worked," as Jacques Rancière has argued.[36]

If the word *translatio* is a bearing across, a transfer, and, in a manner, a passage, then it inevitably entails that which breaks down and remains enfolded within the abyss of the break. Hammad's poetry announces a loss that the translation carries forth. Apter, citing Alain Badiou, sees the failure of translation as "an enabling mechanism of poetic truth."[37] In the Darwish poem Hammad evoked earlier, the poet set a limit on poetic words as passages, even as he celebrated their creative power. Darwish writes:

> I said to the words: be the crossing of my body with the eternal desert
> . . . .
> this is my language and my miracle . . .
> the sacred of the Arab in the desert
> who worships what flows from rhymes
> like stars on his cloak
> and he worships what he says
> it is necessary for prose then,
> it is necessary for divine prose for the prophet to triumph . . . [38]

Darwish seems to wrestle the poetic word from the sacred past and to connect it to a future. The poetic gaze that can only see the past is not prophetic. And here one recalls the association of *shi'r*, the Arabic word for "poetry," with prophetic vision. As *dīwān al 'arab*, or the register of the Arabs, however, it is connected to an ancient heritage. Poetic language is seen as the only possible triumph not only over time but also over inherited ways of establishing identity. And language is a way of guarding off disappearance "that does not disappear," as Darwish proclaims in the poem. The language of this poem, especially in this passage, recalls the language of the Qur'an in its rhythms and its words. The idea of language as miracle is one of the paramount claims of the Qur'an. As Adonis points out, the Arabic language becomes sacred with Islam, adding even more import to a language that had its poetic weight in pre-Islamic times.

The word "prose," *nathr* in Arabic, also means scattering, dispersal. Prose in its dissemination will also guard against absence. And it is here that Hammad attempts her translation, in this space of dispersal and dissemination of a tradition of Arabic poetry, in this new age that demands new prophets and new languages.

Jacques Derrida reminds us nonetheless in *Monolingualism of the Other* how rare it is to find such a passage. He writes: "the miracle of translation does not happen everyday; sometimes there is a desert without a passage."[39] And yet poetry is sometimes such a passage, and sometimes it delivers on such miracles.

If Hammad in her evocation of Darwish has emphasized the creative power of dispersion, of passage to other languages, poetic forms, and subjectivities in order to belong and to be restored to self, Liana Badr's poetic journey of homecoming has revealed the real historical impasses facing the political and gendered subject. In her poems, Darwish's poetic journey is extended through time and through a gendered voice, intersecting with Badr's journey in its desire for home, for belonging. Badr, foremost among Palestinian and Arab women writers, recounts a voyage of a passage, of going home, in her exceptional collection of poetry *Zanābiq al-daw'* (Lilies of light).[40] Badr is known for her novels, including *Būsala min ajl 'abbād al-shams* (*A Compass for the Sunflower*, 1979), *Nūjūm Arīḥa* (The stars of Jericho, 2002), *Samā' wāḥida* (One sky, 2007, in which she evokes the poetry of Mahmoud Darwish), and *'Ayn al-mir'ā* (*The Eye of the Mirror*, 2009, a work she dedicates to the poet). It was only Mahmoud Darwish, she relates, who took particular note of her poetry.[41] It is noteworthy that she has also produced a volume of novellas, *Shurfa 'alā al-Fakihānī* (A balcony over the Fakihani, 2007), in which she evokes Darwish's poem "Aḥmad al-Za'tar."[42] Badr has directed several films and documentaries, extending her creative abilities through different media in returning to the same literary preoccupations around experiences of women, war, dispersion, and displacement.[43] She has also written a book of criticism on Mahmoud Darwish, dedicated to Darwish and entitled *Taghrīdāt al-shāʿir: Athar al-makān ʿalā al-hawīyya fī aʿmāl Maḥmūd Darwīsh* (The song of the poet: The trace of place on identity in the work of Mahmoud Darwish, 2013).

In the poem "A Voyage in the Mediterranean," originally published in 1994, the beauty and lyricism of the language render more poignant this painful homecoming and the complex state of being suspended between a past that has been left behind and a future that is uncertain. Like Darwish's voyages, it is a sea journey, an ancient poetic motif of exile since at least Homer. The poetic voice tells of the journey back "to the orchards of the ancestors on the land," "to vine groves," "to Jerusalem,"

> where my siblings have siblings
> and my children have their own
> . . . to the walls of my mother's house on the 'shoulder of the valley.'"[44]

In this voyage in the middle of the sea where the past recedes and the future harbors no arrival, she will not be able to return to Jerusalem nor to her mother's house. What she left behind is one last exile, a hospitable refuge in Tunisia, the "golden light" (122), the "air ripe like wheat" (123), which is far behind her now: "A thanks to the warm [*ḥanūn*] refuge," "a sea from almonds" (124). The poetess writes: "I want to awaken so that I can think of the pure dawn" (125), as if this has all been a dream and the reality is one of endless exile and of elusive homecomings: "I am afraid that my heart will transform to a pile of clothes and a pile of bedding, running from one exile to another" (127).

She joins Darwish's poetics in her motifs of exile, and desire:

> When will I awaken from the night's flames,
> traveling to the sunflower fields?
> . . . .
> When is a dream built, o mother?
> Gardens seen after gardens,
> Waves after waves
> From the burning sand in the middle of the water hills. (129)

The collection reflects the progression of the journey, beginning with lyrical love poems, rich in mythological and daily details to the "return," sparse, arid, without reaching home. The final two poems address being at checkpoints and attempting to reach Gaza and Jerusalem. At the end of the collection, the poems are imaginative but the tone is more expressive and more anguished at the injustice and absurdity of not being allowed to visit a place of birth, not being allowed to visit a nearby city.

In the poem "Salālim al-samā'" (Scaling the sky), she recounts being held back at Eres Checkpoint, the entry point to Gaza, and the closing of the entrance:

I try to pass through Eres Checkpoint . . .
it is the exit against the times.[45]

The hardship of the wait is evident:

the elements send the copper light
into our eyes
we listen to the whimpering of water
in the closed bottles. (134)

This interminable waiting, this regular disappointment, is a refrain; the only visible passage without obstacles is that to the sky:

For years and years
it was a temporary life
and despite the long extended ladders to the sky
the gypsies never climbed to the sky. (135)

At the end of this journey, one that attempts a crossing into Gaza, she sees no passages home:

Awake like an owl
searching
for the entrances to my house. (138)

The poetry of Badr is imbued with two exiles from home: from place and into gender. Throughout her writing, it is the woman's voice that expresses the experience of women in war, in love, in life. There is an insistence on women's lives that also stems from a disenchanted knowledge of the expected gender roles that seem arbitrary and trenchant and have unsavory consequences. She writes in a poem ironically entitled "The Horoscopes of Man and Woman":

> The old woman found me
> She, the lady of her tribe,
> Who carries a cane of long days.
> . . . (She speaks to me:) you will know one day
> that you are a girl.[46]

Liana Badr's poetry, like her fiction, evokes multiple experiences of dispossession. In poetry, the lyrical voice affirms itself, its belonging to itself, its possibility to take flight against the waiting and death of Dido, whom she evokes in these poems.

She celebrates instead Ur-Nina in the poem songs included in this collection, a prima donna singer in the Mari empire in the fourth century BC whose statue, Badr notes, stands in Damascus Museum, playing the lyre as she prepares to dance. These poems are dedicated to her, so that she figures in the paratext (dedication and note) and within the poem as a figure who illuminates the journey of the poetic voice, "knowing I will not lose my way on my own, and the Jasmine alone will lead me to my mother's."[47] Jericho is the city evoked as a refrain in these poems and where the poet grew up. The mother-city home whose loss the poet evokes as a desire for an end to travel ends these lines.

This forceful and elegant poetry is fittingly filled with light illuminating a dark experience. Liana Badr's interest in poetry extends to other poets, especially to Fadwa Touqan, the renowned Palestinian woman poet. Badr's film *Fadwa* (1999) poetically and lovingly documents the life of the poetess, her development, her encounters with other Palestinian poets, and her influences on them. In this film, Darwish pays tribute to the force of Touqan on his generation of poets.

If Liana Badr's poetics, like that of Darwish, has emphasized the journey as perpetual dispersion and exile that does not arrive into true homecoming, Ghassan Zaqtan highlights the impact of such violent departures on the subject—a state described so well by Darwish of being suspended elsewhere while another lives one's life. Like Badr, Zaqtan could also be said to be in a state of passage somewhere between the "national" and "diasporic." He was born in Beit Jala and now lives in Ramallah, but he has lived in Lebanon and Tunisia as well as Jordan and Syria. His works of poetry include Ṣabāḥ mubakkir: shiʻr (Early morning, 1980), Tartīb al-waṣf: mukhtārāt (Ordering descriptions: Selected poems, 1998), Istidrāj al-jabal (Luring the mountain, 1998), Ashtar (Ishtar, 2005), and *Like a Straw Bird It Follows Me, and Other Poems* (2012). This last collection, which was translated by Fady Joudah and which won the prestigious Canadian Prize for poetry and the Griffin Poetry Prize in 2013, will preoccupy our analysis.[48]

As Fady Joudah notes in his "Translator's Preface" to *Like a Straw Bird It Follows Me*, many poets and critics agree that Zaqtan is foremost among Palestinian poets; he charts his own path, supported by eminent poets like Darwish, and expresses his own unique poetic voice. Joudah writes: "There are many out there who feel strongly that Ghassan Zaqtan is the most important Palestinian poet writing today. Among them . . . Mahmoud Darwish himself, as he stated in an interview before he died."[49]

In an interview with Jeffrey Brown for PBS, Zaqtan discusses the importance of poetic language as memory, given dispersion and exile, and how memory has a special significance for him in that it is inextricably linked with history, as it was for Mahmoud Darwish and the other poets discussed here: "For this uncertain place, for this uncertain life, . . . we have to protect our history. An entire people has lost its future, has lost its place. And, obviously, poetry is one of the most expressive forms to reach the people. This is why the poets were the first to remind people of their identity."[50]

Zaqtan describes a daily life marked by dispersion, departure, absence, death, and disruption. In the poem "Wolves," which evokes Darwish's verses that were reworked by Hammad, he writes:

The birds' departure from his heart
leaves the plains white
where the story is white
and sleep is white. . . .

. . . .

the voices of those who left long ago.[51]

The poem names itself a lament, "a reckless lament" (31). It is reckless,
for the absence is an endless passage, "the absence that never stops" (32).

Zaqtan evokes Darwish in "The Gambler's Hymn" and in "Wolves,
Also," but Darwish ruminates elsewhere as well in a poetry that is uniquely
Zaqtan's. In the preface Joudah insists on the efforts of the younger generation to chart their own poetic path, given the imprint of Darwish and the
previous generation of poets on Arabic poetry: "Zaqtan and a few other
poets of his generation found themselves in the shadow of a poetry largely
concerned with gathering identity fragments of the individual in a collective mode. And they began to look elsewhere. Zaqtan, through quiet lyric,
focused on . . . palpable daily cares" (ix).

One can argue that Darwish's later poetry also turns more consciously
inward and toward daily cares, and that younger poets have had to contend with a divided self, as has Darwish in his poetry. In the poem "The
One You Accidentally Found in the Mirror," Zaqtan shows the mirror
images of the self and the other, also suggesting a divided self. He reveals
the power relations that are engendered between the self and its other and
the mirroring and reversals of that relationship:

The one you accidentally found in the mirror

. . . .

was there alone thinking of you

. . . .

You used to call him and he'd come

. . . .

Now you recall all this

. . . .

staring at the mirror

. . . .

as he sits in your chair

. . . .

calls to you and you come[52]

Joudah reads this poem as an instance of a divided self as well, where the self is a witness to itself, as if estranged from itself. And yet one could argue that the very image of a mirror, of an identity interrogating itself, is mythological. Zaqtan's poetry, according to Joudah, "moved away from mythologizing exile . . . and honed in on the poem as textural movements, visual and tactile, whose reservoir of everyday things became endless projections that sculpt (or crumble) sound and form" (ix). This poem also recalls Darwish's "As He Draws Away" from the collection *Why Did You Leave the Horse Alone?*,[53] which evokes a poetic voice that finds an image of the "enemy's daughter" in his mirror, the girl with the thick eyebrows living his life for him.

Furthermore, Zaqtan will recall the famous verses of Darwish that he spoke when he returned to Ramallah, evoking precisely exile and home, and appropriately valorizing the home itself over the endless passage: "the house is more beautiful than the path to the house."[54] Zaqtan reworks these verses in his long poem "Alone and the River before Me":

We left, as exiles leave, houses more beautiful than the roads.

. . . .

We dreamt, as residents dream, of roads more beautiful than the
    houses.[55]

In Zaqtan's reworking, he also recalls the other meanings in Darwish's poem, mainly that exile and dispersion are also within the home and that the exilic journey was not for naught. In Zaqtan's verses, the collective predicament is one of being in exile and one of being at home, not unlike Hammad's vision. As Joudah suggests, it is Darwish who published "Alone and the River before Me" with another long poem, "Pretexts," and apparently even gave the title to the poem (x).

In the notes of *Like a Straw Bird It Follows Me*, the translator explains that in "The Gambler's Hymn," the phrase "the poet" refers directly to

Mahmoud Darwish. The verse itself in which this reference is made evokes a famous Darwish poem, "The pigeons fly/the pigeons descend": "written in 1984 and . . . one of [Darwish's] more famous love poems."[56] The Zaqtan verses read as follows:

"the pigeons fly"
which is what the poet said
or
"the pigeons descend."[57]

"Wolves, Also" makes reference to the Darwish poem "As He Draws Away." In this evocation of Darwish's poem, Zaqtan writes:

The enemy comes to drink our tea at night
and leans his Tommy submachine on the wall
The poem was it Darwish's

. . . .
The enemy's daughter was in the shadows
she had thick eyebrows. . . .

. . . .
a voice sprinting out of sleep and a scent of leaving.
. . . .[58]

Darwish's poem "As He Draws Away" is itself a reworking of a poem Darwish wrote decades earlier, "A Soldier Dreams of White Lilies,"[59] in which the soldier decides to leave, for he cannot identify with the image of the nation that is being imposed. In the poem, he is not seen as an enemy.

Zaqtan, evoking Darwish's "As He Draws Away," also envisions an "enemy" who approaches in "An Enemy Comes Down the Hill." The enemy is identified in the poem as a "settler," for those living on hills are living on settlements in occupied Palestine: "and by his being not 'us'/ . . . / death begins."[60] It is precisely this settler violence that requires a forced dispersion of the inhabitants of the land, a complete negation of the other, that is expressed in the man coming down the hill to a town or a village, where numerous people have their livelihood, their history, their connections to place, and are required to be removed (35). Place is being disfigured, the verses suggest, but what is timeless about a place remains.

The newcomers have left no imprint except on the main roads, and they abandon the place "without effort," leaving behind them a trail of losses. In the place there is a continuity that is immutable; the historical disruption will not disfigure the features of the place:

> From the mountain edges, all the caves will appear peaceful
> and the road will seem as it were. (36)

In a very poignant poem that also recalls Darwish's "Fallen House," but that has a power and beauty all its own, Zaqtan's "A Picture of the House at Beit Jala," describes what it means to lose a home, what it means when there is no passage back, when there is no return. Zaqtan begins the poem by announcing a painful feeling that commands a return in order to complete what's been left uncompleted, to restore what has been torn apart, to find some normalcy in the face of loss: "He has to return to shut that window."[61] The stubborn insistence on that specific window, on a life interrupted in its daily tasks and routines, violently marks a trauma:

> It isn't entirely clear whether this is what he must do,
> Things are no longer clear since he lost them. (98)

The poem inscribes a certain disorienting impact of loss on life but also a certain relation of loss and what grounds being. It reveals the destabilizing effect of loss. And it engenders the notion that the lack of certainty ("no longer clear") is also one of loss. The loss that also engenders a lack of clarity creates a void that cannot be situated, filled, or sealed; it engenders the exhausting work of trying to suture the fractures "somewhere within him" (98). Even memory begins to betray one with loss "watching the dust that seems, since he lost the things,/to lure his memories into hoax and ruse" (98). The experience of such devastating loss of home creates other losses, whereby the abjection of that first experience, its sheer magnitude, also distances well-meaning friends:

Since he lost them he stays with friends
who become fewer. (98)

The home is evoked simply as "there" in the poem, that is to say, in
its distance, in not being here, whereas the title of the poem "A Picture of
the House in Beit Jala" names a singular place that is the poet's first home.
The title further specifies that it is a question of a reproduced image, that
the loss has already taken place and is further removed, as if the picture
seals the original loss. The picture itself seems to also be lost, for the evocations of loss in the poem is in relation to "things" in the plural, juxtapos-
ing the loss of that singular home: "Things are no longer clear since he
lost them."

Zaqtan ends the poem by emphasizing how the magnitude of loss
leaves meaning behind and an internal emptiness:

Since he lost them
the day's small
purposes are also no longer clear. (99)

Zaqtan's poems have been described as "melancholic," but this evalu-
ation almost attributes some failing on the part of the one who experiences
the loss, as if the person subjected to loss is unable to accept and to move
on. However, when certain events are of such magnitude, the loss is irrecoverable. That the poet creates beauty out of such pain is a testimony to
him and to a certain refusal to be reduced to the pain of that loss.

A poetic of dispersion unites the poets, as a consequence of a historical experience of rupture and loss, and as a creative promise.

2

"A Coming to Language"
The Cinema of Elia Suleiman, Hany Abu-Assad, and Rashid Masharawi

Like the poetry of Mahmoud Darwish, which innovates within a tradition of Arabic poetry, the cinema of Elia Suleiman, Hany Abu-Assad, and Rashid Masharawi creates a new visual language as it simultaneously situates itself both within world cinema and within local poetics. And it does this most compellingly through ironic humor. Humor becomes a response to the collective predicament of loss and recalls the ironic and the absurd often present in Darwish's poetry. Darwish's work is imbued with complex irony. Edward Said, in *After the Last Sky*, has noted how irony is the dominant Palestinian mode. Said invoked Emile Habiby as well as others who, in their novels and short stories, have "put Palestinian irony on the world map."[1] Palestinian cinema is a visual language that has successfully accessed an international audience, though it fashions itself as Palestinian. The Palestinian films to be discussed are visual counterparts to Darwish's poetics of loss, belonging, dispersion, and dispossession.

In Middle Eastern literatures and cinemas, despite the sometimes solemn subjects, a long tradition of humor exists in which the comic and the tragic intermingle. Palestinian cinema highlights the stakes and place of humor in art and in life. It evokes the following questions: What is film's relation to the political, to power, to representation, to art? Can humor in cinematic art be emancipatory? How does ironic humor face loss? Irony, with its tension with the real and interrogative posture of discrepancies in meaning, has a long history and is particularly suited to examine political realities. If humor signals a certain aesthetic, in sharing with the aesthetic the principles of equality, expressiveness, freedom, and indifference, it also signals a certain anesthetic in its appeal to intelligence rather than to emotion.[2] Is laughter bound to be aporetic?

In the second scene of Hany Abu-Assad's *Al-Janna al'ān* (released in English as *Paradise Now*, 2005), we see Said, one of the two main characters, in a photo shop in Nablus. It is a framing that anticipates and calls attention to the framing of the film and that of Palestinians. Said appears in close-up profile against a synthetic, kitschy background image of what looks like a New England town with a tree in the peak colors of autumn surrounding his profile. Said's face looks serious, in contrast to that of the zealous photographer who insists that Said smile for the photo as he adjusts his subject's position against this imposed background. The stubbornness of both Said, who refuses to smile, and the photographer, who otherwise refuses to take the photo, elicits a comic tension. A matter-of-fact conversation follows about picking up the photo, a photo that will later serve to identify Said after his suicide mission, we later find out. Somehow everything is arranged. The photo and the film come to life in a space of dissension.

Although these early twentieth-first-century films directed by Palestinians center on loss, violence, and death, they strikingly employ humor in its various forms (especially irony, parody, the absurd, and dark humor) to complicate and nuance their representation, as if to portray first and foremost a fundamentally human experience and to reclaim and salvage selves long lost to given representations and tired meanings. They do so also to mark a certain kind of death in life that inhabits those lives the films depict, both from the violence that delivers death and from the deadening daily routines of oppression. Humor emanates precisely from this death, from the mechanical that generates it; humor seems to call for a work of mourning and gestures toward art as a refuge for politics. Analyzing films that were made since 2005, I wish to explore the modalities of humor and the effect of representation on the possibilities for politics in recent Palestinian cinema. I focus on three films produced under Israeli occupation: *Laila's Birthday* ('Eid Mīlād Laila, 2008), directed by Rashid Masharawi; *Divine Intervention* (Yaddun Ilāhiyya, 2002), directed by Elia Suleiman; and *Paradise Now* (Al-Janna al'ān, 2005), directed by Hany

Abu-Assad. In these films, humor opens into politics in its preoccupation with communal life and with freedom.

In *Laila's Birthday*, Abu Laila, a judge turned cab driver, has strict rules for his passengers but faces a typical day of chaos, contradictions, and lawlessness under occupation when he finally breaks down, assumes his judicial role, and passes judgment. In *Divine Intervention*, an image of a Palestinian fighter used as target practice is transformed into a flying female ninja that wages a mythical battle against Israeli Defense Forces, spanning the history of the struggle in a replay reminiscent of video games and popular global action films. In *Paradise Now*, two friends are preparing for a suicide mission. The first friend, to be videotaped in a typical fashion with a prepared speech, is frustrated when he discovers that the video recorder has broken down and did not record his solemn speech; on the third retry, he interrupts his delivery and advises his mother instead on the best place to buy water filters.

These films consciously reflect on the act of representation, on its aesthetic and political dimensions. In representing what seems to defy representation, humor plays a key role, pointing the way to the possibilities and limits of cinematic representation. Humor resists any foregone conclusion or easy interpretation. It also renders all the more haunting the situation depicted. Humor sometimes reaches an aporetic function in constructing and deconstructing meaning, all the more to bear witness to a grave historical reality. The following questions will concern us: Can humor, and cinematic art, allow for a surpassing of "deadening political realities" and offer an "emancipatory aesthetic?"[3] If, according to Jacques Rancière in *Dissensus*, very little if any politics exists today, is art (and specifically film) the displaced space for it?[4] To what extent does humor and loss, often present in Palestinian films, open into politics? Are these filmmakers reconfiguring what is generally meant by art as (true) politics? And if they are, is it no longer art? How are the senses of the individuals under occupation affected? How do these films signal this influence? To what extent do they reproduce, counter, or reconfigure the assault on the senses? These questions are not, of course, limited to Palestinian artists. As I will show, in these films humor evokes a promise of a new communal life, even as it signals limited freedom.

Films have provided a certain visibility to Palestinians in the face of their historical invisibility and the distorted and imposed representations of their identity. Edward Said, in the preface of *Dreams of a Nation*, writes: "Palestinian cinema provides . . . a visible incarnation of Palestinian existence in the years since 1948 . . . by trying to articulate a counter narrative and a counter identity. These films represent a collective identity."[5]

It is this contested collective identity rather than a lack of film production that has contributed to the invisibility of Palestinian cinema and to "a lack of a comprehensive film history."[6] Writing about the Oscar nomination of *Paradise Now* in 2006, Felicia Chan indicates that the controversy around the film "dramatizes the tensions in operation as a cultural identity seeks a political one."[7] Palestinian identity is in fact a political one, given the scattering of a nation. Recent films by Elia Suleiman and Hany Abu-Assad, along with others, have gained international recognition.[8] As coproductions, often financed by European nations, they complicate the notion of "national cinema" and starkly reveal the tensions between national narratives and transnational forces.

Hamid Naficy maintains that Palestinian cinema is "one of the rare cinemas in the world that is structurally exilic, . . . made either in . . . internal exile in an occupied Palestine or under the erasure . . . of displacement and external exile."[9] This heterogeneous corpus nonetheless shares a quest for "nationhood," according to Chan.[10] Hamid Dabashi writes about Palestinian cinema's *statelessness*, what he calls the "geographical absence" that haunts the history of Palestinian cinema to become "the creative core of Palestinian cinema, what has made it thematically in/coherent and aesthetically im/possible."[11] This diversity in content is also reflected in form. Although I focus on three features of Palestinian cinema, cinematic production has ranged from documentaries to experimental films to art video and video installations.[12]

Humor as Intervention

According to Henri Bergson in *Laughter: An Essay on the Meaning of the Comic*, the comic also has to be considered within "the nature of art" and its relation to life, including politics. For Bergson, the comic cannot be entirely situated in either the realm of art or life.[13] It is utilitarian insofar as it aims for improvement, and it is aesthetic insofar as the comical emerges from a certain freedom, "when the society and the individual freed from the worry of self-preservation, begin to regard themselves as works of art" (20). Other writers also argued that freedom was essential for the comic. And yet what happens when there is no such fundamental social or political freedom?

Although laughter signals, as Bergson writes, "a slight revolt on the surface of social life" (200), it nonetheless focuses our attention on mechanical gestures rather than on intentional acts, on missed freedoms.[14] It is precisely the "breakdown" of these gestures into free acts that the films open up and that is considered here.

Laughter, which is not necessarily subject to will, and which is fundamentally *human*, as Bergson has noted,[15] is more significantly a response to a certain mechanism that we witness or that we elicit. The comical is characterized first and foremost by *"mechanical inelasticity"* (10, emphasis in original), whether "introduced into nature" or into the "regulation of society" (47). Bergson writes: "A really living life should never repeat itself. . . . This deflection of life towards the mechanical is here the real cause of laughter" (34). So we laugh when someone living resembles something mechanical or when something mechanical is at the heart of someone living. Ultimately, all humans are prone to rigid habits that turn them against themselves and others (130).

Laughter, then, which can signal a certain aesthetic, in sharing with it the principles of equality, expressiveness, and indifference, also signals a certain anesthetic in that it appeals to intelligence, not to emotion. Bergson speaks of an *"absence of feeling* which usually accompanies laughter," a laughter that "demands something like a momentary anesthesia of the heart" (4, 5, emphasis in the original). Indifference and a social environment are prerequisites for it, even when this social complicity is imaginary: "Our laughter is always the laughter of the group" (6).

If humor's aesthetic qualities open it to the political, in the sense of disrupting the consensual, its social dimension seems to do so as well. Bergson writes: "Laughter must answer to certain requirements of life in common. It must have a *social* signification" (8). Humor, however, proves aporetic. This same social aspect seems to close humor from the political, however, in demanding conformity and consensus. For although a social environment inevitably creates difference, this difference is corrected by laughter in a society that insists on conformity. Social maladaptation and "a *growing callousness to social life*" are sources for laughter (133–34, emphasis in the original). Laughter inevitably implies a relation to power: "Laughter cannot be absolutely just. . . . Nor kind-hearted either. Its function is to intimidate by humiliating" (198). At least since Aristophanes, then, laughter has touched on politics and society. Since then too, comedy has been connected to aesthetic expression and to fantasy.

Rashid Masharawi's *Laila's Birthday* (2008)

Rashid Masharawi's film is not simply a "social satire" that aims to expose and to correct; it is also, to borrow Bergson's language in reference to Mashrawi, "laughter [that] . . . encounters a void" (85). The film was lauded and described as "cinema of the absurd and [a] sociological exposé," as having an "exasperated fidelity to a chronically malfunctioning city," and as a "dark urban comedy,"[16] one that does not "address politics or document holy war."[17] In each of these descriptions, the film is rendered in a depoliticized urban space and its comic aspects separated from any politics, as if Ramallah simply suffers from municipal mismanagement rather than from occupation and the continued dispossession of a nation, as if the film is simply a study of a social group in a random urban setting. In the face of such erasure of the political, it is as if the film itself can be credible and worth watching only if it showed the Palestinians not as occupied people but as persons trying to survive in the midst of corruption that is not attributed to anyone in particular. Such mystification is also evident in the literal translation of the film, the subtitles, which turn the political prisoner, who appears in different scenes as a protester, witness, and emblem of a larger conscience, into a "convict." It is important to distinguish clearly between the social and the political, as Rancière does, "between those who are regarded as capable of taking care of common problems and the future, and those who are regarded as being unable to think beyond private and immediate concerns. The whole democratic process is about the displacement of that boundary."[18]

The film seems to present in the character of Abu Laila subjects who attend to common problems and what those problems may indicate for a common future, as well as to more familial daily matters.

Events of the film take place in one day, which implicitly represents a "typical day": asked by his wife at the end of the film how his day went, Abu Laila, responds, "As usual." And thus his trials signal an extended existence under a singular occupation. His name alone signals a comic tension: rather than his given name of "Jalal," which means reverence, he chooses Abu Laila, a suggestive parody on the patriarchal practice of taking on the name of the firstborn son. The feminine name of Laila evokes the nocturnal world of fantasy. Abu Laila awakes before dawn to a shattering noise, an intrusion from the outside into his home, where evidently he cannot find full refuge. He takes stock of his silent surroundings, opens the balcony and surveys the quiet city, anticipates another day, walks to his daughter's bedroom, returns anxious as he looks at the camera, where a mirror image of himself appears, after which the bustling of the new day begins with preparation for work and school and an announcement of Laila's birthday celebration in the evening, where the father is expected and will oblige.

The workday begins with the useless, ritualistic morning visit to the Ministry of Justice after dropping off the daughter at school. We learn that the entire ministry has recently been replaced, though the concern remains about the decorative aspects of justice, as evidenced by the preoccupation with the replacement of office curtains. As a former judge, a "returnee" seeking to help build a nation, Abu Laila is now a taxi driver. The figure of the returnee reminds us of those who have not returned, and it highlights how the nation is "partially scattered," and by extension that "rights and obligations extend beyond boundaries of nation-states."[19] He establishes strict laws for his taxi, contra the situation in Ramallah, where essential lawlessness, injustice, chaos, and uncertainty reign. These laws, which constitute the basis for comical situations, include not going to the checkpoint, not allowing smoking or weapons in his taxi, and not letting amorous teenagers loiter in the taxi for lack of a private space. The absurdities he encounters include being stopped by a policeman simply because the policeman wants to purchase his taxi for extra income. He services a very limited area, bound by checkpoints, revealing the constrained life under occupation.

In our consideration of art and politics, and how both redistribute the field of the sensible, the film shows how the senses of individuals under occupation are assaulted and saturated, especially by sounds of shelling, helicopters, gunfire, traffic, cell phones, and so on. Laughter is a release that counters this assault. The assault on the senses heightens some senses but not others, signaling a process of dehumanization, an effort at survival, and an eclipsing of the political. The film alludes to this dynamic in many different episodes. One such scene of disorientation is when the main character watches the TV news in a café with a group of men. All are listening and begin to speculate about the images of destruction presented to them, about who the soldiers might be and where the event may be taking place. Is this the work of the Israeli occupation or the American occupation of Iraq? More than a sign of solidarity and a sense that all occupations are alike, the scene seems to point again to the mystification of political oppression through representation, even to those undergoing occupation. Ironically, mayhem breaks out amid the viewers when a shelling occurs in the immediate vicinity, coinciding with their speculations. The shelling breaks down the divide between their reality and the representation on TV that distances them from themselves, framing the limits of representation and the errors of misrecognition. Again, even as they take shelter under a table while they hear more shelling, speculation ensues about whether the shelling is from the Israelis or from internal factional fighting, forcing a sordid and violent collapse between the event and its representation. As Judith Butler points out in *Precarious Life*, "for representation to convey the human, then, representation must not only fail, but it must *show* its failure."[20] All this culminates in a central scene of the film in which the regime of representation and of humor breaks down.

In this scene at a gas station, Abu Laila emerges from his absurdly decorated-for-a-wedding taxi. The appearance of the cheerful car contrasts with the grim toll that the day has apparently taken on him. Standing in a distracted fashion, as the curious worker who fills his car with gasoline watches, Abu Laila becomes increasingly conscious of how his senses are assaulted by the chaos around him, by the previous shelling and the ordeals of a day under occupation. As the noise of traffic, blaring horns, and helicopters becomes intolerable, he takes a loudspeaker—significantly, from a police car that is also filling up at the gas station—to speak out and address his fellow compatriots and the occupiers. He loses control as the tragic seems to coalesce with the comic. He tells two men in stopped cars who are creating a traffic jam to move along, he tells the pedestrians to move onto the sidewalks, he tells the young men carrying arms that they are neither soldiers nor policemen and that if they want to carry arms their place is with the resistance and not among women and children. He does not forget the Israeli helicopters and bitterly lauds their military might. Like the regime of representation in which he is implicated, he breaks down in protest to deliver a judgment, to breach an opening into something new.

The breakdown transforms the mundane space of the gas station into a scene of political protest, of dissensual speech, of judgment. Abu Laila

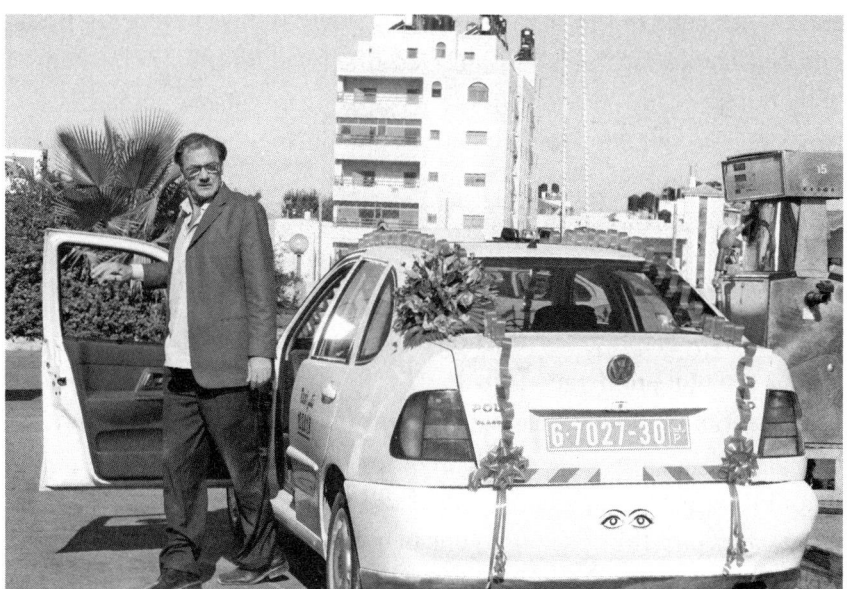

4. Rashid Masharawi, from his film *Laila's Birthday*, 2008, reproduced with permission from Sweetwater Pictures and Rashid Masharawi.

finally passes judgment and assumes the role of judge. His pronounce-
ment brings temporary order. The quest for freedom is articulated,
freedom from incursions of Israeli planes, from chaos, from the dysfunc-
tionality of the everyday in a condition of occupation where authority
has signaled simply policing the everyday. The scene counters the daily
assault on the senses (among other things) with its own assault: first with
speaking out and rupturing the normalcy of the abnormal, then with the
return to the domestic, harmonious sphere. It sets up a new sense of the
aesthetic as political.

On the one hand, the return to the familial sphere becomes an active
way to resist the assault on the senses; on the other hand, instead of pur-
suing the possibilities of this breakdown, the film privatizes it into a family simply coping with the everyday and trying to survive under singular
political circumstances, as if the struggle has been reduced to one simple
form: to endure each day. Andrew Horton and Joanna Rapf write in the
Companion to Film Comedy that comedy, which reflects complex sociopolitical problems, "celebrates the human capacity to endure rather than
to aspire and suffer."[21] Humor in this film is connected to daily endur-
ance. The scene of the "breakdown" also suggests that humor lends dignity and complexity to those subjected to a condition that robs them of
both. In *Divine Intervention*'s ironic appeal to "the fantastic" or in *Paradise
Now*'s regime of contingencies, failures are pursued to their logical end.
In all three films, however, the insistence on the absurd—as that which
is disharmonious and out of joint with *propriety* or reason—brings the
Bergsonian conception of humor to Rancière's notion of *dissensus* as the
disruption of consensus.

In this geography, the reduction of politics to policing is evident. Palestinians, a plural proliferation, abiding by a principle of unity through common experience, political claims, and historical grievances that promise to
extend into the future, are caught between the policing of the Israelis and
that of their leadership. The scene of the breakdown, however, momentarily transforms this space from one of policing to one of politics, albeit a
threatening transformation, as evidenced by the reaction from Abu Laila's
fellow men. As Rancière stated in relation to the general depoliticization
of the public space: "The police . . . say[s] . . . there's nothing to see and so

nothing to do but move along. . . . Politics, by contrast, consists in trans-forming this space of 'moving along', of circulation, into a space for the appearance of a subject: the people, the workers, the citizens. It consists in re-figuring space."[22]

Politics in this film emerges as intimately linked with justice, and with a particular speech act performed as a breakdown of all oppression, pro-visional as this may be, when those excluded or subordinated speak out.[23] This speech act is significantly humorous, a corrective and an index for a life torn apart. Humor insists on common speech. In order to get any-one's attention Abu Laila has to use a loudspeaker, competing with the helicopter noise, the blaring horns, and the numbing indifference, lest his voice be crowded out. Humor here mitigates the pathos that all too often defines the reality of occupation and that becomes the all-too-common representation of the victim. As Rancière indicates, politics is not simply about governance or the proclamation of the "Rights of Man":

> Politics begins when those who were destined to remain in the domestic and invisible territory of work and reproduction, and prevented from doing "anything else," take the time that they "have not" in order to affirm that they belong to a common world. It begins when they make the invisible visible, and make what was deemed to be the mere noise of suffering bodies heard as a discourse concerning the "common" of the community. Politics creates a new form, as it were, of *dissensual* "commonsense."[24]

Like aesthetics and politics, humor creates new realities, "invents ways of . . . seeing, and saying, engenders new subjects, new forms of collective enunciation."[25] However, the danger of retreating into the private realm is to deny Palestinians the status of political beings, to relegate them to a domestic space as a group: "If there is someone you do not wish to recog-nize as a political being, you begin by . . . not understanding what he says, by not hearing what issues from his mouth as discourse. . . . Traditionally, in order to deny the political quality of a category—workers, women and so on—all that was required was to assert that they belonged to the 'domestic' space that was separate from public life."[26]

Before the breakdown scene, Abu Laila takes a woman who has just lost her husband home from the hospital: the scene of silent grief is juxtaposed with the later scenes of the wedding celebration, the anticipated celebration of Laila's birthday, and the many comic scenes ahead. Comedy and tragedy intermingle, as they do in life. The comic, then, is linked to loss and allows for maintaining a certain dignity, which is precisely the first casualty of occupation, rather than falling into banality, senselessness, or being overwhelmed by injustice. Associations of loss and mourning are reinforced throughout the day: the birthday cake to Laila was originally a gift from the wife to her (now dead) husband, whom she thought was simply recovering in the hospital. The structure of substitution and continuation around loss evokes solidarity and community in the face of dispossession. Such a scene of mourning structurally opens onto the possibility of politics in the breakdown scene. Humor and mourning both become responses to loss.

Butler argues that mourning, which necessitates acceptance of a transformation, may open onto politics, for "without the capacity to mourn, we lose that keener sense of life we need in order to oppose violence."[27] Grief provides a sense of community: "If my fate is not originally or finally separable from yours, then the 'we' is traversed by a relationality that we cannot easily argue against."[28] The experience of loss and mourning is one that could inspire solidarity and justice. As Rancière also argues, loss promises a "new form of individual and community life" through an art that could be available to everyone. And the art that engages loss also holds a promise in that it is democratic, even as the promise cannot be altogether fulfilled, as aesthetics remains distinct from politics.[29]

Humor, which also faces loss in these films, does so to pierce through oppressive realities and open possibilities for new realities. Like Masharawi's film, Suleiman's *Divine Intervention* creates new ways of seeing a colonial structure in its painfully absurd effects. Humor allows for seizing the tangible in the everyday in its most profound truth. The human struggle to survive is both elevated and held to unforgiving scrutiny. This poignant chronicle of love and pain, as Suleiman subtitled his film, is a testament to the power of the imaginative to interrogate the real in the ironic marshaling of the fantastic that elicits the film's most memorable humor, and the power to imagine beyond the violence.

At the Limits of Representation:
Elia Suleiman's *Divine Intervention*

The effect of humor on representation can be seen in Elia Suleiman's *Divine Intervention* in the ironic interruption of the "effect of the real" and the introduction of the "fantastic" precisely to question the nature of reality under occupation. Although this film does not present a classic depiction of the fantastic as the supernatural, it does elicit a certain hesitation regarding the status of the real and a certain questioning of the nature of the present reality depicted: one critic asks whether these fantastic scenes express ironic wish fulfillment or bitterly allegorize a history of struggle.[30] By its humorous fantastic imaginings, the film stages and complicates cinematic representation and the national narrative. The introduction of fantastic elements seems to highlight through irony, dark humor, and parody a sociopolitical reality marked by the absurd, where the absurd is henceforth an index for power and for violence, a manifestation of the state of occupation. Suleiman's film starkly reveals the tensions between national affirmations of identity and globalized representations of them. Inspired by global cultural influences—the film is often evoked in relation to the work of Buster Keaton and Jacques Tati in its negotiation of the serious and of humor, in its reflection on humor, and its place—the film represents the political in the mundane and insists on transnational cultural connections in the face of internal rifts in the relations between the self and other.

The film is preoccupied with loss and dispossession. It asks, as does the film scholar Gonul Dönmez-Colin: Is memory enough when making a film about "people and places that are disappearing"?[31] It also asks: How does one represent differently? And, as Butler posed the question, "How does the diasporic 'inform/disrupt' ideas of the national?"[32]

Presented as a chronicle, *Divine Intervention* is a mosaic in which everything is in a liminal state since the present is one of struggle and continual loss. Events seemingly lack coherence and happen without any context, which creates a poignant effect, both comical and alienating, and which the introduction of the fantastic amplifies. The visual narration, the use of a static camera and wide shots, suggest stifling tedium in Palestinian life and create the effect of the absurd that the film depicts as everyday sociopolitical reality. Such a state of loss is ritualized into everyday social interaction, so that all relations between the self and the other are violently constrained within this state's bounds. The narrator, E. S., portrayed as a filmmaker and a silent witness to his own life, has to meet his lover at the Ram checkpoint since they live on different sides of it. As such, they both witness and therefore endure daily Israeli harassment of Palestinians. The film begins in his birthplace, Nazareth, and ends in Jerusalem, thereby encapsulating his own life and that of Palestinians from the Nakba of 1948 to the occupied present.

Suleiman's work significantly employs fantastic images, eclectically borrowed from video games and films; these original images seemingly escape the confines of Palestinian national identity only to reaffirm them. Three scenes constitute the intervention of humor through the fantastic. The first shows E. S. driving to see his ailing father. As he finishes off an apricot, he throws the pit out the window, striking and blowing up a military tank with it. The second shows his female friend crossing the Ram checkpoint on foot against the orders of the Israeli soldiers, which causes the guard tower to fall. The scene I am concerned with is the climax of these episodes and of the film. It involves a female "ninja" figure facing Israeli armed men. The image of the Palestinian that serves as target practice is transformed before the eyes of the attackers into a fighting and flying ninja, "essentially casting the Israelis in the role of Goliath."[33]

Significantly, the incorporation of the fantastic is a humorous staging of representation.[34] If the fantastic is what presumably departs from the real and calls it into question, the real itself has become in the film a theater of the fantastic. In this final scene, the fantastic consists of a representation, an image coming to life and becoming a reality. It is this incongruity of a flying ninja in this typical West Bank landscape juxtaposed with the familiar militarized figures that elicits laughter and is emblematic of the absurd. The frame of the ninja scene, which begins with an image

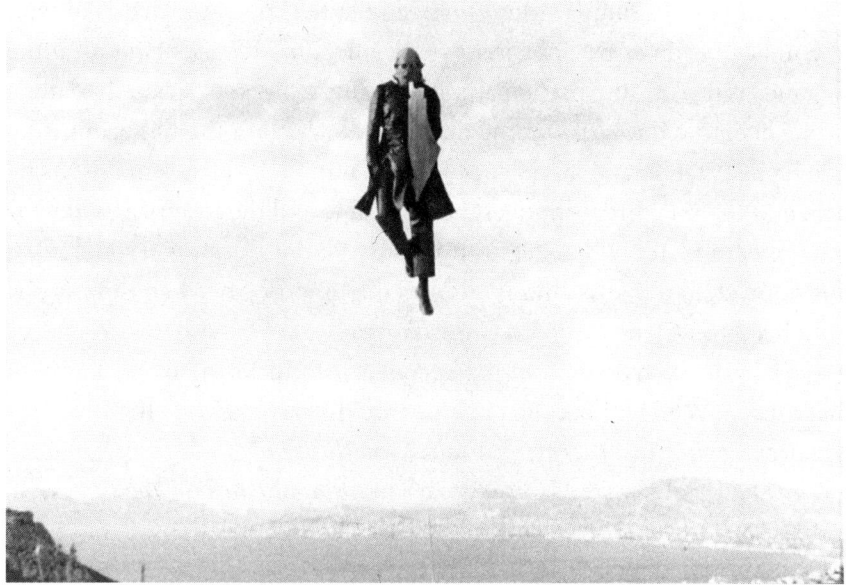

5. Elia Suleiman, from his film *Divine Intervention*, 2002, reproduced with permission from Elia Suleiman and Pyramide International.

of a female ninja and returns to that same image after the confrontation, presents the conflict and face-off as one of representation and hence of political existence: it signifies who has the power to represent, who creates images of others, who diffuses these images. In a parody of multiple genres, the escalation of the violence spans the history of the conflict. The ninja, head covered in a *kuffiyeh* and dressed in black, begins in response to throw stones, then Molotov cocktails, and then throws an Islamic crescent at her opponents, who are using heavy military weapons.

Everything is mediated by the image. The scene stages dominant representations about Palestinians that presumably "justify" more violence against them. When the image of that same Palestinian serves as a target of violence and comes to life as a female ninja figure, it shows the effect of representation on reality. At the same time it presents the struggle of Palestinians against overwhelming force in affirming a national identity. At the end of the scene, the Israeli commander stands alone in a desolate landscape, oblivious to the image of the Palestinian as militant that he projected onto the ninja. More than simple testimony to what is absent, the image becomes part of a struggle, challenging representations on the ground, as it were, and participating in forging a different space. The ninja scene becomes the focus for the disparate elements of the film, rupturing the representation and its violence that are imposed on Palestinians.[35] The real and the imaginary connect the mundane and the historical, whereby film offers a memory that begins from a particular Palestinian standpoint, draws on shared myths, and is addressed to a more global community. If film becomes a repository of a certain memory, in Darwish's work, poetry, especially in its lyric-epic form, becomes a form for memory. Darwish has asked: "Who will narrate our story, we the passersby . . . the banished from place and from myth."[36] From *Limātha tarakta al-ḥiṣān waḥīdān?* (*Why Did You Leave the Horse Alone?*) to *Athar al-farāsha* (*The Butterfly's Burden* or *A River Dies of Thirst*) a reflection on the relationship of poetry to history is never absent.

Poetic memory shapes "cultural identity for a people fighting for its identity."[37] Darwish writes: "Memory . . . can anchor a place in its place, not only because place is in us even if we're not in it, but because hope is the weapon of the weak."[38] Poetic memory is a song that is related to a people without an effective home.[39] Darwish's questions, "What does it mean for a Palestinian to be a poet? And what does it mean for a poet to be Palestinian? . . . The first and second questions are one, undivided, and at the same time do not altogether meet,"[40] have now translated into artists reflecting as well on what it means to be an artist and Palestinian, but also what it means to be Palestinian in the diaspora.

The fantastic highlights Suleiman's cinematic language, which "juxtaposes two versions of reality—one present and the other absent, each concealing yet exposing the other."[41] The tendencies of the fantastic seem to also be those of dark humor: Probing "disparate concepts without attempting to reconcile them, favoring the fantastic, . . . [revealing] the 'gap' between appearance on the surface and reality underneath."[42] Dark comedy, which characterizes the work of Elia Suleiman, involves using *irony* "to attack an apparently absurd universe." This irony in Suleiman is not unlike that of Darwish. It is marshaled against the senseless.

It constitutes a critical vision of history. Moreover, it is an irony invested in the present. It carries a distant vision and an intimate pain. It employs violent images in which "there is little sense of hope," as we witness in the ending of this scene and the ending of the film.[43] It is through the fantastic that Suleiman achieves a dark humor, allowing him to focus on the process and consequences of representation, on how representation serves as an essential component of the political conflict and as a challenge to his cinematic endeavor.

We see this tendency of dark humor in the use of symbols in this scene, such as the map of Palestine, the colors of the flag, the crescent and star, the halo of bullets. Nutith Gertz and George Khleifi argue that Suleiman's use of symbols is double edged, introducing the historical symbols of the struggle and placing them in a virtual space. While Suleiman "exposes . . . the fictitious status of these symbols through the use of parody, absurdity, and humor, he also searches for the truth behind them and renews their lost significance."[44] Through these symbols, the intervention of the fantastic renews Palestinian struggle and its affirmation of national identity.

In borrowing from biblical myths and visual popular culture, Suleiman articulates an ironic expression of identity that escapes the narrow confines of nationalism but manages a necessary articulation of self in the face of an aggressive negation and appropriation. Besides being the most spectacular and the most sophisticated scene in the film, the ninja scene testifies to violence under occupation.

The fantastic also becomes a way to face the anguish of loss. Sobhi al-Zobaidi argues that "poetic and imaginary means . . . provide Palestinians with the virtual worlds they need in order to negotiate their loss and confinement . . . [they are] driven towards virtual worlds in search of continuity."[45] It is this unexpected distance from reality, or the collapse of reality into the fantastic—where an apricot pit, for example, is able to blast a military tank, and where the driver continues on nonchalantly—that elicits the laughter. The all too real violence of everyday military occupation is reworked and transformed through the imaginary into a virtual response that calls it into question and defies it.

The fantastic—and dark humor—attempts to achieve what is impossible in reality, to bring together what has been torn asunder: "to break down the stifling blocked borders . . . to reunite the fractured space and to rejoin the divided identity."[46] In response to Gertz and Khleifi, Zobaidi compellingly notes, however, that it is not simply a question of breaking down roadblocks but also of facing the effacement of Palestinians and their claim to the land: "Palestinian cinema . . . goes beyond 'roadblock movies' around which identities clash, power is practiced, and struggles take place . . . it is not the roadblock that presents the crisis, but memory itself."[47] Through humor and fantasy, *Divine Intervention*, which ends on a foreboding note that amplifies the seriousness of the Palestinian predicament under occupation, allows for the possibility of overcoming cinematic obstacles in creating another space in cinema.

Suleiman enacts a nuanced and compelling cinematic representation by means of the introduction of humor and the fantastic. In going against prevalent narrations of Palestinian identity, the film reveals the real possibility that politics will rupture consensus in the face of continued fragmentation of geography, people, and memory. In this act of representation that borders on testimony, Naficy writes, "Suleiman . . . gives voice to the film—with all the muteness, inarticulateness, and trauma of coming into language that are the hallmarks of his work."[48] It is in this innovative cinematic endeavor that Suleiman offers fantastic humor to *present* what eludes *representation*.

Hany Abu-Assad's *Paradise Now* (2005)

Paradise Now, which takes place from 2000 to 2005 during the second Intifada in Nablus, historically a key site of resistance to the Israeli occupation,[49] tells the story of two friends, Said and Khaled, who have signed up for a suicide mission together. Living under occupation and working precariously in a garage to support their families, their future is uncertain. Said's father was executed, presumably for being a collaborator, when Said was only ten; Khaled perceives his father as capitulating in his struggle against the Israelis in the first Intifada. The two young men undergo a change and come to radically different decisions regarding the suicide mission. Whereas Said wavered and Khaled was convinced, a reversal takes place with the introduction of a contingency. Together the two positions constitute a chiasmus and a political impasse.

At the heart of the film is the possibility of contingency, which becomes the source of humor and its unraveling: something inexplicably goes wrong. The contingent leads to the breakdown of representation and of the operation itself in the scene of Khaled's repeated speeches. Yet it also allows for humor and representation. This contingency offers an innovative aesthetic and possibly a new politics. Politics, as Rancière has suggested, is predicated on a "radical contingency."[50]

This early scene introduces contingency in representation through its malfunctioning when the video recording fails, leading to other complications. The humorous and sober scene is a deconstruction of a genre of representation around suicide bombing. The scene opens with a photographer facing us, the viewers, as if he is about to take a photo of us. Behind him are a group of men watching, including Said and Jamal, the facilitator of the mission. We are situated by the camera in the place of Khaled, who is about to give a speech before he carries out his mission. Then the photographer takes a video camera and begins recording. The camera now frames Khaled. There is a gradual close-up of Khaled as Said looks on gravely. Khaled begins his speech solemnly with familiar recitations from the Qur'an; he addresses his father and mother in formal Arabic, which is itself incongruent and deflates the solemnity. When he has finished, he asks: "So how was it?" This naïve concern about his performance given the reality of death that waits is both comical and startling. The photographer indicates nonchalantly that the camera had not recorded anything. Something went wrong. Repetition ensues, this time with an audience eating sandwiches. It is a repetition that unhinges unreflecting discourses of heroism. Once again, we are being photographed and videotaped, and Khaled's performance comes to a stop as before. The camera is not working again. In the third try, we now see the back of Khaled and the front of the video photographer. We are still in the film, framed on the side of Khaled. Khaled suddenly stops after he launches into his prepared speech and offers his mother some advice about the best place to buy water filters. It is as if this faltering performance will unhinge many things, among them the resolve of Khaled.

The breakdown of representation is highlighted in the film, indicating representation's power and shortcomings as well as the need for alternative visions. Late in the film, Said tells his story in an effort to convince the organizer to let him carry out his mission. He represents himself against what he perceives and what he proclaims as the occupier occupying all roles, leaving none for the occupied, an echo also of the Darwish verses in which others live his life instead of him.

Said's recorded performance is much more solemn, as if to signal how humor also risks falling into the senseless, risks robbing the dignity of living beings. Said's words launch the visual preparations of the body with the participation of the sounds of Qur'anic recitations. The camera moves in a continuous circle, which seems to be in harmony with the space in which Said and Khaled find themselves. As it circles, a shift signals the advancing of the purification ritual to prepare the bodies for burial (usually performed after the bodies are dead). The camera creates a visual rhythm to the sounds of the Qur'anic recitation that come to a closure with an image reminiscent of the Last Supper in Bunuel's *Viridiana*. We see a large wooden table with Said and Khaled at the center and the group of men next to them sitting for lunch. The idea of the martyr (and witness) in this scene transcends their religious identities. The emphasis seems to be on fluid, harmonious, creative art even as the film portrays a scene of preparation for death, a death out of joint with nature and custom. The scene is highly aesthetic with its visual tableaux, rhythmic Arabic of the Qur'an, circular and continuous camera movement, juxtaposition of Said's solemn words and images of the purification rites for the dead. A recurrent motif in the film is that "life is death under occupation." As Said and Khaled reiterate, "under occupation we are already dead" and "in this life, we are dead anyway."

Said describes occupation as "life imprisonment." Among its crimes, he states, is that "it breaks any resistance, it ruins families, it destroys morals and people." It is in this sense that collaboration is the principal drama in the family life of Said and the others. The popular consumption of videos of executions of collaborators, as we see in one scene, is indicative of this destruction. In addition to showing the abject violence of occupation, and of some of the responses to it, the film shows how the struggle is political first and foremost. No one can maintain a neutral position, not even the viewer who is framed at several instances within the bounds of the film and who is confronted by the gazes of the characters in the last scene. The viewer is not allowed the luxury of aesthetic distance. In the emphasis on loss of life and ravages to the family, the film differs from the resilient vision in *Laila's Birthday* where the family is the bedrock that allows the individual to endure.

What strikes one about this film that treats such a thorny political issue is its beautiful aesthetic, especially its visual elements, which perhaps serve to highlight the beauty of place and a way of life often forgotten in the damage to daily life. Two different worlds are portrayed: the old city of Nablus, with its Ottoman stone houses and ravaged vestiges from the violence of occupation, is juxtaposed with images of modern and prosperous Tel Aviv, less than an hour away, that depict the semblance of a "normal life." The separation of political narrative and aesthetic is deceptive. A complex relation exists between them, as is evident in many of the scenes.

Paradise Now, which is not only a "buddy story" but also has elements of a "romantic comedy," presents what seems like a sardonic reflection on cinema and the Palestinians in an early scene. As Suha asks Said about his hobbies one night at her house, she wonders if he likes to go to the cinema. Said explains that there is no cinema in Nablus, that he and his peers burned the Cinema Rivoli ten years ago in protest against Israel for not allowing Palestinian workers into Israel. Suha asks: "Why cinema?" Said responds: "Why us?" Said asks a question that has plagued Palestinians politically from the beginning but it has not found a hearing. The question implies that the regime of politics has been elsewhere and that Palestinians have borne the burden of history.

As she continues her questions about his possible preferences in cinema, she asks, "What genre?" He responds, "The kind that frustrates." She: "Like what?" He: "Like life." Whereas art always takes on a life of its own, not being solely bound to external constraints, excising life from Palestinian art is not innocent. A discussion follows around struggle and the many ways of resistance. For Suha resistance should always be "nonviolent"; for

Said, the forms of violence that are imposed already determine the nature of the struggle. There are different positions in the film regarding struggle. Khaled tells Suha that she is changing a political struggle into an ethical one: "You want to change the struggle into morals; Israel doesn't have morals." He seems to concede to her point of view later in the film when he becomes skeptical about the suicide mission. A distinction between the political and the ethical, however, need not lead to a political struggle that negates ethics.

Austere in its aesthetic, elegant in its cinematography, the effect of the film is nonetheless political rather than simply the pleasurable, technically innovative, or beautiful. The film is an art of experience as well as an art of expression. Like the other films discussed, it sets up a new sense of the aesthetic beyond pleasure and beauty: political scenes reframe the aesthetic as political. In fact, the film announces this intent to reframe. Said worries that the effect of his story may be "entertaining people whose lives are a little better." Indeed, he muses, "the world watches indifferently."

In the final scene, each principal character looks at the camera, looks at us, finally, then the camera goes to a close-up of Said's eyes looking at us. Then white. This scene captures *dissension*, an aesthetic that breaks the regime of representation and reconfigures the field of the sensible: it looks back, implicates us, and refuses to repeat the violence.

The three films, similar to other recent Palestinian films not discussed in this chapter, use humor as a critical lens through which to assess daily life and loss under occupation and as an index for a political impasse. More than that, humor, in its ability to "partition the sensible . . . the visible and the sayable," can be aligned not only with aesthetics, as Bergson has argued, but with politics as well, as Rancière demonstrates.[51]

Such humor proliferates and has received a warm welcome from its audiences, following the literary tradition of Palestinian authors such as Mahmoud Darwish and Emile Habiby, and there is no indication that such filmic engagement with humor is fading out, given the recent short films of Abu-Assad and Suleiman's latest film, Al-Zamān al-bāqī (*The Time That Remains*, 2009). One notes a proliferation of programs on Palestinian television incorporating humor as well.

Although Palestinian film may not be the most viable arena for politics, it has significantly allowed for it in its absence elsewhere. Film has emerged as a space of dissent, one with multiple voices and visions. Through the filmmakers' innovative (if provisional) dismantling of a familiar regime of representation, the films discussed in this chapter push through humor and beyond humor to reconfigure the assault on the senses and lives delivered by occupation and by discourses that maintain it, to an aesthetic that neither harmonizes the violence into a simple effect of the beautiful nor falters on its innovative possibilities. Humor opens into a space of critique and affirmation of the self's aspirations for freedom. In their responses to loss, specifically through the ironic and the absurd in the tradition of Palestinian writers like Habiby and Darwish, the films provide an uncompromising terrain for politics.

3

A Memory for Disappearing Archives
The Visual Art of Contemporary
Palestinian Artists

In the past decade, Palestinian aesthetic production—local and diasporic—has been gaining increasing visibility and recognition on the
international scene. In addition to writers and artists such as Suheir
Hammad, Ghassan Zaqtan, Elia Suleiman, and Hany Abu-Assad, Emily
Jacir's prestigious Hugo Boss Prize in 2008 and Sharif Waked's exhibits
in the Tate Modern and the Guggenheim are but the latest examples
of the growing appreciation for Palestinian artistic expression. In addition to the long and distinguished careers of Kamal Boullata and Mona
Hatoum, artists such as Steve Sabella, Khalil Rabah, Raeda Saadeh,
Rula Halawani, Taysir Batniji, Zeyad Dajani, Rana Bishara, Sandi Hillal,
Hani Zurob, Raeda Saadeh, and many others have also gained international recognition.[1]

These artists are also *"visual counterparts"* to writers such as Mahmoud Darwish, Ghassan Kanafani, Emile Habiby, and to film directors
such as Rashid Masharawi, Elia Suleiman, and Hany Abu-Assad.[2] Indeed,
this has been the main purpose of the book, to show how artists in different media and in different corners of the Palestinian diaspora innovate
uniquely and join the poetic legacy of Mahmoud Darwish in reassem-
bling a disappearing homeland. Let us now turn to this struggle against
erasure. Memory testifies to a belonging that cannot be denied, against
efforts of effacement. Palestinian cultural expression is marked by unique
images, language, and a "defiant memory."[3] Like the poems of Darwish,
this art ultimately transforms and reinvents tradition through medium,

image, and language.[4] It also transforms prevalent notions of identity and belonging, ultimately inscribing new visions of "home."

The recognition of these artists is crucial to the dissemination of an artistic experience that has historically remained on the margins and points to a wider and more extensive experimentation that is taking place in the Palestinian cultural scene. Have the 1990s heralded a new period of creativity in the wake of Oslo and "as a result of the decentralization of the Palestinian political scene," as Ilan Pappé argues?[5] Kamal Boullata notes the number of women among the leading innovators and points to the challenges of tracing developments in Palestinian art "across disconnected territories and different cultural environments."[6] Likewise, Gannit Ankori writes: "More recently the Palestinian artists—notably Vera Tamari, Samia Zaru, Samia Halaby, Tina Sherwell and Bashir Makhoul—have continued to dominate the fields of art commentary and historiography."[7]

Palestinian artists, transnational, local, and diasporic, are creating new artistic forms and articulations of self in the way they employ performance art and media.[8] "Performance" indeed becomes "a necessary concept in understanding artistic responses to power."[9] Henceforth, it is "dislocations" that will inform the notion of "belonging."[10] As diasporic identities, Palestinian artists are "constantly producing and reproducing themselves anew."[11] These artists are situated at the intersection between different places, languages, and art forms.[12] Boullata writes: "Place is an incessant factor that often predisposes the formation of art and how each period in art's development unfolds in the context of its association with the different place in which the art creativity has been undertaken."[13]

Yet the study of the contribution of these artists remains in its inception. Kamal Boullata's *Palestinian Art: From 1850 to 2005* (2008) is a seminal text. Gannit Ankori's *Palestinian Art* (2006) was the first substantial book in English dedicated to art in the Palestinian context. Several other books have appeared that touch on Palestinian art, such as Fran Lloyd's *Contemporary Arab Women's Art: Dialogues of the Present* (1999), Nada Shabout's *Modern Arab Art: Formation of Arab Aesthetic* (2007), and Irit Rogoff's *Terra Infirma: Geography's Visual Culture* (2000). As Kamal Boullata has indicated in *Palestinian Art*, this lack of documentation has to do as well with the relatively marginal status of the visual arts in Arab culture. Historically, it is the poetic word that has been privileged above all. Palestinian art remains marginal in the art world globally,[14] which has led to challenges in constituting a historiography of this art. Kamal Boullata writes of the "difficulties in tracing developments amidst ruptures, fragmentations, discontinuities and displacements across disconnected territories and different cultural environments. . . . Poetry continued to be revered as the supreme form of self-expression. That is partly why the interpretation of metaphors and allegories in Palestinian art could only be understood in the context of the popularized images that have first been articulated verbally."[15]

Boullata distinguishes between those artists who stayed and those who remain in the diaspora. He argues for "a correlation between artistic style and 'proximity to the land,'" suggesting that artists who remain in Palestine tend to espouse figurative art, whereas those who live in exile adopted the language of abstraction, although this divide is increasingly being bridged when one considers local artists like Tayseer Barakat, exilic artists like Steve Sabella, or diasporic artists like Eman Haram.

Marked by its diversity, whereby dispersal and rupture, which began in 1948, become points of inscription, this aesthetic corpus does not relate a unified story of the Palestinian experience. Narratives about Palestinian art tend to locate its beginning in 1948, although many acknowledge that a vibrant art movement existed before the Nakba and is now difficult to trace, since much of the artwork was lost to looting from homes after their inhabitants fled.[16] Whereas Jerusalem was the art center as well as the cultural capital of Palestine pre-1948,[17] today it is difficult to locate a center for Palestinian art.

The diversity of the artists is evidenced by their individual vision; each of the artists "grapple with his or her personal identity or concerns vis-à-vis gender, home, genealogy and national identity in a different way."[18] As Edward Said has noted in *After the Last Sky*, it is impossible to compose a single narrative of the Palestinian experience.[19] Ankori emphasizes the recent proliferation of works: "Given the scope of this tragedy, it becomes understandable why, even among Palestinians, attempts to narrate the story of Palestinian art have been few and far between, gaining momentum only during the last decade."[20]

Although each artist interrogates the notion of "identity" in his or her own manner, it is the negotiation of the personal and the collective, the historic and the aesthetic, that they seem to share.[21] The artists resist efforts to make them *representative*: "These women artists are not representative of Palestinian artists or other women . . . Arab or otherwise . . . nor are they . . . outside of the historical and the particular."[22] Boullata demonstrates how the concept of "identity" is complicated and nuanced for these artists who are uneasy with fixed demarcations of identity, whose "work derives its lucidity and power from personal experience and the specificity of time and place . . . wherein the personal and the political are entwined . . . a process where each [artist] developed her own strategies of resistance to mainstream conventions."[23]

Boullata argues that "memory of place" unites Palestinian artists of the post-Nakba period, despite their dispersal.[24] Not only is the medium, in its diverse use by these artists, preoccupied with memory, but it becomes itself a "defiant memory," to use Said's term, which articulates a "logic of irreconcilables . . . unwilling to let go of the past" while being marked by change.[25] Loss and the need for memory transcend the particularities of identity without eclipsing the historical.[26]

More than individual visions, the works reveal a tentative, uncharted community of creation and reconfiguration of identity. They still convey local cultures imbued with changes and are "actively involved in the creation of specific . . . identities."[27] Palestinian art has incorporated aspects of global culture to affirm its national belonging and has addressed itself to international audiences, which "raises questions about . . . the roots of these relations and ideas."[28] Palestinian exilic artists contest, remember, and transform as they remain deeply rooted in Palestinian life.

Like the poems of Mahmoud Darwish, Emily Jacir's visual artwork *Where We Come From*, included in Emily Jacir-*Belongings: Arbeiten/Works 1998–2003* (2004); Eman Haram's photo exhibits *Iconographies* and *Involuntary Memory* (2006), as well as photos available at Saatchi Gallery; Mona Hatoum's and Sharif Waked's recent artworks; and Till Roeskens's *Videomappings: Aida Camp, Palestine* (2009), as well as Rehab Nazzal's art, inscribe a memory—intimate and plural, fluid, and *performative*, across many displacements—that resists systematic erasure of collective history and a loss inherent in any displacement.[29] It is a memory that spans many transformations. Rather than simply preserving a memory of what was, before any displacement or loss, these artists present an artistic reenactment of the process of effacement of collective memory, all the while presenting an art that sutures the ruptures by its enactments and gathers the shards of lives. Loss is no longer of an event passed, but emerges as a continual experience of dispossession. One notes a dynamic search for form that could speak to the loss. These artists offer an aesthetic that expresses profound experiences of displacement, fragmentation, belonging, and transformation. No longer simply a postmodern tendency, loss is very much a result of history.[30] Boullata writes that grouping these individual artists across this fragmentation is important to fully understanding how their work responds to their present and reflects their cultural heritage; it entails "finding lineages where discontinuities prevail and recognizing affiliations across fragmentation."[31] Although Said has long noted the fragmentary mode of Palestinian narratives, "the essence of fragmentation has penetrated the art-making process itself, effecting its syntax, style and poetics at the very core."[32] Fragmentation in fact permeates these artworks: "Everywhere in these texts and images we find maps that separate and fragment and embody conflict while the foods and soaps and laundry blueing across the lines of imaginary belongings."[33] Their production reveals how the political need not be at odds with the aesthetic. If the political is reconfigured, as it is in the productions of Palestinian artists, as the concern for the other and the insistence on the human experience, then their art may well be political.

Emily Jacir's Private Archives

Emily Jacir's visual artwork *Where We Come From* speaks of the fundamental link between memory and loss, life and art, personal exile and collective displacement in order to express a belonging to a place, to a past, to a people with a claim: the piece, she writes, "[comes] from my experience of spending my whole life going back and forth between Palestine and other parts of the world."[34] At the heart of her work is the question of belonging, just as it is in Suheir Hammad and other artists examined thus far. Jacir says her work "is about passing through places. It is my lived experience wherever I am."[35] One art critic also reiterates the importance of home for Jacir: "Here, stories testify to a life of longing to be at home, as well as to a place—Palestine—that may not be a nation but is nevertheless a *powerful state of belonging for a displaced people.*" It is a belonging that persists against "that sense of fractured geography."[36]

Where We Come From performs both the displacement of Palestinians, the restrictions on their movement, and the will to reconnect and overcome obstacles. The artist herself, an American citizen, is able to travel everywhere. In this work she carries out personal requests of Palestinians who cannot go home or cannot cross certain borders of their country to see friends or family, who ask her to visit particular places and people dear to them. In documenting her visits in photographs, she reveals the absurd and abject circumstances in which Palestinians often find themselves, conditions under which, among other things, they lack freedom of movement. She states: "I have seen the deliberate fragmentation of our lands and the isolation of our people from each other by the Israelis. This is an extreme form of violence. For me, this piece was a dialogue between ourselves across these artificial islands and borders that have been created."[37] Her photos reflect the dispersion that she tries to overcome: images of absence mark incomplete lives, and yet they create links with others.[38]

One personal request is from Jihad, identified in *Belongings*, an Arabic English bilingual text, as "Born in Shati Refugee Camp, Gaza City/ Living in Ramallah/Gazan I.D. card/Father and mother from Asdud/ (exiled in 1948)." The request reads: "Visit my mother, hug and kiss her. . . . Visit the sea at sunset and smell it for me and walk a bit . . . enough. Am I greedy? . . . I left Gaza for Ramallah in 1995 and cannot go back. I also cannot move to any place in the West Bank because of the Israeli restrictions." A note is included at the bottom describing the visit, how they had tea, how the mother inquired after Jihad. The color image next to the text shows the back of the artist as she holds and kisses the mother, who is closer to the viewer.[39] Jacir's work testifies to irrecoverable loss and to a belonging that persists against all fragmentation.

Ultimately, her images are a "memorial to untold stories":[40] "anti-images, unspectacular private pictures," "a self-portrait which also speaks collectively of a people," a "personal archive as a proxy for the disappearing archives of Palestine."[41] Edward Said has written that archives are often subject to destruction in conditions of conquest because they indicate a history.[42] The artist nonetheless recognizes certain paradoxes of her art project: "*Where We Come From* is a failure in some way. I am not sure how to reconcile the notion that non-Palestinians are being entertained by our sorrows and dreams."[43] Consequently, she is no longer allowed to go to Gaza and to certain parts of the West Bank: "Jacir could not create this work today."[44]

Calling her work a "poetic commemoration, . . . at once politically engaging and life affirming,"[45] critics also see it as "a self-portrait which also speaks collectively of a people that remains waiting interminably at the airport."[46] Loss is seen as fundamental to her art, which resists it.[47] Referring to Jacir's performative work, *Change/Exchange*, John Menick asks: "And isn't something here lost as well, albeit not as precious as land or human lives, but perhaps, as in the case of Palestine, as frustratingly irreclaimable?"[48]

Material for a Film continues the work of commemorating loss and visually inscribing the otherwise forgotten lives. Here, Jacir returns to history, to the targeting of Palestinian intellectuals. More than "a traumatic repetition,"[49] it is a tribute performance to commemorate the assassination of the Palestinian intellectual Wael Zuaiter in Rome by Israeli intelligence agents in 1972 in retaliation for the killing of the eleven Israeli athletes at the Munich Olympics. Michael Wise questions the basis for this targeted killing: "Palestinian factions vigorously denied it, and subsequent accounts by investigative journalists have also raised doubts that he was involved in those killings."[50] Although *Material for a Film* was initially performed and filmed at the Sydney Biennale in 2006, where Emily Jacir shot a gun at a thousand blank books, it is a film in the form of an installation that premiered at the Venice Biennale in 2007.[51] Commenting on her artwork, Jacir seizes on a detail in the original assassination where one bullet hit the copy of *A Thousand and One Nights* that Zuaiter was carrying with him, showing that what is targeted is not only the lives of Palestinians but also their stories, their histories, their cultural work, their claims to belonging:

He was killed by 12 bullets at close range to his body, but there was a 13th bullet which struck his copy of "A Thousand and One Nights." Wael's dream had been to translate "A Thousand and One Nights" directly from Arabic into Italian. . . . This alone inspired an entire performance in which I shot 1,000 books each with one bullet using the same gun the Mossad had used to kill Palestinians in Europe. The books were white, and they were blank and symbolized the thousands of stories that have not been written and will not be written.[52]

Jacir reveals the volumes of blank pages that were to be filled with a thousand stories, reviving the story of Zuaiter's life and contesting his untimely and excessively violent death:[53] "He was the first target and an innocent man. . . . He was also a pioneer in trying to tell our story to the outside world. Wael Zuaiter was a poet and a translator who despised all forms of violence."[54]

And yet Jacir resists the impulse to narrate, the impulse for stories to substitute for lived lives, and tries to protect the vital present of these lives: "If all we have left of ourselves are stories, then in some ways we are already dead."[55] The limits to commemoration are signaled in the white pages and in the white walls of the installations: they "acknowledge the irrecoverable nature of the significance of his life, as much as its unfulfilled potential."[56] If Hammad had been "born to tell this story," Jacir recognizes the necessity and the limits of this storytelling in the face of loss.[57] Sharif Waked in the video installation *To Be Continued* will return to the *One Thousand and One Nights* and the life-giving promise of stories in the face of political death, as I will show later in the chapter.

Eman Haram's Art and Memory

In the exhibit *Iconographies* at Nabad Gallery in Amman on March 22, 2013, Haram's second solo exhibition there, she reflects on memory, oblivion, amnesia, the self, interminable waiting, belonging, and on iconography as a "discipline of creating meaning through images."[58] The image *In the Presence of Absence* openly evokes one of Darwish's poetic works by that title and reflects on the predicament of the divided self. It suggests that this inner division is historical, given the symbols associated with Palestine found in the image, such as keys. This division is mirrored so it also reflects on the viewer, and so the divided self and the viewer are connected precisely in that process of fragmentation.

Memory as "revisiting and bridging with the past" is conceived as "an act of resistance to counter the systematic erasure of the colonizer . . . a will to be."[59] Haram distinguishes between oblivion, or the possibility of "re-birth or renewal," and amnesia, which for her is "tantamount to death." Her focus is precisely the struggle against amnesia in this artwork of reconstruction and excavation:

> Haram . . . attempts to reassemble a vanishing homeland . . . blurs the boundaries between photography and other print media . . . explores the physical and metaphysical states deriving from this banishment. She reclaims familiar iconic symbols and narratives that are historically connected with Palestine, and layers them with added significance to reach a new vision of a denied homeland beyond the concrete, to the mythical and spiritual. The recovery of a vanishing homeland becomes a return to beginnings, where all narratives converge.[60]

The suspended state of waiting is suggested by the image *Waiting ii*. The image captures a woman in midsentence. In fact the image frames only her mouth and her body in a certain posture of waiting. She is speaking and yet her voice will not reach us. She is far from the "voiceless refugee" one sees transmitted in the media; everything in her and about her speaks. The image seems to echo Kanafani's story "Men in the Sun": When the men speak, are they heard? The perched bird resting on her hand is in a similar posture of anticipation and of voicing, in this dream of veritable flight into freedom, into true home. In many of Haram's images, the hands figure prominently. The elderly woman in this image is sitting on an outdoor step, her hand on her knees. One is reminded of the Palestinian laborers' hands, or the strong hands of women in the villages who work the land. This gesture, common to older women who rest their hands on their laps, palms down, is familiar, imposing order and repose on a world that may not have those qualities. The hands are in a gesture of waiting. Her dress is vibrant, the flowers become organic and blend into her and into the bird. And yet her face, like the many faces in Haram's works, is chalk white: a certain death inhabits this suspended existence of a people routed and rerouted, severed from past and place, targeted, incarcerated, met with mistrust and harassed wherever they find themselves. The face, it can be argued, "a primary inducer of memory," "is one of her primary icons . . . faces, transformed, reworked and distorted . . . are placed within other icons such as picture frames, clocks, embroidery, traditional costumes, keys and birds."[61] On the woman's face runs a red-blue color of untold violence and of death. The colorful composition indicates a certain ability to have withstood being perverted by this violence, precisely from a strong conviction of the injustice of this historical experience, of the communal bonding that stems from this catastrophe, and of this desire to tell, to create, to not be silenced. She sits on a stone step, like many *fallahas* are bound to do, where the outside and inside are precarious boundaries for a certain generation, often dictated by the seasons. The posture of the woman indicates the weight of the years, the history, a certain reconciling with the unmoving fate in order to survive.

In *UNRWA Unit 10401*, we are presented with an image of a very humble room that we can guess is in a refugee camp, as the title also suggests. The room, it seems, serves as both a bedroom and guest salon. The semblance of a home is intact: a framed picture of a beloved relative, a picture of the Dome of the Rock in Jerusalem, a prayer rug, and cushions lend dignity to the inhabitants of the dwelling, even if the walls and floors are in a decrepit state. Nevertheless, the title of the image depersonalizes it as unit and number, highlighting that a refugee's existence is precisely linked to relief organizations and is depersonalized, forgotten, dehumanized, and that the home is a camp, an incarceration, despite the efforts of these relief organizations. The image of the room itself suggests attempts at the re-creation of a home in a suspended state of waiting. The image gives a general impression of homes in Irbid Refugee Camp in Jordan, in Al Yarmouk Refugee Camp in Damascus, and in the humble homes in Zarga, Jordan, where large Palestinian populations have settled waiting to return. The image, quite familiar, is of a makeshift existence that would

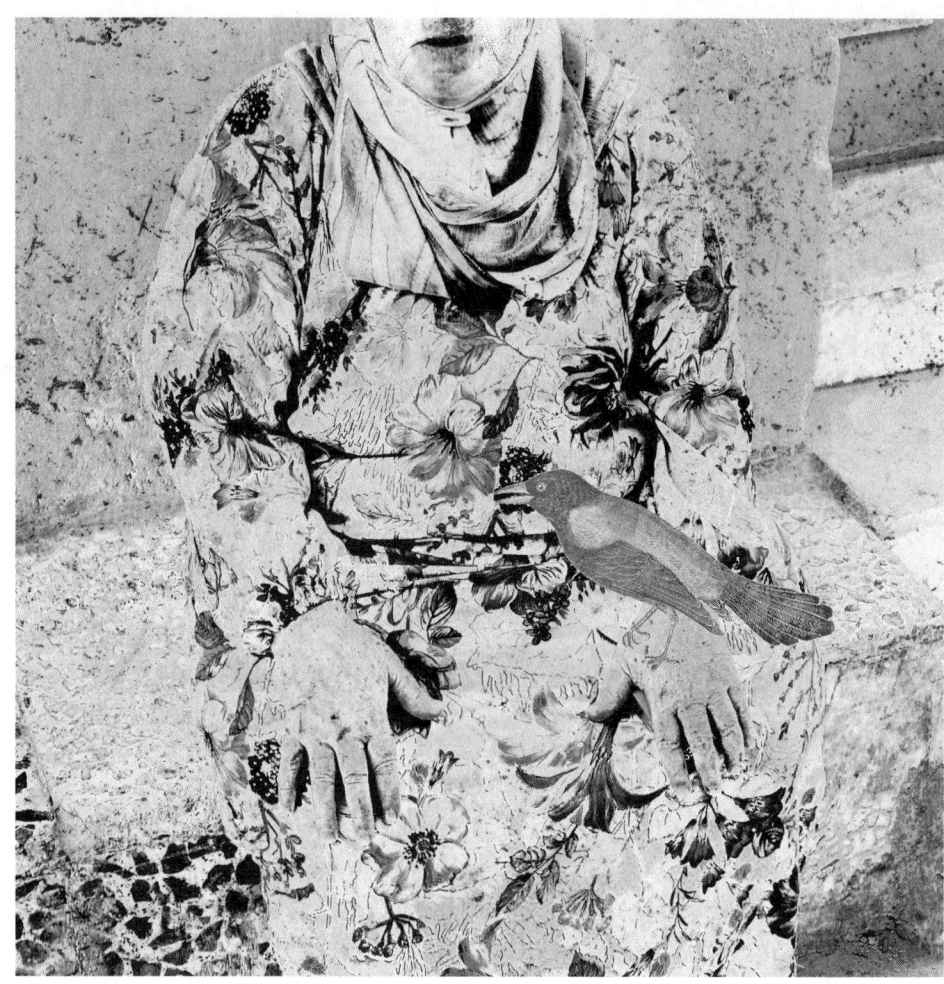

6. Eman Haram, *Waiting ii*, also entitled *The Waiting, UNRWA Unit 10109*, 2013, archival pigment print on organic Awagami bamboo paper, varied ed. 1/7, 56 x 76 cm, reproduced with permission from the artist.

allow the inhabitants to pack to another destination at a moment's notice, always to another place.

In Haram's *The Fall*, recurrent images of fallen oranges, of traditional dress, of keys becoming undone in a "necklace of doves," of a red bird, a *hanthala*-like witness, of earthy brown and red color, and of a white background offer a beautiful if melancholic composition that speaks

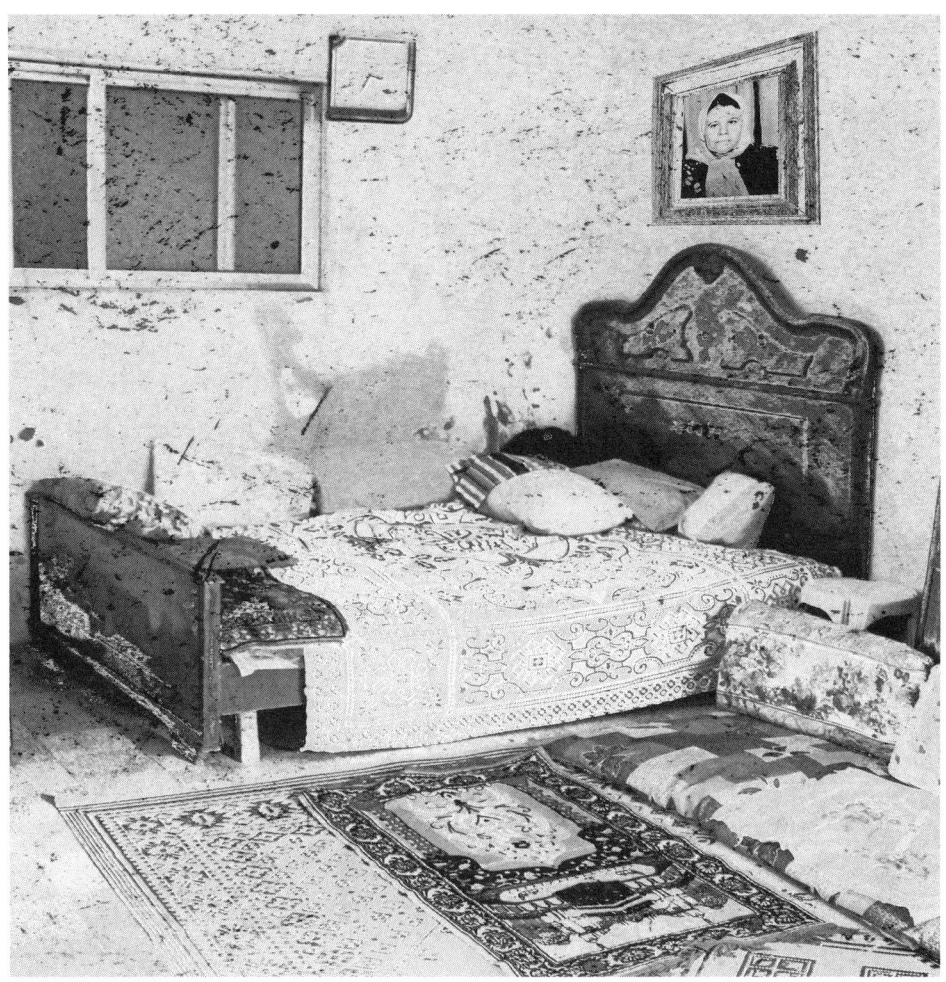

7. Eman Haram, *UNRWA Unit 10401*, 2012, archival pigment print on organic Awagami bamboo paper, varied ed. 2/7, 56 x 76 cm, reproduced with permission from the artist.

defiantly of loss. Oranges blend with the dress, the dress is as if on display, a relic, a memory. And yet Palestine is not just memory and relic but is an open arena of struggle and of everyday tangible existence for millions of Palestinians, as Haram's artwork shows. The figures wear necklaces of metal keys that weigh down. The many keys indicate many displacements and a loss that has become constitutive of identity. The images give the impression of colored x-rays that distance us in time from that reality. *The Fall* is an imposing life-size image (36 x 72 inches), evoking both the historical rupture and the severed connection with an insistence on the need for new stories.

Palestine becomes an ongoing and open-ended assemblage of symbols and images reinvested with meaning and power. The tree, for instance, is a recurrent and powerful image in Haram's work. Haram indicated that "trees are metaphors for people," in the violence that is inflicted on them, in the resilience they show.[62] Trees have the power to renarrate. In *The Melancholy of the Olive Tree*, the image on the cover of this book, she evokes the nobility of the tree, its association with the sacred, its role as witness. The image (a varied edition; 26 x 46 inches) is of an ancient tree in the sacred garden, the Garden of Gethsemane, a protected site in Jerusalem.

Her images seem to interrogate the meaning of being Palestinian. Haram asks: "Why return to it?: Palestine is not a fate that can be escaped, if one is born into the world with the slightest connection to this bruised land. I return because my fate is unquestionably intertwined with the fate of my double rooted there; the sacred olive tree."[63] Although a sense of urgency characterizes the Palestinian predicament, the artwork is more than an ethical imperative or a statement of identity. Ultimately for Haram, "the work is and has to be motivated by that which transcends the political and the ethical in order for it to become."

In a more recent artwork that is still in progress as of this writing, a textured photograph series of seven images that began in 2010 and that resembles pencil etchings, she incorporates Darwish's verses in the images *Study-Mapping Amnesia ii 1/7* and *Study-Mapping Amnesia iii 2/7*. In both artworks, a juxtaposition of two images occurs. In the third image, we see a framed torso of a woman with scientific inscriptions. On the dress and in the background one finds writing in Arabic, though it is mostly difficult to decipher. One can sometimes discern words like "my father," "land," "I," "life," "absence," words one can easily attribute to Darwish. While one wonders about the relationship of the gendered subject to the poetic words, one can also imagine the critical gendered subject/ object and subject of the analysis, formed by and forming her words. In

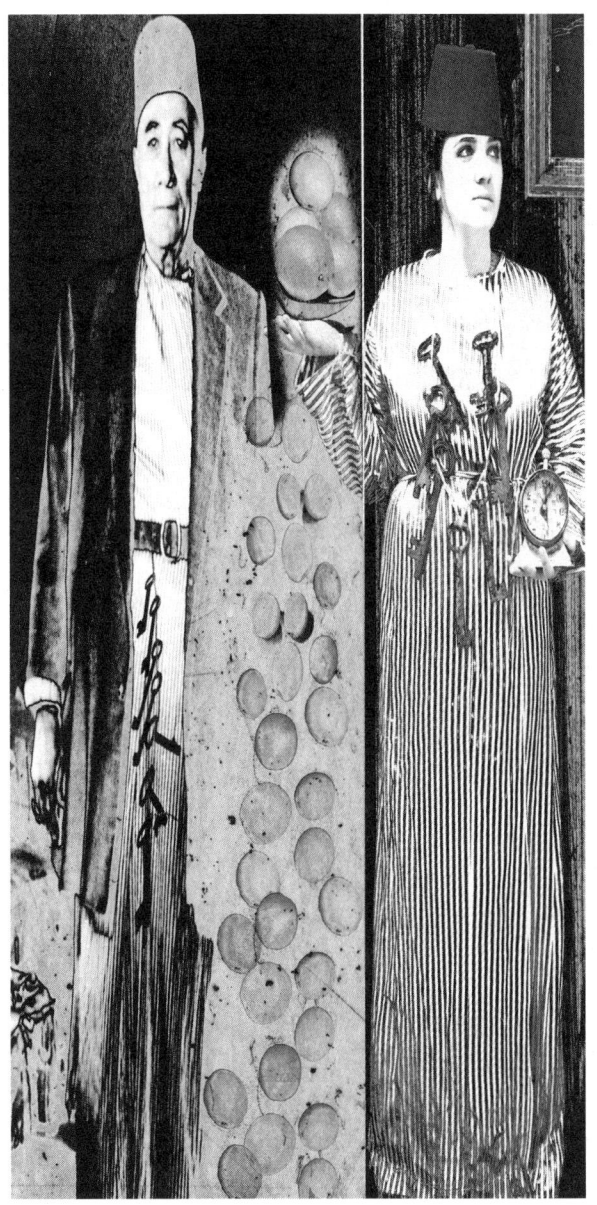

8. Eman Haram, *The Fall*, 2012, archival pigment print on organic Awagami bamboo paper, varied ed., 36 x 72 in., reproduced with permission from the artist.

the second image, the background is almost black but we have only Arabic letters with some English letters and some numbers, as if the language is yet forming or is dissembling.

Haram's *Involuntary Memory* also ruminates on the process of loss, but as *erasure*—sometimes due to the nature of memory but more significantly as historical effacement, a process whereby memory nonetheless also persists as a basis for belonging. Historical erasure is a deliberate attempt to deny the presence of what exists, but no erasure takes places without a remainder. It is from this that Haram begins. Involuntary memory represents "the more indirect and deep sense of personal experience (times, places, feelings, and situations) that are not subject to immediate recall but instead are involuntarily triggered by objects or events associated with that experience."[64] Calling her photographic experiments "ongoing explorations" and "disconnected lives," Haram suggests in this series that history is intimately at the heart of her art, where the self also issues forth a collective experience, where memory recalls a forgetting. Her photos expose the effacement, and by so doing also resist it.

Untitled (composite digital photo, 2006) uses language in conjunction with image to clearly evoke historical erasures of identity, of the past, of collectivities. The fading, blurred images of faces recall the inscription of effacement. The black and white image seems to evoke the past, as the image's grainy quality evokes a negative of a receding original. The words too are faded to differing degrees: "colonized" and "erased" alluding to the past, whereas "occidentalized," "occupied," and "justified" in bold suggest the present. The word "erased" echoes with each historical violence named. An accusation and a judgment frame the words "colonized . . . erased . . . occidentalized . . . erased . . . erased . . . occupied . . . justified." Language provokes by what remains essentially unsaid. The rhythm of language coincides with the image and forcefully drills against that vanishing. Just like the suspension points, the image remains an overture rather than a foreclosed conclusion. The English words target an audience. The word "occidentalized" is used rather than "Westernized." Such use further performs this process of erasure in the layering of identities: The Palestinian American artist now living in Francophone Montreal (having lived previously in the United States, Syria, and Lebanon) and spending half the year in Amman has infused the English she uses. The artist's language occupies the position of "in-between" many languages, revealing a critical posture and "the continuous quest for a language of self- expression." This "in-between . . . the dominant English-speaking art world" and the "Arab matrix" reveals an "'alienated' awareness," an "unmasking of the 'foreign' language."[65]

All the Erased Faces Haunt My Remembrances (constructed digital photo, 2006) reveals the blurred images of women's faces turned to the viewer as they advance forward. In contrasting black forms to white heads-carves, the remembrances have clearly turned to haunting, and the group of passersby strangely inhabit the self. The haunting of collectivities in both images are projections of the intimate self, the past that continues to inhabit the present. The haunting of that which should no longer be there seems to work counter to the erasure, even while defining its nature (i.e., that the haunting is that of all erasures of selves, whether political or social). The encompassing word "all" embraces a collectivity of women without losing the singularity of the self.

In *Erasures* (composite digital photo, 2007), schoolgirls are photo-graphed from the shoulders down, in uniform clothes and postures. As education is primarily concerned with the mind, the absence of heads implies effacement by a process of education. As in the artist's history of attending a Protestant school, education is linked to Western missions.

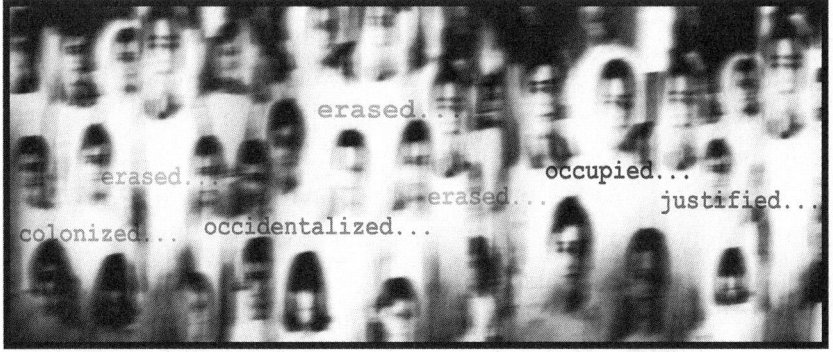

9. Eman Haram, *Untitled*, 2006, archival pigment print on 100% cotton Arches paper, 28 x 60 in., 7/18, reproduced with permission from the artist.

The x-ray dimension of the image exemplifies a photographic exploration of the self in which the object becomes elusive. Memory captures a searing image. One panel bordered and colored arbitrarily marks a self.

Erase the Oblivion (constructed digital photo, 2006) presents a likely family photo and a seemingly natural process of fading away juxtaposed to the torn borders between the women, as if in panels, and the angst of the appeal to "erase the oblivion." The series seems to enumerate various erasures—from the historical and the social to the seemingly natural—that occupy the self.

Art as Dissensus: The Subjective Mappings of Mona Hatoum

Rancière reminds us that politics is "the cluster of *perceptions* and practices that shape this common world . . . *a way of framing, among sensory data*, a specific sphere of experience, . . . *a partition of the sensible, of the visible and the sayable*."[66] Politics emerges also as a particular speech act performed when those excluded or subordinated speak out in "a struggle to have *one's voice heard and oneself recognized*."[67]

Mona Hatoum, *The Negotiating Table* (1983), enacts a politics of remembering and belonging. A powerful, macabre, and visceral image reveals a corpse shrouded and lying on the surface of a wooden table: murdered, possibly tortured, and yet it breathes—a living death. Absent political figures are missing on the opposing empty chairs; the installation announces art as preoccupied with death in its violent forms and with the death of politics. Hatoum, speaking about *The Negotiating Table*, explains: "I was lying on a table, my body covered with entrails, bandages, and blood and wrapped up in a body bag. There were chairs around the table and sound tapes of speeches of Western leaders talking about peace. It was basically a juxtaposition of two elements, one referring to the physical reality and brutality of the situation and the other to the way it is represented and dealt with in the West."[68]

What is common life becomes this mutilated body; what is on the table and what cannot be easily ignored is precisely this violence, and yet it is not addressed by the rhetoric of official political speeches that pretend to be the only viable discourses. Rancière highlights how dissensual speech

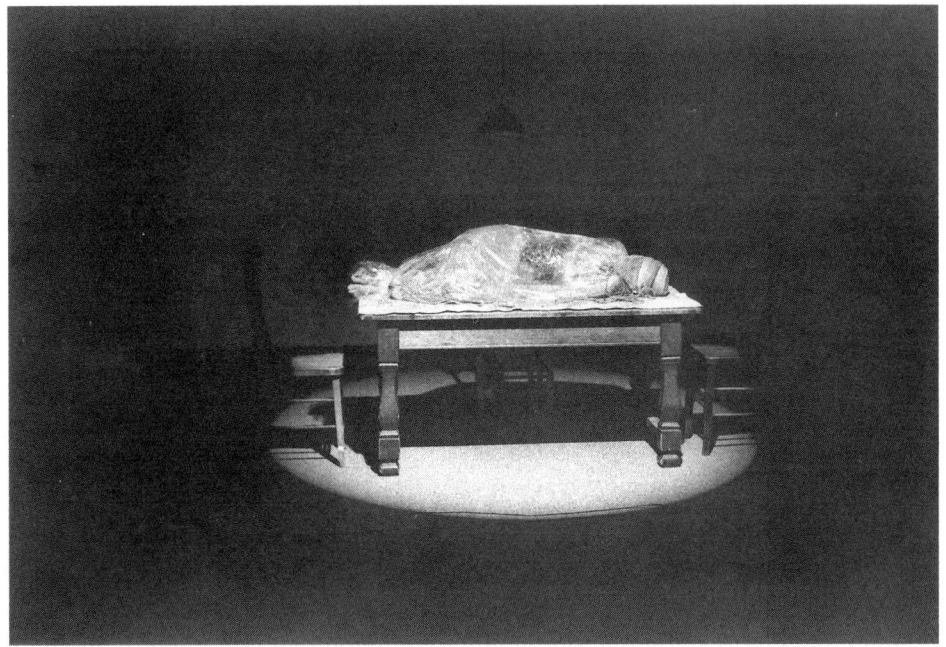

10. Mona Hatoum, *The Negotiating Table*, 1983, The Western Front Vancouver, © Mona Hatoum. Photo: Eric Metcalfe, Courtesy White Cube.

is transformed into private noise and excluded from the political space, a predicament of being "loud and muted," in the words of Suheir Hammad.[69] Rancière writes: "If there is someone you do not wish to recognize as a political being, you begin by . . . not understanding what he says, by not hearing what issues from his mouth as *discourse*."[70]

The Negotiating Table evokes a primary language that announces there is violence, there is death, there is loss in the present, which has to be acknowledged and addressed before any real negotiation or dialogue can take place, and which the art will not allow to be covered over with official discourses. Hammad expresses in her poems the predicament of those asked to adopt a language in contradiction to their lived lives: "We no longer know language," she writes in *Breaking Poems*.[71] She suggests that the very discourse about Palestine is occupied: "humiliate a people distract the rest/ . . . / . . . new world old words/this ain't living/words are against us/there is a math only subtracts" (19). Hammad demands a new language, a "break into language insurgent" (39). The poetic or artistic experience becomes an antidote to a discourse that has served as a math of dispossession. She writes: "language can't math me/i experience exponentially" (23). This art of experience (as well as of expression) counters this "math a myth wa language a lie" (35). Dispossession as a math of subtraction was rendered a sacred myth, perpetuated by consensual political discourses that separate and classify into hierarchies of identity and power. This art by Hammad, Hatoum, Haram, the refugees of Camp Aida, Hany Abu-Assad, Elia Suleiman, Sharif Waked, Emily Jacir, and others is one that names the violence, pierces through the din of discourses.

Hatoum made this performance in the wake of the Sabra and Shatila massacres of September 1982 perpetrated by the Lebanese Christian Phalange forces under Israel's watch. Hatoum calls this horrific event "the most shattering experience of my life," and Ankori links Hatoum's image to the "traumatic expulsion of the Hatoum family from their home, in the wake of the Dir Yassin Massacre."[72] One could also fast forward and consider this image in relation to the period after Beirut, especially in relation to the politics of the Oslo Accords, where such speeches continued and were amplified at the same rate as that of increased aggressive settlements.

Hatoum, who was born in Beirut and lives in London, combines the visuals of the absent political partners in the wake of dreadful violence and the sound of empty speeches about peace and negotiation. Hatoum's art makes a claim on the present and is in this sense a thing of the future. *The Negotiating Table* becomes a commencement and a commandment, "a new way of framing a specific experience."[73]

Hatoum's installation *Present Tense* (1996) reinscribes common loss in the *present*, rendering what has been made "invisible visible."[74] It refuses to locate the fragmentation and dispossession simply in a historical past. It introduces subjective mapping as a *dissensual* intervention in the official mapping that serves as continued erasure of geographies. Hatoum began this work in Jerusalem in 1996 when she traveled there for the first time. Using the famous Nablus soap, she decided to make it the foundation for this map. Placing the different soap cubes on the floor of the Anadiel Gallery, she then inserted tiny red beads into the soap to outline the fragmented territories that were supposed to be handed over to the Palestinian authority, according to the Oslo Accords. Hatoum explains:

> On my first day in Jerusalem I came across a map divided into a lot of little areas circled in red, like little islands with no continuity or connection between them. It was a map showing the territorial divisions arrived at under the Oslo Agreement, and it represented the first phase of returning land to the Palestinian authorities. But really it was a map about dividing and controlling the area. . . . I decided that I would like to do something with this local soap made from pure olive oil, and the work came together. . . . I ended up using little glass beads which I pressed into the soap. . . . I saw that particular soap as a symbol of resistance. It is one of those traditional Palestinian productions that have carried on despite drastic changes in the area.[75]

The soap is highly evocative of Nablus, a longtime site of resistance against the Israeli occupation, of the persistence of tradition despite the erasure, of the fragility of the fragmented map that threatens effacement, of the indifference toward this erasure in the washing of one's hand of it, of the more disturbing settlement policies that touch on ethnic cleansing. Moreover, Jack Persekian of the Anadiel Gallery noted that the beads appeared like "blood drops" that reinforce the sense of the violent erasure at work.[76] Many of Hatoum's critics have noted the powerful dissensual effect of her artwork. For instance, Ankori writes: "Mona Hatoum forces us to see, to feel and to think of the familiar as unfamiliar," an unsettling perspective that in the words of Edward Said "offers neither rest nor respite."[77]

If a certain order has prevailed for decades through ruthless force that has translated to dispossession and exile for different generations, forging a nation one family member at a time, this art not only testifies to this phenomenon but it also turns upside down this order that pretends to dehumanize and render abject in the name of the loftiest human values.[78]

As early as 1988, in *Over My Dead Body*, we see continuity in the preoccupation of her art. Mona Hatoum is no doubt influenced by the explosion of TV images of Palestinian youths and families facing military tanks with nothing but stones during the Palestinian uprising of 1987–89.[79] In

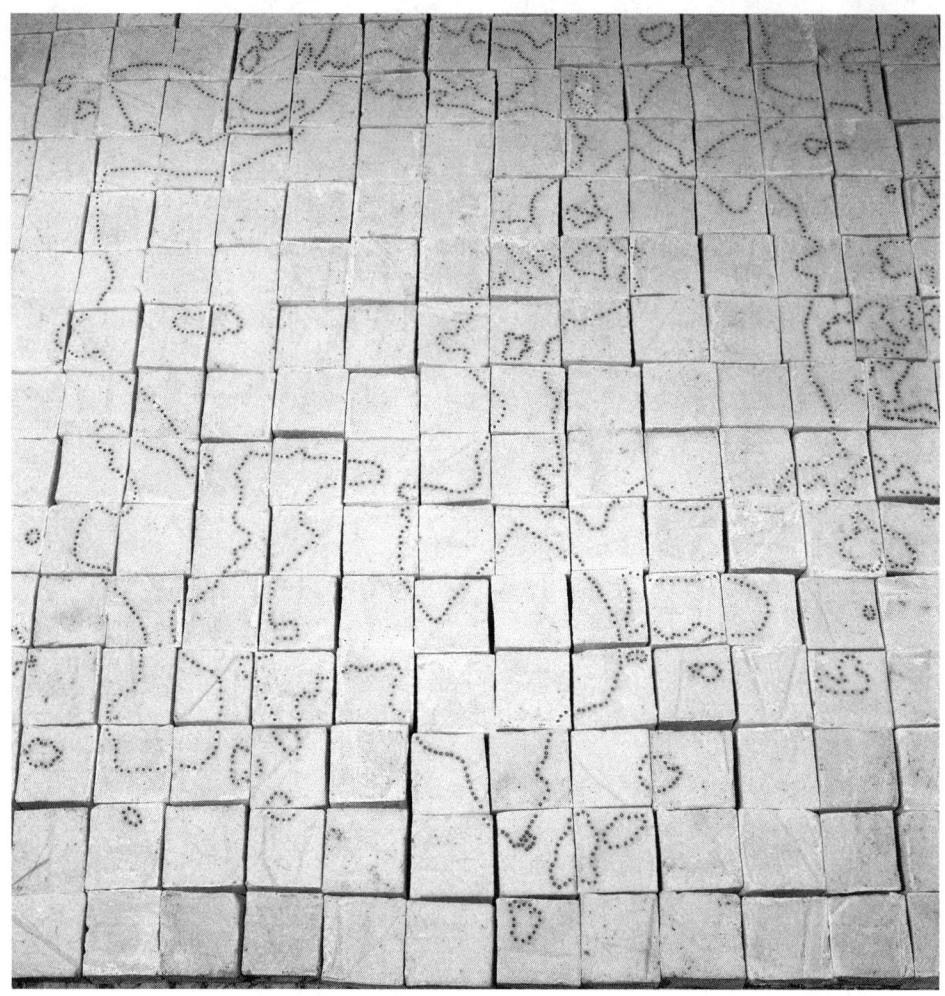

11. Mona Hatoum, *Present Tense* (detail), Installation, Anadiel Gallery, Jerusalem, 1996, Soap and glass beads, 1¾ x 94⅞ x 117¾ in. (4.5 x 241 x 299 cm) ©
Mona Hatoum. Courtesy White Cube and Anadiel Gallery, Jerusalem.

this image a very small soldier figurine is perched on the nose bridge of
the artist, his rifle pointed at her. She looks at him with anger and defiance. The contrast between her large size and his very small one turns the
tables around on military might in the face of strong defiance. One notes
her youth and her aliveness, whereas the soldier is a tiny and inanimate
miniature toy. The face-off is between his military tool reduced to nothing

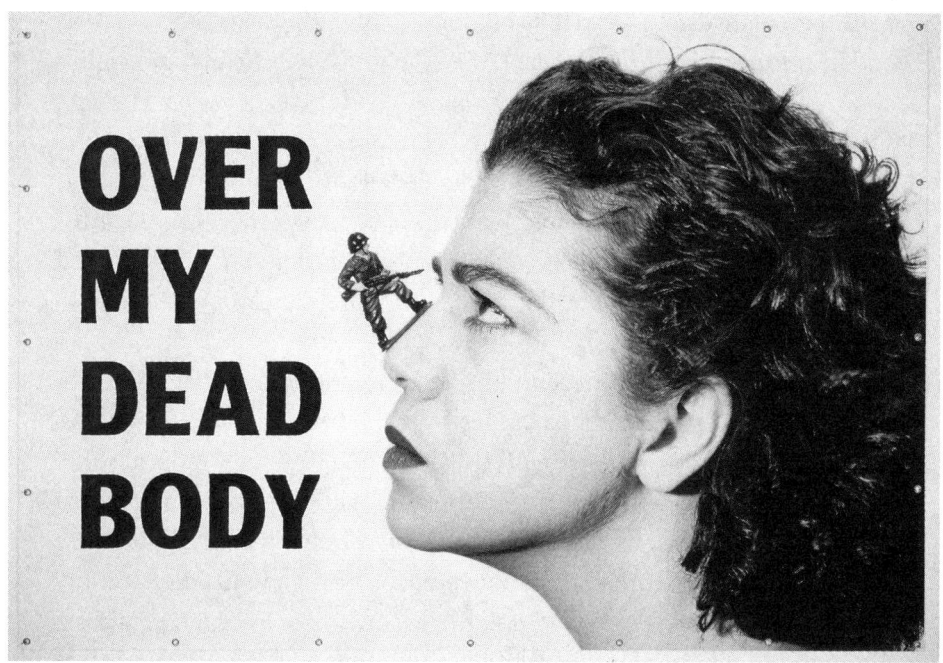

12. Mona Hatoum, *Over My Dead Body*, 1988–2002, inkjet on PVC with grommets, 80½ x 120 in. (204.5 x 305 cm) © Mona Hatoum. Photo: def image. Courtesy Galerie Max Hetzler, Berlin, and White Cube.

and her bare face. It is as if the image insists on justice, creativity, and determination, which can overrule historical imbalances of power. The phrase "over my dead body" is also a statement on the power of nonviolent resistance of the first Intifada. Twenty years later in *Round and Round* (2007) we see the same soldier figurine as the one in *Over My Dead Body*, linked to other identical figurines who point the gun, and this pointing links them in a vicious circle.

Increasingly, Hatoum's work will reveal a preoccupation with home, as evidenced by the number of works that refer directly to "home," especially from 1999 onward: *Homebound 2000, Mobile Home 2005, Suspended 2011*, etc. It is home as *disorder*, a state of not being "at home." Evocations abound in her art here and elsewhere of globes, cities, maps—fragile maps, maps that swing, maps of cities, maps that disappear, the precariousness ensuing from maps, subjective mapping as a way to contest official maps with the creative act—as well as of violence and of war in *Bunker* (2011) and in *Nature morte aux grenades* (2006–7). The linguistic play in English and in French of the words "pomegranates" and "grenade" is apt enough, since the pomegranates of home have been transformed to existential grenades of disappearance and violence due to colonial dispossession that has yet to end. Art and death are intertwined. Art faces violence, like the artist faces the armed soldier in *Over My Dead Body*: "Hatoum has transformed familiar, every-day, domestic objects . . . into things foreign—unhomely—menacing and dangerous."[80]

Jaime Lanaspa lucidly identifies the concerns of the artist as including "suspension and instability" as well as "the fragility of the assurances and bonds that keep us together."[81] Likewise, Edward Said indicates that Hatoum's art, like Hammad's, is preoccupied with the fracturing of identity, "the *presentation* of identity as unable to identify with itself, but nevertheless grappling with the notion (perhaps only the ghost) of identity to itself. Thus is exiled *figured and plotted* in the objects she creates."[82] The fissures are there in the fabrics of the home, whether it is familial or national. Catherine De Zegher writes that her art "serves to interfere with, yet never quite obliterate, familial abandonment, ethnic rejection and national disinheritance."[83]

And so she reassembles, remembers, and recollects through her art the home that is no longer there, that is no longer familiar: "Only by recollection could she adapt to her losses, estranged as she was from her embattled homeland, 'at the crossroads of dispossession.'"[84]

Hatoum's work gets read as a mark of trauma ensuing from national displacement, social restraints, and separations: "Trauma concerns the loss of connection to the self, to the others, to life, to nature, to beauty. . . . Together we have the obligation to heal and restore these broken connections."[85]

But what if her artistic creation is also that of connection, precisely because her art touches those who may have been far from experiencing historical dispossession, because the art lends meaning, form, and continuity to senseless historical violence, fragmentation, and exile:

Though Mona Hatoum has used a great variety of media, she has inventively maintained a continuity in the issues addressed, among them the mapping of reality at the fringes of vision; a problematization of our understanding of alterity; space and time; the subversion of the formal properties of works of art, a procedure based on an economy of loss; and the reformation of female imagery. Mainly in Hatoum's work the irresolvable pain and enriching beauty of being an exile . . . is embedded overtly displaying the implements with which to unhinge the paradox enfolded in it.[86]

Till Roeskens

Till Roeskens's artwork *Videomappings: Aida, Palestine* (2009), for which he was awarded the Grand Prix of the French Competition at the International Documentary Festival (Marseille, 2009), is likewise preoccupied with subjective mapping. This young Franco-German artist asks Palestinians living in Aida Camp to draw maps of what they see around them on their daily routes. Aida Camp, located near Bethlehem, borders the Israeli-built wall and the Gilo settlement. The drawing process that is recorded on video involves telling the stories "related to those subjective geographies." The tellers appear behind a paper screen. We hear the voices of the tellers and the sounds of drawing but we cannot see the faces as they trace on paper the routes of their daily lives inside and outside the camp. We glimpse their life at the refugee camp and the way they handle obstacles they confront. Roeskens considers this artwork *a collaborative one* and calls it "*a tribute to resistance by going around obstacles, in times when the very possibility of that resistance seems to be vanishing.*"[87]

The videomapping screens six maps, representing different life stories, some by women, others by children or by men. Those recounting them trace their daily passages. Neither they nor the places they draw can be seen. By denying the gaze that may not see beyond the workman's poverty or the woman's ethnic clothing, where the grief of the other is then abstracted into something that risks becoming acceptable, the voices that recount and the hand that re-creates their world beyond their confines are rendered legible, tangible, visible, intimate. Roeskens comments on the drawings that "unfold a topography": "*Where are these voices? Behind the sheets (of paper). Of course, but where else? Nowhere: that is precisely what the voices are trying to say. Or rather, because even nowhere persists on taking up some space, they say that they are in Palestine."*

The voices in Roeskens's art render a certain visibility possible when images of Palestinians proliferate in and saturate the media and documentaries, and yet Palestinians remain abstract, distant, alien, and invisible. As Rancière reminds us, "politics begins when those who were destined to remain in the . . . invisible territory of work and reproduction . . . take the time that they 'have not' in order to affirm that they belong to a common world."[88]

In the video *A Trip to Beersheba,* or Bi'r al-Sab', a young man's voice recounts his trip to see a girl, essentially risking his life to cross into Israel. His story allows us to see how he experiences the world, which is not without a certain humor and improvisation. His voice is in tandem with the lines he draws, becoming more animated as obstacles unfold and more monotonous as he traces the routine pathways.

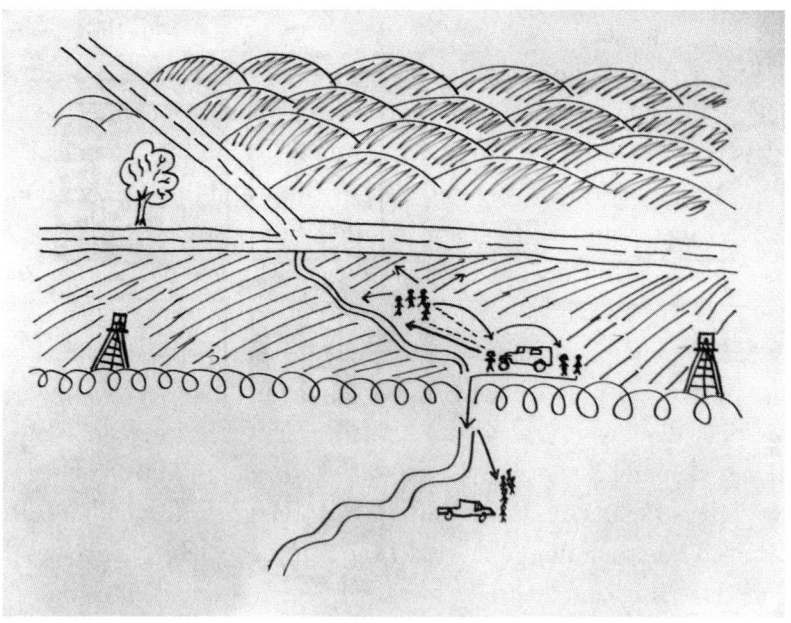

13. Till Roeskens, *Drawing 5,* from *A Trip to Beersheba,* video, 2011, reproduced with permission from the artist.

The trip from Aida Camp to Bi'r al-Sab' passes through Hebron and some Bedouin villages. Mahmoud Issa, the young man recounting and drawing, describes the difficult roads he has to take to avoid the checkpoint. After an incident in which soldiers begin shooting at them and round up some of his fellow travelers, the men manage to cross through other roads. Returning, he scopes the scene, asking others, "Is there a road?" as if the road exists one day but not another, meaning, "Are the roads open?" which is precisely the precariousness of their making way in a territory militarily demarcated to bar their passage, to keep them out. The day he returned from Bi'r al-Sab' there was a bulldozer attack in Jerusalem, he tells us. The army is everywhere. After walking for a long distance, they encounter soldiers. When the soldiers begin shooting, his companions run despite his previous instructions not to do so and are rounded up. He, however, stands still, as bullets fly around his legs. In his mind, he says, he sees his life passing by as if on a video screen. He laughs, all for a girl. He's told to lie down. He asks why? His simple questions interrupt the mechanic operations of interrogation and temporarily break them down.

As the soldiers check his papers, a dialogue with one of the soldiers ensues: he explains his trip, that it was just to see a friend, that he means no harm, believes in peace, etc. His unseen friend who listens as Mahmoud draws laughs at this familiar discourse, at this rehearsed performance. The soldier too rehearses, explains himself; he's a man of peace as well. "You could have killed me," our narrator tells him. "I would have killed you long ago if I wanted to," the soldier answers. The soldier says that Palestinians are like "mice": "we close here . . . and you find a way there." More laughter from the narrator can be heard, and from his friend who listens to the story. "They just want to work," explains the narrator; "these men are not trying to blow themselves up. They just want to earn a living." "I know," the soldier says, but he is under orders. Orders are not to let anyone in. Orders are to kill. "You've just crossed a border," he tells our narrator. But crossing borders is not a crime under international law. And of course neither the occupying state nor its occupied territories have internationally defined and recognized borders. The voice changes as he traces the map of return to the sounds of lines mapping lives.

In this subjective mapping, Roeskens offers a dialogue between a soldier and a Palestinian trying to cross to Bi'r al- Sab'. The nature of this individual dialogue is an opening and a limit, just like the road and its blocks that the young man faces traveling from Camp Aida to Bi'r al-Sab'and back. In a system of policing that violently demarcates positions as "border guard" and "infiltrator," the dialogue reveals that knowledge of the other does not seem to be an obstacle, that individual dialogues do take place in unlikely circumstances, that insurmountable differences are not of a cultural nature. The man undertaking the trip does not participate in Israel's economy, which anticipates each crossing to be that of a suicide bomber, nor in the Palestinian economy, in which desperate men seek work in Israel.

Here dialogue takes place between individuals caught up on either side of a system of violence. It is up to the individual benevolence of the soldier to act or not act on the orders. It is up to the individual Palestinian to respond in a way that ensures nothing less than his very survival.

The act of subjective mapping in the face of a diminishing geography creates paths where there are obstacles. The military mapping of the occupied territories creates zones of nowhere, camps in limbo for decades, where movement is restricted by traveling and fixed checkpoints, where walls separate what recently was a more integral territory. Childlike drawings of these individual maps document the violent realities, re-creating and pointing to ways of overcoming. It is an art that stages public discourses that mystify this experience of dispossession. It renders public the private voices, their intelligibility undeniable. This art does not remove or obfuscate the violence, the living death that is on the table. If dialogue is indeed an intensely risky encounter, must we not invent a new language for any promising dialogue, as Darwish's poetic language has done and as the artworks seem to show? Must we not transform language to speak to this reality without risking a double erasure, one that we inflict this time? And how can we get ahead of a politics of dispossession in Palestine and in Israel if not by a politics of dissension that, like the art, creates new realities, "invents ways of . . . seeing, and saying, engenders new subjects, new forms of collective enunciation?"[89] This artwork does not allow the grief to become acceptable or overwhelming. The real dialogue begins effectively with subjective mapping. It commences and commands a veritable opening.

Palestinian artists have often been uneasy with the interpretation of their work in terms of "identity" and "liberation politics." Mahmoud Darwish, for instance, resisted his "public consecration as Palestine's poet." At the same time, he warned against eliding the political dimensions of his poetry "as a way out of it." He was also critical of the turn in the Arab world "to an unnecessarily opaque . . . aestheticized form of poetic writing with grandiose claims of subversion and liberation from the tyranny of the classical Arabic meter."[90] According to Abdelkebir Khatibi, "these compositions of forms and signs, these metamorphoses of the visible," pose a fundamental question to the viewer concerning the possibility of "laying the poetic and artistic foundations for a nation in exile."[91]

Uneasy, then, with solely political interpretation of their work, Palestinian artists also resist the eliding of its political dimensions. Although art may contribute to healing social and historical wounds, Palestinian artists are vigilant to the way art can be easily recuperated for the enjoyment of others without registering the protest.[92] This art, a "defiant memory" marked by change, has in its very constitution challenged such recuperations.[93]

This art is also fundamentally transnational. Maymanah Farhat writes: "transnational art . . . is perhaps one of the most complex narratives gaining visibility today." Maurice Merleau-Ponty has described art as a "transnational phenomenon" that "transcends spatial and temporal differences to bring . . . together in a single effort, a single accumulative history—a single art or culture. Although there are certain universal elements in art, *one could also argue that there are more significant, relative ones.*"[94]

Rehab Nazzal's Sounds

Rehab Nazzal, a Palestinian artist living in Toronto whose work connects personal memory, lived experience, and archival documents, centers on the violence of colonialism on the body, on the home, and on the belonging to a home.[95] Nazzal's work can be situated at the nexus of art and activism, art and documentary. Her art reflects on representations of and connections to war, how "we connect in the absence of images with each other."[96] *At Home* is a multichannel video installation that that was featured at the Toronto CONTACT Photography Festival in May 2012. The installation uses still and moving images and sound. It engages with the present, documenting the daily toll of the Israeli occupation.[97] *At Home* includes five short videos, *A Night at Home, Target, Mourning, Bil'in,* and *One Thousand Palestinian Political Prisoners.*

What is most intriguing about Nazzal's work is her use of sound, especially given the absence of images, or sometimes the oversaturation of images, to represent violence. The use of sound is even more significant given "the silence surrounding violations of international law." Such representation engages the viewer as a "witness" to this silence. *At Home* intertwines "still and moving images, images in the absence of sound and sound in the absence of images."[98]

At Home re-creates life under occupation and all that entails: imprisonment; the assassination of intellectuals, leaders and activists; military incursions into Palestinian towns and villages; restriction of movement and of making a living owing to the wall and the numerous checkpoints. Four of the videos loop "without the demarcation of a beginning or end. . . . This absence of a distinct start or end can also be representative of the prolonged struggle of the Palestinians."[99] Furthermore, the artist uses videotapes in black and white to reinforce the documentary feel of what is represented.

The silent videos *Mourning* (2012) and *Target* (2012) address the assassination of Palestinian intellectuals, activists, and leaders. *One Thousand Palestinian Political Prisoners* (2012) includes a portrait of one thousand Palestinian prisoners that the artist photographed from the streets of the West Bank over a period of five years, during public protests or while the prisoners were on display in public spaces. We only glimpse each image for a few seconds before it disappears again, followed by another image: "This bombardment of images depicting prisoners of all age groups and gender" is meant to depict the extensive imprisonment of Palestinians and the prevalence of this experience in their lives.[100] Some photographs show women holding framed pictures of their imprisoned children. In one arresting image, we see the inscrutable expression of a mother's grief as she half turns away from the camera and we note the force of her hands as she tightly holds the image of her son to her body, but as the image faces the viewer it is turned away from her. The framed picture is the only thing she can hold on to.

The image in the video Bil'in (2010) is made opaque by tear gas and emulates the lack of visibility ensuing from a gas attack; it "dispatches the sound of . . . peace activists fleeing tear gas attacks . . . in the village of Bil'in, located in the West Bank." In *Walking under Occupation*, Israeli soldiers prohibit photography, having deleted the images on the memory card and forbidding any photographs of security checkpoints.

A Night at Home (2009) is recorded footage that opens on a scene that is completely black with the sound of loud gunshots and sleepy voices inquiring about the shots. Nazzal indicates that the video is a document of an incursion of Israeli forces at night: "In the absence of light, the camera captures only the sound of shooting and the whispers of a son, mother, and grandmother posing unanswerable questions." One critic writes: "You hear ominous crashes, you hear a family's frantic whispering, you hear gunfire, but you see almost nothing. . . . The piece is Nazzal's attempt to convey some of the terror of war."[101]

The video juxtaposes the intimacy of night, of sleep, of a family home with the violent intrusion of the occupation forces that may attack at any time. It is mostly the son who asks questions of the mother, and the mother who questions the grandmother. The grandmother seems to be the one who lives there permanently and is more familiar with the intrusions. The son seems to be unaccustomed to it and his distance allows us to have a removed perspective about the nature of these incursions and how complicit the international community is in allowing the occupation to continue. The grandmother's perspective highlights the ordinariness of this kind of violence. The mother straddles both worlds. She shares her son's perplexity and the weariness of the grandmother. The art documents and brings a reality that has been rendered invisible to visibility. It makes us listen to what has been systematically muffled in its play on visibility and on the stifled voices trying to grasp the overwhelming violence disrupting their lives. Home is neither safe nor inviolable in this work.

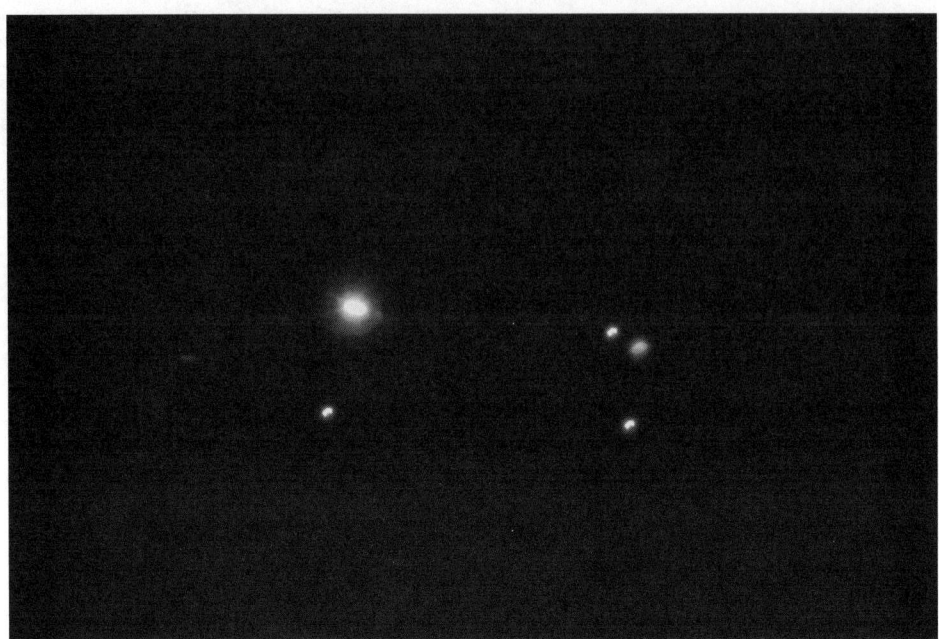

14. Rehab Nazzal, from *A Night at Home*, video, 2009, reproduced with permission from the artist.

Nazzal's art calls attention to the everyday reality of occupation, which includes being subjected to violence at any time of the day or night. The prisoners are also being awakened gratuitously at night at the Naqab prison for a military exercise to raise morale. Nazzal describes the personal circumstances that led to the creation of the video. She recounts a terrifying experience when late on the first night of their visit Israeli forces fired sound bombs on the town. They awoke frightened, bewildered, and uncomprehending as they listened to the shooting:

> Turning the lights on meant becoming the target of Israeli snipers. Recording that event in the dark and through the window resulted in the capture of some flickers of light. However, recording sound waves did not require light, and the sounds were captured entirely by the video camera. The absence of light means the inability of witnesses to capture evidence, . . . Darkness often offers a cover . . . when invading Palestinian towns and villages and while conducting house searches.[102]

Nazzal valorizes sound for its artistic effects as well as for political possibilities. The technique is innovative, since the audience may be saturated with visual images of violence and desensitized to the suffering of others: "in the absence of visual expressions [sound] can strongly evoke a sensory response, without necessarily identifying the source of sound. This . . . gives it a universal dimension that visuals do not possess."[103]

Although Nazzal's work innovates aesthetically, it does so by linking the aesthetic to the ethical. The responsibility for this artist is to document, to respond in a way that makes reality visible and heard, to bear witness through art, as if art cannot simply appeal to the "beautiful" or the "new" but is forced to arrest the viewer, to make the viewer see reality in situations in which one has been saturated with news images about Palestine, the saturation making image even farther removed from reality. Through Nazzal's artworks, however, we look in a new way and access new perspectives; new alignments of image and sound make what is represented close to us, its reality becomes our reality. Her method denies us the contemplative gaze that can be later left behind after the viewing. The images and sounds stay with us. We are jolted to the sound of the first shot as if we are there, and we ask the same questions. We wonder when the morning will come. David Paterson aptly writes: "Sometimes in art, it's what you don't see that's important. That's certainly the case with *A Night at Home*."[104]

Sharif Waked's Humor and Video Art

Sharif Waked's video art is tremendously innovative and shares with Rashid Masharawi, Elia Suleiman, and Hany Abu-Assad the ability to create with humor from contentious matter. Among his works, *Beirut, an Apple*, from the series *Melancholia* (1998), evokes directly Darwish's verses in "Madīḥ al-Dhill al-ʿĀlī." It shows a fading white-washed wall riddled with bullets and two gaping openings that reveal images of faraway landscapes and people, evoking a destruction of home and a dispersion of people. His artwork *To Be Continued* is reminiscent of a scene from *Paradise Now*, in that one expects a suicide speech in the posture of the presenter, but like Emily Jacir's artistic treatment of *One Thousand and One Nights* for her video work *Material for a Film*, the presenter instead reads from this fantastic work. As in Darwish's poetry, and as the work of all of these artists show, to tell one's story is to fight against death, loss, erasure, and absence. One can also read Waked's *Beace Brocess* as an extension of or juxtaposition of Mona Hatoum's *The Negotiating Table*, in that it parodies the spectacle of a peace process that has no substance. One notes also the connections between Nazzal's art and Waked's *Chic Point*, for Nazzal reclaims the archival footage, and through sound she is able to reverse the perspective and reclaim the story from the other side. Waked's parody of fashion tailored for crossing checkpoints calls attention to the stark reality of settler colonialism coexisting with the veneer of civilization, affluence, and high culture.

Waked's works include *Melancholia* (1998), *Zoom* (1999), *Jericho First* (2002), *Chic Point* (2003), *Tugra* (2008), *To Be Continued* (2009), and *Beace Brocess* (2010). They are now part of the permanent collections of many prestigious cultural institutions, including the Guggenheim Museum (New York), the Sharjah Art Foundation (UAE), Fondation Louis Vuitton pour la création (Paris), the Israel Museum (Jerusalem), and many others.

Video is a dynamic, hybrid, and complex form that is essentially *democratic*: "it has drawn on a diverse range of art movements, theoretical ideas, and technological advances, as well as political and social activism."[105] Mona Hatoum's short black-and-white video art *Changing Parts* (1984) is often considered one of the first Palestinian experimental video arts. In the video Hatoum contrasts her home life in Beirut and in London, thus contrasting war with ordinary life.[106] Video art has its roots in the late eighties and gained its prominence in the late nineties:

> With the eruption of the first Intifada in the late 1980s, many Palestinian filmmakers and artists used the medium to document the brutality of occupation and the destruction it inflicted on Palestine and Palestinian society. Many videos were produced during this period; however, due to the nature of the films, which are categorized as political activism, they have not been archived or documented by art practitioners or art centres. As a result, many of these efforts have gone unrecorded.[107]

Video becomes a valuable and effective medium for Palestinian artists like Waked for experimentation and for calling into question representations of Palestinians, offering their own creations.

In *To Be Continued*, Waked presents a video performance of a suicide bomber's last broadcast. Instead of reading from the Qur'an as is habitual, he reads from *One Thousand and One Nights*, "thus avoiding the horrific denouement" in this foregrounding of the role of representation.[108] In these tales, Scheherazade narrates to King Shahrayar one story that she interrupts at daybreak and continues the next night, and the next, thus saving herself and her kind. In a seeming parody of the "living martyr" videos, Waked also points to the importance of the imagination to deliver us from cycles of violence, valorizing the life-giving possibility of narration, fiction, and fantasy: "Through this unending process of reading and narration, the 'living martyr' eternally delays the seemingly inevitable occurrence of death and mortality. The 'living martyr's' existence in a permanently suspended state becomes a site to ponder the thin line between the political and the existential."[109]

Sharif Waked's short video *Chic Point* (2003) evokes gender dynamics in a colonial context, particularly in the daily reality of Palestinian men crossing military checkpoints under Israeli occupation. Although women and children also cross checkpoints, the proliferation of these checkpoints and the ever increasing restriction on movement has turned this into a predominantly male experience of surveillance. Palestinian males are often subjected to strip searches, including being asked to lift their shirts so they can show their stomachs to Israeli soldiers, who suspect suicide bombers.[110] The video stages this crossing as a male fashion show, parodying the projections of fantasy and desire and bringing the reality of settler colonialism a little closer to home. One after the other, we see male fashion models on the catwalk moving to the sound of a heavy musical beat as they display their clothes. This is no ordinary fashion show, however, since the clothes are made to facilitate the "security check" at the checkpoints without the men having to take their shirts off. So the clothes include holes in the abdomen and stomach area, sometimes heart shaped, sometimes meshed, other times zippers or button are involved. The tone is light

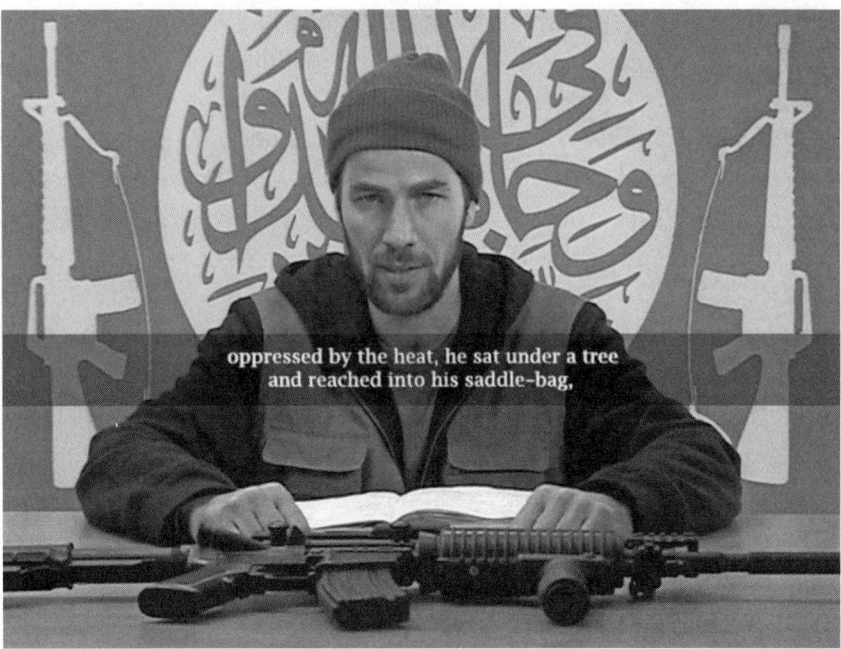

oppressed by the heat, he sat under a tree
and reached into his saddle-bag,

15. Sharif Waked, from *To Be Continued*, video, 2009, reproduced with permission from the artist.

and humorous in this first part of the video. The show mitigates a humiliating power dynamic by highlighting it. It reveals the contrast between a market-driven world that stages male fashion shows and celebrates handsome men and an existence that cannot be divorced from the politics of dispossession and a culture of humiliation. The video seems to suggest that a colonialism sedimented from a foregone era can present itself as a cutting-edge laboratory of military practices as well as of cultural trends.

Under occupation, the video seems to say, there are only vulnerable bodies subject to military interrogation and pointed guns. The play with seduction in the first part of the video is humorous precisely because an encounter at a military checkpoint between armed soldiers and suspected bodies can only be devoid of any erotic element. An extreme usurpation of power, which is by definition illegitimate, can only be compared to a violation, to a rape of power; and it would be misguided to see the later in terms of a play of eroticism. The artist described his work in these terms: "*Chic*

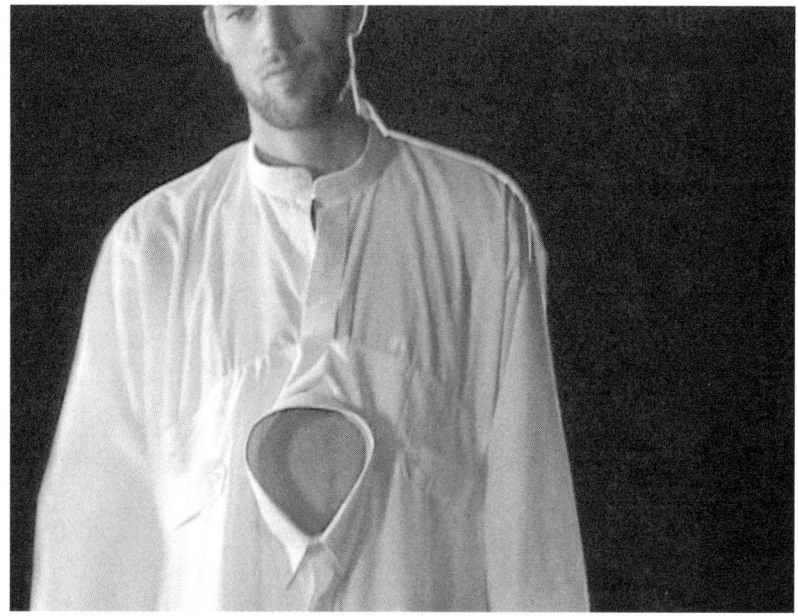

16. Sharif Waked, from *Chic Point*, video, 2003, reproduced with permission from the artist.

Point bares the loaded politics of the gaze as it documents the thousands of moments in which Palestinians are daily forced to nude themselves in the face of interrogation and humiliation, as they attempt to move through the intricate and constantly expanding network of Israeli checkpoints."[111] Moreover, the men who are forced to undergo security checks at checkpoints are necessarily Palestinian, and they can be visually identified as such by what they wear rather than by the way they look. For instance, one of the models in a dark suit cut off in the middle carries, in an ironic twist, not a briefcase but a grandmother's plastic mesh bag in bright blue, which identifies him as Palestinian since these bags are everywhere in the villages of the West Bank.

Ariella Azoulay also argues for an encounter between a sovereign state and a dispossessed body. She writes that this work "offers a glimpse into the new visual field born at the checkpoints, a visual field in which the sovereign's junior proxy looks at, examines, and does as he sees fit with the Palestinian subject."[112] Moreover, the "visual field" created by these checkpoints and highlighted in the video places the spectator in a complicit position with the militarized gaze: it "manages to place the spectator in a position that slowly reveals itself as a paraphrase of the gaze at the checkpoint . . . the checkpoint marks the Palestinian body."[113] The spectator who also watches this exposed body engages in a power dynamic: "At any given moment the sovereign's junior proxy can demand the Palestinian's body be exposed. At any moment he can set up . . . a mobile kit for passing judgment and sealing fates. . . . The Palestinian's body . . . serves as a pretext for drawing a border from which he may be observed."[114]

The ending of the video, which documents Palestinian men crossing checkpoints, is extremely significant and sober: it mitigates from any erotic element one may wish to attribute to the scene. As one critics has argued:

> The videotaped fashion show ends suddenly in black silence and afterward . . . after the stylized noise that preceded it—a series of still black-and-white photographs appear on the screen. These show men, singly or in groups, exposing their naked bellies and chests to soldiers at military checkpoints, each photograph with the name of the place and year it was taken: Bethlehem, Beit Sahur, Ramallah, Nablus, Jenin, Jericho, 2000, 2001, 2002, 2003. . . . Most of the men in the photographs are neither young nor well built. . . . In a few of the photographs, the arms of those who are walking toward the soldiers are frozen in clumsy positions, as though they are wondering whether to keep them in the air. . . . Here, the darkness surrounding the models—whether used to make them stand out or to swallow them up threateningly—is replaced by bits of landscape and scenes of wretched human existence.[115]

In fact, as this critic argues, the scene is precisely about "the nature of Israel's military control over 3 million Palestinian civilians." The artwork accomplishes its objective through the performance, documentation, and representation of occupied reality in an innovative aesthetic and through dark humor, "*attracting attention—by force of surprise and challenge to the habits of the usual sensory reception—to the vulnerable body,* both covered and revealed."[116]

It is in this context that the desire to read the video as a "queer encounter" needs attention. To read the scene as an expression of homoerotic desire is to neutralize the political violence taking places at checkpoints, to displace the reality of that experience into a universal application of queer theory onto violent contexts of power. It is only possible to read the scene as a predominantly "queer encounter" if one renders symmetrical and equates the ending of the video (historical photos) and its beginning (fantasy fashion show), arguing for a blurring of the boundaries between the two segments. In fact, the separation between the two segments is abrupt and stark, as if to jolt one out of the realm of fantasy, reminding us of a system of settler colonialism that has not been superceded. Although Sharif Waked plays on the homoerotic gaze in the video, it is precisely to parody it and subvert it, to call attention to the problematic projection of desire in contexts of subjugation and to the abject reality of what it means concretely to be under military occupation. For the conclusion one draws from these "encounters" at checkpoints is not inevitably about homoeroticism. The aim of the scene is also to make fun of any spectator who can be drawn to the plight of the oppressed only if they are packaged as "sexy."

Although Waked does complicate the representation of the Palestinian to go beyond that of a perpetual victim, and works against familiar representations, seeing the Palestinian male as "an object of desire well aware of his desirability" has its limits. The Palestinian male of course does not suffer from a crisis of his own desirability. If anything, the nature of the military gaze that objectifies the male body is to attempt to disarm the Palestinian of his own masculinity and of his humanity. Although Palestinian artists do complicate and nuance and render multiple representations of Palestinians, at no point do they mitigate the power of the political critique of occupation.

Arguing that Waked offers "a new, and *explicitly homoerotic, interpretation, presenting it as a means for Israeli soldiers to 'check out' Palestinian men, who 'dress up for the occasion,'*" risks effacing the checkpoint set up by the Israeli military, bringing closer the occupier and occupied, but not in any politically effective way of democratic coexistence that would necessitate an end to the occupation.[117]

The humor in the video only highlights that an usurpation of power is involved in daily encounters at checkpoints. There is nothing erotic about crossing policed checkpoints or militarized borders, whether homoerotic or heteroerotic, even if the erotic may be marshaled as a form of facilitating crossing or simply for its own ends. There is nothing nonchalant about the performance.

Sharif Waked, then, like the other visual and performance artists, highlights memory and its nexus with dispossession, loss, and belonging.

4

"All We Have Is the Song"
Music and the Poetry of Darwish

Art changed after Oslo, according to scholars who follow Palestinian artistic expression, but so did the very meaning of the terms "engaged art," "resistance," and "politics." Keen to establish themselves as artists first and foremost while engaging their art with reality, rather than displace the art onto realities divorced from their present, Palestinian artists were able to innovate aesthetically and to highlight the need for a different kind of politics. Performing well and accessing international audiences became in themselves acts of resistance. Mahmoud Abu Hashhash insightfully indicates why Israel has always clamped on Palestinian creative and cultural expression: "Israelis never wanted Palestinians to express themselves in a creative way. . . . We did not have any fine art department before the Oslo agreement, because this was not allowed. . . . Because to Israel . . . the most dangerous thing is to start seeing the Palestinians as artists . . . who can express and convey the spirit of the times."[1]

As with other creative expression in occupied Palestine, music has long been censored and musicians targeted: their material was banned, they were harassed, imprisoned, and exiled. "Stern censorship of musical activities before the early 1990s is among the most frequently told stories by Palestinians."[2] Music follows from the legacy of Darwish and connects itself to Palestinian poetry. It is an expression of protest and a struggle against dispossession. If the form of oppression is one of fragmentation of geography and of people, then this is an art that connects artists and their audience from Gaza, the West Bank, Israel, and the diaspora. If the form of oppression is erasure of Palestinian identity, then this performance enacts

Palestinian presence in the international arena. If the form of oppression is internal and external displacement, then it is an art that articulates a belonging against all exclusion and negation.

Mahmoud Darwish's lyrics have been put to music, his legacy canonized, his birthday declared by the Palestinian Authority a "national day of the culture of Palestine," yet his legacy still needs to be studied as well as celebrated. Darwish's lyrics are rendered in the songs of Marcel Khalife, in the musical compositions and interpretations of the Trio Joubran, in the more recent work of Sabreen, Reem Kelani, Sami Jundi, Reem Talhami, Jen Marlowe, Elayyan, Sameeh Shuquair. Other Palestinian musicians who have also rendered Palestinian poetry in music and have innovated while staying close to Palestinian musical traditions include George Qirmiz, Mustapha al-Kurd, Said Mourad, Reem al-Banna, 'Issa Boulos, and many others.[3] The influence ranges from incorporating a few verses to interpreting entire poems in music. Trio Joubran was the only group to my knowledge who joined Darwish in some of his poetry readings and interpreted his verses to music as Darwish recited his poetry. One of the Joubran brothers, Samir Joubran, speaks about the trio's performance with Mahmoud Darwish in 1996, after which they performed with him until two weeks before his death: "We had a concert in Arles. . . . Mahmoud Darwish is everywhere in our music, also in the name of the tunes. . . . Our latest CD is in tribute of Mahmoud Darwish."[4] Likewise, Darwish's poetry has also been rendered as a staged musical. In an interview with Heather Bursheh, Reem Talhami indicates that her lyrics are incorporated from Mahmoud Darwish, Samih al-Qasem, Rashid Hussain, and Tawfiq Zayyad: "I was asked to take part in the production *Jidariyyah* by Mahmoud Darwish, as both singer and actress. . . . The play toured the world for some years."[5]

The popular group Sabreen, who perform internationally, also set music to lyrics by Darwish and by other poets such as Hussein Barghouthi and artists such as Sobhi Zobaidi. Established in the early 1980s, Sabreen has introduced a "creative fusion of musical styles from traditional Arab genres, Palestinian folk, and modern Western traditions like jazz, pop, and rock-and-roll."[6] Like other Palestinian groups of diverging styles who employ recurrent themes of struggle and identity, the group's "intentionally 'distorted' and 'eclectic' styles and expressions [are] a deliberate musical response to Palestinians' harsh economic and political realities."[7] Sabreen is seen as cosmopolitan by many critics, "less encumbered by exilic nationalism, folk preservation, politics, and aesthetics."[8] The group's innovative music allowed for new expressions of the Palestinian experience and is believed to be an emblem "of the Palestinian musical future."[9]

In their music too, a certain tension between the national and the transnational emerges: Palestinian musicians like Simon Shaheen and others and like Palestinian filmmakers and visual artists, both local and diasporic, express and complicate the concept of the "national" through the transnational and diasporic while becoming "an integral part of the global circulation of world music."[10]

Collaborations between musical composition and lyrical text are especially complex and rich in Palestinian music. Most memorable is Marcel Khalife's songs, which call attention to the vitality and centrality of the poetic text in music. One recalls specifically the controversy that ensued when Khalife set Darwish's famous Joseph verses, themselves interpretations of verses from the Qur'an, to music: "he was under fire not for the music but for the texts, which were, however, not written by him. Music as the conveyor of text was regarded as more subversive . . . than just the poems as printed or as read. Part of the calamity was . . . that the original words were . . . from the Qur'an."[11] Indeed, in this case, Marcel Khalife endured censorship just like Palestinian musicians have been enduring.

Many ethnomusicologist and critics have identified text as "a vital element" when it comes to Palestinian music.[12] Dalia Cohen and Ruth Katz argue, for instance, that the text "plays a role not only in defining the structure of a simple song, but also in shaping the structure of a complex work (such as the *nuba* and the *waslah*, as well as the Iraqi *maqam*). . . . The text is actually the central pillar of the genres."[13]

Palestinian music, which has often been regarded as one of struggle and resistance, reflecting the history of Palestinians themselves, cannot be dissociated from other Arabic music, even as it guards its distinctive sounds. Whereas Cohen and Katz have argued for affinities between Palestinian music and music of the Levant generally, others have recalled the influence of music from Cairo and Beirut, which itself drew some of its influence from Western music: "Egyptian popular songs of ʿAbd al-Wahhab and Umm Kulthūm in the mid-twentieth century—heavily influenced by European functional harmony, orchestral setting . . . —have had a significant impact on the post-1948 political struggle in Palestine, explicitly linked to notions of Arab unity and the liberation of Palestine."[14]

One can detect this influence in the musical instruments themselves, which include the ʿūd, the durbakke, the daff, the nāy, and the qānūn, often accompanied by Western instruments such as the violin, electric organ, and drums.[15]

The Palestinian musical tradition spans back to the nineteenth century and much earlier. The period after the occupation heralded political songs "that promote the spirit of resistance and struggle," whereas the Lebanese War in 1975 created "support of Palestine by non-Palestinian musicians,"[16] for example, by the Lebanese Marcel Khalife, Fairuz, and the Rahbani brothers. Since Palestine was seen as an Arab cause that served as an emblem for solidarity and the quest for freedom, it became ever present in all creative and intellectual endeavors, including in music. Beginning in 1985 "protest songs have been . . . disseminated quickly through audio-cassettes and other mass media."[17]

Although a long history of musical expression exists among Palestinians, critical studies have only begun to study it in a considerable manner very recently. These musical performances and daily practices of everyday life have influenced the poetry of Palestinian poets including Darwish, for they too carry memory and emotion.[18] Joseph Massad's 2005 essay is a notable example of scholarship that since the late nineteenth century shows "a textually and musically rich tradition, and one so old that some people even maintained that it reflects to a certain extent the poetic activity manifested in the Song of Songs . . . these scholars have provided us with a corpus of songs attesting to a well-entrenched tradition."[19] Cohen and Katz trace Palestinian scholarship of Palestinian music, and particularly folk songs, to the 1970s and attribute the effort to a desire "to identify with it and save it from oblivion."[20]

Although musical differences abound in Palestinian music, the political history of Palestine has helped "coalesce the local tradition."[21]

Palestinian musicians also have collaborated with others to create new fusions and transform received tradition.[22] The Palestinian folkloric musical tradition has been considered as mostly oral, vocal, and improvisational.[23] Cohen and Katz characterize it as primarily improvisational: "creativity is manifested in improvisation." They identify the following genres for songs, attributing them also to Arabs in the region, including: *shurūqī*, *'atābā*, and *mījānā*; *mu'annā*, *ḥadādī*, and *mhrabe*; and *far'awī*, *shubās*, and *zajal*.[24] One thinks of such songs as "Yā Zarīf al-Ṭūl" or "'Alā Dal'ūnā" or "'Atābā" as part of this folkloric heritage. One also thinks of such musical groups as Firqat al-'Āshiqīn (whose repertoire includes songs of *'atāba, dal'ūna, zarīf al-tūl*) or other groups such as *Baladna*, led by Kamal Khalil, who also set his music to the verse of Darwish and to Tawfīq al-Ziyad, Ibrahim Nassrallah, and Samih al-Qassem. McDonald writes about the contributions of such groups as *Baladna*: "The combination of well-known contemporary and past Palestinian poetry with modernized sha'bi folk song created a new style at once indexical of contemporary themes and issues while rooted in Palestinian history and practice."[25]

Folk music has had a continuous presence inside and outside Palestine, though as McDonald argues, "the PLO spent . . . on . . . music performance . . . as a means to reframe Palestinian identity around a new generation of revolutionaries working . . . to reclaim the homeland from 'outside,'. . . . With the expulsion of the PLO from Lebanon . . . nationalist energies were refocused back 'inside.'"[26]

If folklore or traditional music is inextricably connected with Palestinian identity and history, Chuen-Fung Wong calls attention to how even innovative music that is more transnational and less traditional is one of resistance and struggle, since the technical aspects of the music reenacts the beat of the occupation: "Such stylistic newness is often conceived as a new means for struggle, in which musical features such as imbalanced phrases, unsteady rhythms, and inconstant beats are iconic of the experience of occupation among Palestinians. . . . Musical devices and techniques that are transnational and global in nature are often consciously deployed by Palestinian composers and musicians as artistic weapons."[27]

Other musical institutions in the Palestinian Territories are anchored at once in tradition and in Western as well as transnational musical trends, including The National Conservatory of Music, considered the most important institution for music education, which became the Edward Said National Conservatory of Music in 2004 after his passing away. Another important institution is al-Kamanjāti (The Violinist), established in 2002.[28]

The emergence of Palestinian rappers in the last decade, including DAM, SAZ, AREPAYAT, MWR, ABEER ZAINATY, and AWLAD EL HARA, has, however, created scholarly interest and tremendous popularity for that genre in the Occupied Palestinian Territories and elsewhere. Massad situates rap in a tradition of revolutionary Arab political songs since 1965. Groups such as DAM have claimed inspiration from a tradition of poetry from Darwish to Samih al-Qasem and others. As Helga Souri-Tawil has indicated, these groups began inside Israel "rapping about Israeli discrimination against Palestinians, and widened their repertoire to a range of 'angry' political expressions, from being slighted by Arab nations to addressing internal social problems such as drug-use and misogyny. . . . Rap has become . . . a vehicle for political critique and mobilization."[29]

Critics intriguingly consider rap as "a poetics of displacement and protest"[30] and "a space of non-violent resistance," not unlike the characterization of the early poetry of Darwish.[31] Here I focus mainly on the hip-hop groups that have emerged and gained international visibility and popularity. In particular I look at DAM's songs and albums.

Hip-hop has always been more than simply musical expression; "it was created," writes Sunaina Maira, in New York in the late 1970s "by African-American, Caribbean, and Latino (Puerto Rican) youth . . . to address everyday experiences of exclusion, criminalization, and impoverishment." It is an eminently affordable youth form and subculture that does not require economic resources. It is composed of musical and nonmusical elements: "rapping (MCing), deejaying, producing the beats, graffiti art, and breakdancing." It is a political form with a vision and a stance: "The 'heavy reliance on lyricism' makes Hip Hop a genre that can be powerfully used for social and political commentary."[32]

Palestinian hip-hop emerged with Tamer Nafar and his small group of three—Tamer Nafar, Suheil Nafar, and Mahmoud Jreiri—from Lyd, "one of the most dangerous, drug-addicted, and crime-infested cities in the Middle East."[33] The acronym DAM refers to "Da Arabian MCs" but also has connotations in Arabic of enduring, of blood.[34] Palestinian hip-hop began with '48 Palestinian artists, specifically Palestinian artists from Jaffa, and proliferated with such groups as SAZ, ABEER ZAINATY, ARAPEYAT, MWR, AWLAD EL HARA, and it has spread to the West Bank and Gaza and to the Palestinian diaspora. Maira writes: "'48 Palestinian youth were the pioneers of Palestinian hip hop and have inspired much of the hip hop movement in the West Bank, Gaza, and in the Diaspora, generating a transnational network of artists and fans."[35] In the West Bank, one can name Palestinian Street, Rami G.B., Boikutt, and Stormtrap, while in Gaza artists include PR (Palestine Rapperz) and MC Gaza. In Jerusalem, new Palestinian groups emerged such us G-Town, OC Soldiers, Ejtiyah, and Underground. In the Arab world, the spread of hip-hop groups can be noted from Morocco to Lebanon: Haked, Soultana, M.B.S, Lotfi, Double Kanon, S.O.S., Fareek al Atrache, Aksser, El Rass, Rayess Bek, Malikah, Ramy Donjewan, Mohammed El Deeb, MC Amin, Arabian Knightz, Ibn Thabit, and Khotta (Plan) B. Maira enumerates as well the groups in the diaspora such as the Philistines in the United States; Narcicyst in Canada; La Caution in France, and Shadia Mansour in Britain.[36]

Tamer Nafar, in the film *Slingshot Hip Hop*, acknowledges the power and influence of poetry, specifically that of Mahmoud Darwish, on his art: "We've learned from Arab poets how to use metaphors. Instead of stealing them from books, we develop our own images using our street slang." In the film, he names additional influences such as Edward Said, Nizar Qabbani, and other contemporary Arab writers: "30% Hip Hop music; 30% literature; and 40% the political situation."[37] DAM's albums, which include *Dedication* and *Dabke on the Moon*, show a variety of other influences, from alternative music to Trio Joubran to the raï tradition.[38] This assemblage of alternative styles is linked through expressions of cultural protest and affirmation. On the one hand, DAM steps out of Palestinian folk music traditions, although not entirely; on the other hand, the group forms part of an international music scene forged by networks of solidarity. Although their music is finally about life and all that defines it, as DAM members remind us, their music has Palestinian culture and political life as its horizon: "DAM's music is not just about the dark times. . . . We have art, culture, history, we sing about all of it . . . we sing about love. . . . In one of the Mahmoud Darwish poems, he wrote about how Palestinians also die from old age. . . . And when we are free, we will continue to sing."[39] Hip-hop is an expression of youth, of identity, and of protest. Tawfiq Zayyad has written: "We sing our songs/As though we were twenty impossibles."[40] Youth and hip-hop are intertwined. Although Palestinian youth, like other youth in the region or globally, tend to be marginalized, seen "as exceptionally troubled . . . due to . . . deprivation of freedoms," despite the desire for them "to experience something other than violence, suffering, and loss," Maira argues that increasingly they are seen otherwise. The upheavals in the region brought about mostly by youth movements have led to viewing Palestinian and Arab youth "as a force of political change."[41]

Hip-hop becomes an expression of new identity. David McDonald asserts that performative arts such as music "have been shown to be constitutive modalities for the construction of national identity formations." All the more so with Palestinian hip-hop when Palestinian identity is constantly under erasure: "In the absence of political, economic, and other material means with which to articulate national sentiment, Palestinians in exile and under occupation are often left only expressive media through which to assert national belonging." McDonald identifies musical performance as "a *primary process* for understanding what it means to be Palestinian."[42]

And yet the meaning of the term "Palestinian" is reworked by Tamer Nafar, who in his identification with the American hip-hop artist Tupac claims him as "Palestinian" and reconfigures and bases the meaning on solidarity: "His ghetto is my ghetto . . . all he talks about is the ghetto, revolution, politics. And he died because he was willing to speak out for his belief. . . . That makes him . . . Palestinian."[43] It's Tupac's historically disempowered subject position with which Nafar identifies, as well as his empowered struggle against it, which takes form in music. More important, Nafar reworks what it means to be Palestinian, from an ethnic or national identification to an emblem of solidarity with the dispossessed of the world and with those who resist oppression. For these artists, such possible reconfiguration is enacted through art; through performance, "a sense of Palestinian identity, or belonging, [is] within ephemeral moments of performative identification."[44]

Edward Said's vision of Palestinian identity as one of contestation helps us to situate music within a larger array of Palestinian art: "When identity itself operates as a site of contestation, the channels through which it is mediated and negotiated—music, art, dance, literature, poetry, and so on—become spaces in which the self is imagined and performed into being and thus become sites of contestation themselves."[45]

In "Hip Hop from '48 Palestine: Youth, Music, and the Present/ Absent," Sunaina Maira and Magid Shihade argue that this new musical art is also a new form of protest against the dispossession, displacement, and the alienation of Palestinians. Hip-hop, according to Maira and Shihade, "reimagines the geography of the nation, linking the experiences of these '48 Palestinians' to those in the West Bank, in Gaza, and in the diaspora . . . producing an archive of censored histories."[46]

Rap also keeps the Palestine question alive and at the forefront of cultural concerns at the same time that this cultural expression forms part of a global youth movement. It, writes Maira, "recreates national cultural imaginaries . . . and become[s] part of a globalized Arab youth culture that is inflected by local traditions and is often mixed with other subcultures." Rap becomes a way to connect with a wider Palestinian and Arab community, to find a common language for its youth who are "deeply engaged in questions about freedom, democracy, and solidarity, and using new generational idioms for cultural expression."[47]

The quest for a new form coincided with a quest for new politics. Most critics situate Palestinian rap in 2000 and embed it in the politicization of youth. Rap artists, writes Maira, are linked to political movements in Israel such as Tajammu. Palestinian hip-hop is "rethinking 'politics,'" which is "not just something external that this youth culture comments on or reveals, but is constantly produced, negotiated, and challenged within youth culture itself."[48]

Hip-hop constitutes a continuous aesthetic experiment for Palestinian artists as they develop a new musical language, but the artistic experience is also a political engagement, more directly so than other Palestinian art forms: "performances opened spaces for feeling as if . . . creating a vital connection, a belonging, to the nation in exile."[49] Musical performances also offer the possibility to withstand and to persist in the face of political oppression, a memory that connects to the past and that echoes intricate structures of feeling.

Certain critics like McDonald consider Palestinian music, in all its forms, as "resistance music," in that it also participates in a larger quest for self-determination. Although it may be so, this vision of Palestinian music tends to gloss over vast differences of stylistic experimentation, developments, and visions. McDonald returns in his analysis to the "Palestinian wedding," which is an old trope for resistance. In doing so, he highlights the importance of wedding music to a continuation of Palestinian music and subjectivity, which is an arena of improvisation and innovation as well: "Weddings were sites of intense nation building . . . were closely identified within a broad-based and diffuse notion of 'resistance,' . . . refracted through the prism of class, religion, gender, and politics . . . the foundational repertory of Palestinian song . . . remained elusive, kaleidoscopically shifting under the duress of overlapping frames of difference.[50]

Outside of weddings, the audiences for Palestinian musical artists are as diverse as the hip-hop genre across international borders. Ammany Jamal raises this issue in regard to the performative slam poetry of Suheir Hammad and concludes that the older generation in the Arab American community would not relate to Hammad's poetry. Hammad's audience, she argues, "like that of her second-generation cohort, is a broader coalition of individuals that includes other minority groups."[51] Of course Hammad's audience is not limited to American audiences and their minority groups, nor are DAM's audiences limited to within the boundaries of Palestine. In fact, their audiences are primarily minorities, diasporas, moving across many boundaries. McDonald emphasizes the disconnect between artist and audience when it comes to hip-hop, although the widespread popularity and inclusion of hip-hop in more mainstream cultural venues seems to point to increasing acceptance: "In calling for the crowd to sing

a famous intifada song . . . Nafar attempted to reposition the group . . .
as . . . [a] new direction in Palestinian protest song."[52] Maira points out,
however, that rappers are often included in programs for major cultural
events in Palestine and so have gained wide acceptance if not popularity.
She writes: "The 'street' or 'the underground' indexes a notion of everyday
experience, and in some instances its own cultural authenticity, that has
always been key to the allure of rap."[53]

Reem Kelani notes, however, that it is generally "ethnic" or "authentic" music that is valorized over diasporic music, not just by the hip-hop
audience but also by the Western audience of her music.[54] Although there
is some argument by Palestinian audiences on the "inside" as to whether
hip-hop is "authentic Palestinian expression," most consider, as one artist
has argued, that there are no borders to art.[55] If it is not Palestinian, then
hip-hop is also not altogether "Western," since it emerged from subaltern
margins of society and since "it interacts with and draws on diverse cultural expressions" and is the site where "youth mix, and recreate, multiple
cultural idioms."[56]

In reaching out to audiences other than Palestinian, especially when
they rap in Hewbrew to Israeli audiences, rappers follow from a tradition
of Palestinian writers and from Darwish. Darwish emaphasizes in *State
of Siege, which is preoccupied with the other,* that the shared destiny of the
besieged and the besieger calls for a search for mutual acceptance and
common ground. He writes while under military siege in Ramallah: "I am
the last of the poets who are upset by that which upsets their enemies/ Perhaps the earth is narrow to its people and gods."[57] He also insists that the
Palestinian poet must contend not only with the predicament of his own
people but also other people: "The search for normal life in this country
has to include a solution for the other. . . . This is the role of the Palestinian poet now . . . to transform enemies into adversaries."[58]

DAM's performances are multilingual: the group performs in Arabic
and Hebrew, and sometimes even in English. The importance of this multilingualism is that the song is both an articulation of a national condition, an aspiration to go beyond it, and a defiance of historical oppression.
In addition to going immediately beyond the national, the song opens
onto a human community and a community with the "other." It is song

as dialogue and communication and reconfiguration of community. It is song as promise.[59] As many critics have pointed out, multilingalism allows DAM to reach different audiences, for Israeli audiences to accept a message of antioppression from Palestinians, and for Palestinian audiences to accept a radically new musical form from Palestinian and Arabic musical traditions: "Though the Hebrew and Arabic verses espoused an antiracism, antioccupation message inside a deeply Palestinian neighborhood, up until this point the Palestinians in attendance looked and acted as though they were the outsiders. Here, by indexing the well-known words of Julia Butrous and Ahmad Qa'bour, employing linguistic signs of the 'folk' and 'country,' Tamer Nafar reached out in a powerful way to his Palestinian audience."[60] For members of DAM, such multilingualism is a necessary pedagogical strategy as well as an aesthetic choice that faces historical realities. Nafar asserts: "We have to educate ourselves, but also the other side. They do not know or want to know what's happening here."[61]

Repeatedly, hip-hop groups emphasize that rap serves as an alternative *education* to the one that artists of '48 received. Music for artists like Nafar signifies the ability to sing despite the harsh conditions of occupation. Music performance is to sing what one lives, to make it known, but also to defy these degrading conditions, to not be reduced to the condition of "occupied," to surpass the fear and the powerlessness that can be internalized. Nafar continues: "We live under a physical and mental occupation. . . . The generation of our parents is full of fear and apathy. . . . We do not accept this. We want to shake things up. We sing about what we see, about the violence, the humiliation we face. . . . We think this is educational in a true sense."[62] What is striking about this statement is its affinity with Ghassan Kanafani's *Resistance Literature*. Music here is "educational in a true sense" in raising consciousness, in having the denied voice pierce through all the discourses about Palestinians that have proliferated while an occupation spans over four decades as of this writing. Mahmoud Jreiri of DAM speaks to the disconnect between one's experience in one's home and an education that is at odds with this experience: "We knew that we are Palestinians, but in school they teach us about Zionist 'heroes,' the same heroes who killed and transferred most of our people. We don't learn about Mahmoud Darwish. You have to figure it out along, and we did figure it out."[63] This sentiment resonates with other youth for whom rap fashions cultural identity: "In schools, they do not teach us about Darwish or about Palestine."[64] Critics such as Maira concur with this pedagogical vision of hip-hop: "Rap has become a pedagogical medium to address the absence of Palestinian history and culture in the Israeli school curriculum, not to mention mainstream Israeli media and discourse."[65] The transnational dimension of rap especially concerns us; in its raising of consciousness it crosses boundaries and links with more traditional music even as it innovates and becomes more global: "The transnational and global scope of such a music education project that is firmly associated with a nationalistic mission reminds us once again that musical sounds are extremely malleable in transcending boundaries they originally signi-fied, a fact that resists any straightforward understanding of the role of music in carrying nationalistic sentiments as simply coherent, iconic, and reflective."[66]

DAM has worked with Israeli artists such as Udi Aloni and Aviv Gefen. Such collaborations not only cross cultural boundaries but also educate politically in the process of music making within a particular nation-state that has censored Palestinian expression. They reveal even more how sub-tle and not so subtle censorship works, but also how their vision of identity and of resistance is open and liberatory. Aviv Geven indicates: "After I saw that our single was simply censored in Israel—it wasn't played on any radio station— . . . I realized how difficult it is to be an Arab Israeli."[67] Udi Aloni edited the video for DAM's best-known song "Min Irhabi?" (Who's the terrorist?). The song responds to a dominant political discourse that casts terrorism as "the manifestation of blind Arab anger against the 'civilized' world." It details the daily toll of the violence of the occupation.[68] In it, Nafar sings:

I am not against peace, peace is against me

. . . .
You can speak out, but not me
Who are you? . . .
Take a look around you. . . .

. . . .

Who grew up free? And who grew up oppressed?
We fight to be free, but our struggle is suppressed
And you call me a terrorist.

Their most famous and popular song is also a landmark song, in that it shows the development and maturation of the group, whose lyrics initially addressed neighborhood concerns involving crime, and went on to tackle larger social issues of discrimination against Palestinians and then to raising consciousness about political issues involving national and transnational claims.[69]

In 2005, DAM toured the West Bank for the first time, "without special permits."[70] The tour itself was politically significant since it defied the prohibition against Israelis traveling to the occupied territories and the disconnection enforced against Palestinians through the fragmentation policies of settlements, checkpoints, borders, and the separation wall: "One of the political interventions waged through the Palestinian Hip Hop is to connect different groups of youth who are dissected by the colonial fragmentation of Palestinian geography."[71]

Just as hip-hop groups have proliferated since the emergence of Tamer Nafar on the Palestinian scene, we see other transnational developments that are more classical in their bent but no less potent in their presence, as at the Edward Said Conservatory in Ramallah, where students are trained in European classical music, which "highlights the cosmopolitan ambition of the Palestinian national music project."[72]

The transformation of Palestinian music, as manifested in such youth forms as hip-hop, highlights the aesthetic project as transnational, multilingual, and intermedial in the way it employs lyrics, music, dance, and visuals, while the political project registers protest and struggle and continues the poetics of earlier Palestinian writers such as Darwish, Samih al-Qasim, Emile Habiby, Ghassan Kanafani, and so many others.

Afterword

When the Poet Becomes an Endless Poem

I have been able to consider only a selection of artists who are increasingly transnational and diasporic and who simultaneously anchor themselves in a poetic heritage, especially that of Darwish. These artists, like Darwish, have endured experiences of dispersion, loss, and dispossession but refuse to lose themselves in loss. Their work, like that of Darwish, expresses a belonging and is preoccupied with an urgent struggle against effacement. Whereas Darwish's voice was practically a lone poetic voice on the international scene for decades, the artists that have emerged for the most part since 1995, or post-Oslo, have proliferated in a decentralized, depoliticized scene. Although their art is preoccupied first and foremost with aesthetic form, the aesthetic is intertwined in innovative ways with politics. I have tried to argue that these artists, like Darwish, and in their own way, are rethinking politics in their art as dissensual and democratic.

In this way, the ideas of Jacques Rancière have been important for my engagement with contemporary Palestinian art. Rancière leads us to consider that in the absence of politics elsewhere, art may be a place of refuge, provisional as that place may be. Rancière presents new ways to think of aesthetic and politics that opens up our consideration of these artworks in transnational and local cultural contexts. The ideas of Giorgio Agamben and Judith Butler have been important in considering new possibilities for politics, ethics, community, and mourning.

I explored contemporary Palestinian art—in its broad sense—in poetry, including spoken-word poetry, cinema, visual and performative art, and music, focusing especially on hip-hop. Given the diversity of the work

129

of individual artists, who create in different cultural contexts and subject positions, they connect to one another in that they are preoccupied with aesthetic and political considerations and produce in the theoretical modalities that I outlined: dispersion, loss, dispossession, belonging, and the struggle against erasure. They connect to other artists outside the Palestinian context as well, which dimension I began to consider in the work of Till Roeskens in collaboration with the Palestinians of Aida Camp and which I would like to pursue further. I would also like to pursue issues that I analyzed in relation to selected artists—such as intermediality, multilingualism, gender, and the diasporic—in the work of other Palestinian and non-Palestinian artists.

I argued that these artists dialogue, or intersect, with Darwish. Some of the artists discussed return to his work repeatedly and reference his work directly, whereas others simply intersect with him and his generation in their artistic visions and preoccupations. If Darwish has always insisted on the poetic qualities of his poems above all, he has done so without mitigating their political possibilities: for to offer political readings of his poetry without attention to the poetry itself is to do an injustice to his poetic project; to eclipse the political altogether is to miss the significance of his poetry. He states: "There is something worse than political poetry and that is the pretention that poetry is above the political, in its profound meaning, which is listening to the present, to the movement of history, and to the collective offering hope in its participation. The apolitical is also political, in a hidden way."[1]

Designated for decades as the "poet of the resistance" with expectations that his poetry adhere to nationalist tropes, he asks: "Is there no other indication for resistance except to say, for example, 'Record I am an Arab,' or to repeat various slogans: I will resist, and I will resist?"[2] Rather, Darwish embraces poetry's horizons while expanding the meaning and force of what the political means: "We wrote life as we lived it and as we saw it. And we wrote our dreams of freedom and insisted on being what we wanted to be."[3]

Darwish bridges the personal and the political in this poetic journey as he does in *Why Did You Leave the Horse Alone?* (1995), a collection of autobiographical poems: "His individual story of loss—including the disrupted childhood, the lost land and lost connection to his extended family, and the perpetual outsider status in adopted countries—is in many ways also his people's story."[4]

Salma Khadra Jayyusi warns us, however, against designating Darwish solely as "a political poet": "His commitment is not solely to a major political issue, but also—in fact primarily—to revelation of the daily human tragedy springing from it. *His primary incentive, then, is to consider the human condition; and it is this that makes him a world poet.*"[5]

Asked about the relation between art and politics, and relating this question to Darwish and poetry, Edward Said responded that he does not see an inherent contradiction between the two. He acknowledges the variety of poetic responses possible, for each poet's relation to his or her present is intimately particular. Invoking Adorno, he argues that lyricism's intimately personal form has an implicit relation to the political, even when it appears most apolitical.[6]

Long resisting categorization of his work, Darwish remarked that "*all poetry is . . . concerned with rewriting the future.*"[7] Darwish has indicated that poetry can only change the poet (and the reader, but not history), so that the nature of the possible transformation for Darwish is henceforth aesthetic, which nonetheless has implications for the individual's humanity: "its role is to resist that which is an obstacle to the reader's humanity, to his being . . . to deepen the idea of beauty in human beings, which leads to the idea of peace: peace between the individual and himself . . . between the individual and nature [his environment]."[8] Poetry changes not through its message but through its act and the affirmation of its voice, it changes through its very existence.

In his poetry, dispossession and aspiration are transformed to an epic, and the lyric embodies loss "at the threshold of presence,"[9] offering a fragile force. He establishes poetry not only as a space of survival but as one of freedom as well, and of possibility. In his poetry, there is a certain "steadfastness in the face of the death of the political project," an undeniable "attachment to a life of freedom."[10] Darwish celebrates the power of the creative endeavor to overcome: "Poetry is a mysterious happiness that overcomes loss and difficulty," he writes.[11]

Darwish has sought in his poetry to protect poetic language, memory, place, and individual voice. Darwish's poetry seeks foremost its own poetic horizon, but it "does not liberate itself from the pressure of its history except . . . through delving into history, not being estranged from it."[12] Darwish was equally conscious of the need to safeguard language, especially given the demands of the historical moment in which he found himself: "It was expected of me in my historical moment to fix a place in language."[13] Poetic language allows for a claim to a future and a defense of one's existence in the past, "so that a poem becomes proof of existence or not."[14] And so the poet, through language, reconstructs from absence: "The poet works alone . . . not only to make the near future less distant, or the distant past more near, but in order to accomplish what is much simpler: to rebuild his personal dismantling world."[15]

The loss is most visibly that of place and the relation to place, and what that loss engenders: the relation to the past, to others, to the self—which was severed in 1948 (and in 1967, 1982, and so on). "Place has been my poem," writes Darwish.[16] As Judith Butler has argued regarding the experience of dispossession, the nature of the tie between self and place is changed, and both place and self are lost, for the tie between them is elusive and enigmatic and shows how the self is constituted by its attachments. Butler writes that loss implies a crisis in relationality and in knowing, it is "losing what we cannot fully fathom": "When we are dispossessed from a place or a community, we may simply feel that we are undergoing something temporary. . . . But maybe when we undergo what we do, something about who we are is revealed, something that delineates the ties we have to others, that shows us that these ties constitute what we are . . . [and so in the process of loss] I become inscrutable to myself."[17]

Darwish's poetics reinforce Butler's argument that grief is not simply a private state, as Rebecca Dyer has noted, but has political implications in opening onto a different future, and that relational ties have implications for theorizing ethical responsibility: grief, Butler writes, "furnishes a sense of . . . *community* of a complex order. . . . If my fate is not originally or finally separable from yours, then the 'we' is traversed by a relationality that we cannot easily argue against." In Darwish's poems a community is suggested with his interlocutors, as Dyer notes, "one that many readers would likely feel themselves a part of. . . . The 'we' in the poem[s] . . . [evoke] also

Palestinians generally—and perhaps includes those who see the situation in Palestine as emblematic of oppression elsewhere in the world."[18]

Rarely named, place surges often in his poetry, a fragile reminder against the threat of its loss. This "articulation of place" is also an opening of a disarticulation, as Jeffrey Sacks argues, since Darwish offers and withdraws the concept of "place" in his poem *State of Siege* in the word "here."[19]

Darwish's writing, which speaks of the fundamental link between poetry and life, memory and loss, personal exile and collective displacement, the individual's existence and the human condition, testifies, in the face of loss, to a belonging that persists against all disappearance, dispersion, and fragmentation. It is a belonging reconstituted by its very disruptions and dislocations.[20] Ultimately this poetry and art become "a proxy for the disappearing archives of Palestine."[21] It resists the systematic effacement of collective history, and loss also inscribes a memory that spans across many transformations.

In one of Darwish's last poems, "La'eb al-nard" ("A Player of Dice"), in which he brings together the existential, poetic, and historical dimensions of his poetry, and in which he presents life as a game of chance, the individual poetic voice addresses a "plural you," proclaiming, "I am like you," even as he mitigates his special role to this collective: "Who am I to speak as I do?"[22] Traversed with reflections on how his life has been inextricably tied to history, he imagines he might not have become a poet had an army patrol not noticed his village, had the place not been broken.

Before his untimely death, Darwish asked: "Is poetry possible?" He stated that even with its diminishing role, "the poet has to cultivate the illusion that poetry is necessary and is able to transform. It may not be possible for poetry to affect change, but it is perhaps possible to change consciousness."[23]

Dispersion, dispossession, and erasure become siege. All sieges suggest the impossibility of journeys and the impossibility of returns. The poet describes this estrangement from home and from self that ensues from perpetual displacement, the real possibility of a solitary ending elsewhere, away from home:

As if I had become happy, I returned.
I pressed the doorbell more than once. I waited.
Perhaps I'm late. No one is opening the door. . . .
I remembered my house keys, and I apologized to myself:
I forgot about you, come in.
We entered. . . . I, the guest and the host, in my house.
I looked around. . . . I found no trace of me. . . .
Perhaps . . . I was never here

. . . .
Where am I?
I screamed to awaken from this hallucination
But I couldn't. . . .
I broke. . . .
A voice rolling over the marble
Why did you return?
I apologized to myself: I forgot about you. Leave!
But I couldn't
Dream rushed toward me
Embraced me
Asking:
Have you changed?
I have changed,
Because dying at home is better than
. . . [Dying] on my way to an empty square![24]

Suspended between an exile that is no longer permanent and a home-coming that is no longer final since his "return" in 1996, a return not to his original home in the Galilee but to Ramallah, Darwish has compli-cated his conception of "exile" and of "home." Our artists in the wake of Darwish are situated precisely between home and exile, between a famil-iar and unfamiliar home, between belonging and dislocation.

In *State of Siege*, the besieged poet, who experience siege as a violent dislocation, paints a long and tragic human scene, which opens onto the unexpected insight: Peace is the apology of the strong to the one who is weaker in weapons but powerful in range.[25] *State of Siege*, but also Dar-wish's poetic oeuvre, is itself part of this "powerful range" of response: "In his early work, Darwish documented the image of the Palestinian 'who is weaker in weapon' rebelling against occupation. At another stage, his poetry represented Palestinian transformations during times of exile. At a later phase, his poetry contemplates the tragedy of hoping for peace with those who do not seek it. In all of these situations, the poet is defending a liberated Palestinian identity and creating a cosmic poetry free from the siege of identity."[26]

Darwish's poetry is for many of his readers and for Palestinian artists experienced as a state of belonging. His poetry surges beautiful and tangible in its simple details, peopled by beings who can still meet across time and place, and is the space where we, his readers, can feel momentarily restored to ourselves. The poet's reflections on the self, love, death, exile, memory, and place has left us a voice that is faithful to place, to a long plural Arabic poetic heritage, to history, and to human experience, a poetry of love and pain that appeals to interpretation tied to freedom, a voice that opens beyond those very limits onto further horizons: "Peace is a song of life, here, in life, on the string of wheat chaff." [27]

Notes

Bibliography

Index

Notes

Mahmoud Darwish and Emergent Palestinian Arts

1. Mahmoud Darwish, "A Player of Dice," 53. This poem was published posthumously in *Lā urīdu li-hādhihi al-qaṣīda an tantahī* [I do not want this poem to end] (Beirut: Dār al-Rayyes, 2009), 35–55. All translations of Darwish and other foreign-language sources are my own unless otherwise stated.

2. Edward Said has called Darwish one of the finest world poets and lyricists. See David Barsamian, *Culture and Resistance: Conversations with Edward Said* (London: Pluto, 2003).

3. Jacques Rancière, *Dissensus: On Politics and Aesthetics*, ed. and trans. Steven Corcoran (London: Continuum, 2010).

4. Thanks to Livia Monnet for this exchange of ideas through e-mail on September 16, 2014.

5. Ilan Pappé, *The Modern Middle East* (New York: Routledge, 2005).

6. Gannit Ankori, *Palestinian Art* (London: Reaktion Books, 2006), 125.

7. See Kamal Boullata, *Palestinian Art: 1850–2005* (London: Saqi, 2009).

8. Judith Butler, "What Shall We Do without Exile," Sixth Annual Edward Said Memorial Lecture, The American University in Cairo, November 7, 2010, http://www
.youtube.com/watch?v =MLgIXtaF6OA (accessed November 30, 2010).

9. Emily Apter, *The Translation Zone: A New Comparative Literature* (Princeton, NJ: Princeton Univ. Press, 2005).

10. Nurith Gertz and George Khleifi, *Palestinian Cinema: Landscape, Trauma, and Memory* (Bloomington: Indiana Univ. Press, 2008); Hamid Dabashi, ed., *Dreams of a Nation: On Palestinian Cinema* (New York: Verso, 2006); Rebecca Stein and Ted Swedenburg, *Palestine, Israel, and the Politics of Popular Culture* (Durham, NC: Duke Univ. Press, 2005); Rasheed Araeen, et al., *The Third Text Reader: On Art, Culture, and Theory* (New York: Continuum, 2002); Ankori, *Palestinian Art*; Boullata, *Palestinian Art: 1850–2005*; Ulf Thomas Moberg, *Palestinian Art* (Stockholm: Cinclus, 1998); Tarif Abboushi, et al., *Made in Palestine* (Houston, TX: Ineri Publication, 2003); Sara Ahmed, et al., *Uprootings/Regroundings: Questions of Home and Migration* (New York: Berg, 2003);

Roy Armes, *Arab Filmmakers of the Middle East: A Dictionary* (Bloomington: Indiana Univ. Press, 2010); Viola Shafik, *Arab Cinema: History and Cultural Identity* (Cairo: The American Univ. of Cairo Press, 1998); Nada Shabout, *Modern Arab Art: Formation of Arab Aesthetics* (Gainesville: Univ. of Florida Press, 2007); and Lina Khatib, *Filming the Modern Middle East: Politics in the Cinemas of Hollywood and the Arab World* (New York: I. B. Tauris, 2006).

11. See Shafik, *Arab Cinema*.

12. Helga Souri-Tawil, "Where Is the Political in Cultural Studies?" *International Journal of Cultural Studies* 14, no. 5 (2011): 467–82.

13. Sunaina Maira, "'We Ain't Missing': Palestinian Hip Hop A Transnational Movement," *CR-East Lansing* 8, no. 2 (2008): 14.

14. In an exchange with Livia Monnet, 2013.

15. Giorgio Agamben, *The Coming Community*, trans. Michael Hardt (Minneapolis: Univ. of Minnesota Press, 1993).

16. I am grateful to Jeff Sacks for these particular articulations in reading my work.

17. Rancière, *Dissensus*, 38.

18. Suheir Hammad, *Breaking Poems* (New York: Cypher Books, 2008), 25.

19. Edward Said, *On Late Style: Music and Literature against the Grain* (New York: Vintage Books, 2006), 84.

20. Darwish, *Fī ḥaḍrat al-ghiyāb: naṣṣ* (Beirut: Riad al-Rayyes, 2006), 114.

21. Interview with Najat Rahman in 2005, in Hala Nassar and Najat Rahman, eds., *Mahmoud Darwish, Exile's Poet: Critical Essays* (Northampton, MA: Interlink, 2008).

22. Translated by Sinan Antoon as *In the Presence of Absence* (Brooklyn, NY: Archipelago Press, 2011).

23. Rancière, *Dissensus*, 145. The next several citations from *Dissensus* are cited parenthetically in the text by page number.

24. Steven Corcoran, "Editor's Introduction," in Rancière, *Dissensus*, 9, emphasis added.

25. Corcoran, "Editor's Introduction," 16.

26. Apter, *Translation Zone*, 6.

27. Shafik, *Arab Cinema*, 211.

28. See Agamben, *Coming Community*, 11.

29. Edward Said, *After the Last Sky: Palestinian Lives*, photographs by Jean Mohr (New York: Columbia Univ. Press, 1986), 34.

30. Edward Said, "The Art of Displacement: Mona Hatoum's Logic of Irreconcilables," in *Mona Hatoum: The Entire World as a Foreign Land* (London: Tate Gallery, 2000), 7–17.

31. Andreas Baur and Roland Wäspe, *Emily Jacir, Installation Shots at the Kunstmuseum St. Gallen* (St. Gallen: Kunstmuseum, Galerie der Stadt Esslingen, Verlag für Moderne Kunst, 2008), 9.

32. Edward Said, *Culture et résistance: Entretiens avec David Barsamian*, trans. Christian Calliyannis (Paris: Fayard, 2004), 186.

33. Ibid., 187.

34. See for instance, in addition to artworks named in previous chapters, Ahmad Natche's film *Two Meters of This Land* (2012), which makes direct reference to Darwish's verses in *Mural*: "Two meters of this land are enough for now. / . . . / For a chaos of brilliant flowers to slowly soak up my body."

35. Lauren Pyott, "Emerging from an 'Age of Defeat': Interview with Poet Ghassan Zaqtan," *Electronic Intifada*, December 7, 2012 (http://electronicintifada.net/content/emerging-age-defeat-interview-poet-ghassan-zaqtan/11978).

36. Darwish, *Fī ḥaḍrat al-ghiyāb*, 114.

37. Ibid., 129.

38. Ibid., 122.

39. Mahmoud Darwish, *Ḥīrat al-ʿāʾid* (Beirut: Riad al-Rayyes, 2009), 156.

40. See Mahmoud Shaheen, trans., *Almond Blossoms and Beyond* (Northhampton, MA: Interlink Books, 2009), 5.

41. Raja Shehadeh, "Mahmoud Darwish," *Bomb* 81 (Fall 2002): 57–58. Cited in Nassar and Rahman, *Mahmoud Darwish, Exile's Poet*, 5.

42. The awards include the prestigious Lotus Prize (Union of Afro-Asian Writers 1969), the Lenin Prize (USSR 1983), Knight of Arts and Belles Lettres (France 1997), and the Lannan Foundation Prize for Cultural Freedom (United States 2001), in addition to the following prizes: the Ibn Sina, the Mediterranean, the Shield of the Palestinian Revolution, the Spanish Library, a special prize from the International Cavafy Committee, the Dutch Prince Klaus, the Sultan 'Uwais, and most recently the Golden Wreath (Macedonia 2007) and the Arab Poetry Prize of the Supreme Council of Culture (Cairo) established by Naguib Mahfouz.

43. These translations include Adonis, Mahmoud Darwish, and Samih al-Qasim, *Victims of a Map: A Bilingual Anthology of Arabic Poetry*, trans. Abdallah al-Udhari (London: Saqi Books, 1984); Ibrahim Muhawi, trans., *Memory for Forgetfulness: August, Beirut, 1982* (Berkeley: Univ. of California Press, 1995); Munir Akash and Daniel Moore, eds., *The Adam of Two Edens* (Syracuse, NY: Syracuse Univ. Press, 2000); Munir Akash, Carolyn Forche, Amira Al-Zein, and Sinan Antoon, eds. and trans., *The Raven's Ink* (Santa Fe, NM: Lannan Foundation, 2001); Munir Akash and Carolyn Forché, with Sinan Antoon and Amira El-Zein, eds. and trans., *Unfortunately It Was Paradise* (Berkeley: Univ. of California Press, 2003); Mahmoud Darwish, *Why Did You Leave the Horse Alone?*, trans. Jeffrey Sacks (New York: Archipelago Press, 2006); Fady Joudah, trans., *The Butterfly's Burden* (Port Townsend, WA: Copper Canyon Press, 2006); Mohammad Shaheen, trans., *Almond Blossoms and Beyond* (Northhampton, MA: Interlink Books, 2009). *Athar al-farāsha: Yawmiyyāt* (The butterfly's effect: A journal) is the last poetic work by Mahmoud Darwish published before his death (Beirut: Riad al-Rayyes, 2008),

translated by Catherine Cobham as *A River Dies of Thirst* (Brooklyn, NY: Archipelago Press, 2009).

44. They include Jeffrey Sacks, *Iterations of Loss* (New York: Fordham Univ. Press, 2014); Khaled Mattawa, *Mahmoud Darwish: The Poet's Art and His Nation* (Syracuse, NY: Syracuse Univ. Press, 2014); Najat Rahman, *Literary Disinheritance: The Writing of Home in the Works of Mahmoud Darwish and Assia Djebar* (Lanham, MD: Lexington Books, 2008); Nassar and Rahman, *Mahmoud Darwish, Exile's Poet*; Randa Abou-Bakr, *The Conflict of Voices in the Poetry of Dennis Butrus [sic] and Mahmoud Darwish: A Comparative Study* (Wiesbaden: Reichert, 2004); and Anette Månsson, *Passage to a New Wor(L)D: Exile and Restoration in Mahmoud Darwish's Writings, 1960–1995* (Uppsala, Sweden: Uppsala Universitet, 2003).

45. Said, *After the Last Sky*, 14.

46. Said, *Culture et résistance*, 185.

47. Jacques Derrida, *Mémoires: Pour Paul de Man* (Paris: Éditions Galilée, 1988), 3.

48. Darwish, *Fī ḥaḍrat al-ghiyāb*, 35.

49. See Judith Butler, *Parting Ways: Jewishness and the Critique of Zionism* (New York: Columbia Univ. Press, 2012).

50. See Agamben, *Coming Community*, 86.

51. Irit Rogoff, *Terra Infirma: Geography's Visual Culture* (NY: Routledge, 2000).

52. Stuart Hall, "Cultural Identity and Diaspora," in *Identity: Community, Culture, Difference*, ed. Jonathan Rutherford (London: Lawrence and Wishart, 1990).

53. Yet Darwish's few prose works, which are nothing less than landmarks in his poetic career, are much less known. The earliest prose work is *Yawmiyyāt al-ḥuzn al-ʿādī* (Beirut: Dār al-ʿAwda, 1973), translated by Ibrahim Muhawi as *Journal of an Ordinary Grief* (Brooklyn, NY: Achipelago Press, 2010). This journal offers a window into how Darwish experienced defeat, loss, and his many exiles. References are also to *Ḥīrat al-ʿāʾid* [The hesitation of the returned]. Two other works followed, written decades apart: Darwish's monumental and most experimental prose work, *Dhākira lil-Nisyān* (Beirut: Dar al-Rayyes, 1987), translated by Ibrahim Muhawi as *Memory for Forgetfulness: August, Beirut, 1982* (Berkeley: Univ. of California Press, 1995); and the last prose work, *Fī ḥaḍrat al ghiyāb* [In the presence of absence: A text] (Beirut: Riad al-Rayyes, 2006).

54. Muhawi, *Journal of Ordinary Grief*, 4, 44.

55. Judith Butler, *Precarious Life: The Powers of Mourning and Violence* (New York: Verso, 2006), 21, xviii. Hereafter cited parenthetically in the text by page number.

56. This prose poem as diary, which is indicated by the subtitle of the collection ("A journal"), appeared in Darwish's *Athar al-farāsha: Yawmiyyāt* (Beirut: Riad al-Rayyes Books, 2008), 35-37, under the title "Al-beytu qatīlan" (A house fallen).

57. Judith Butler and Athena Athanasiou, *Dispossession: The Performative in the Political* (Malden, MA: Polity Press, 2013), 3.

58. Ibid., xi, emphasis mine.

59. Ibid., back cover.

60. Butler, *Parting Ways*, 6.

61. Steve Sabella, "The Colonization of the Imagination," *Contemporary Practices* 10 (2012), http://stevesabella.com/published-essays.html (accessed January 5, 2013).

1. Language's Passage from Mahmoud Darwish to Suheir Hammad, Liana Badr, and Ghassan Zaqtan

1. Mahmoud Abu Hashhash, *Istibāha* (Beirut: Al Mu'assassah al-'Arabiyyah lil-Dirāsāt wa al-Nashr, 2006). He writes in a passage that recalls *Almond Blossoms and Beyond* and *State of Siege* in its use of the tropes of siege and almonds and perseverance against all siege: "All this siege and I did not pay attention to the almonds/ . . . / and women still bury their absent ones with lilies" (31). In another passage reminiscent of Darwish in *Limātha tarakata al-ḥiṣān waḥīdan?* (*Why Did You Leave the Horse Alone?*), he writes: "I was not Eastern nor Western. I was a woman who travels within her body and in it she sleeps" (61). And he writes another poem "Speech of the Red Indian" that recalls Darwish's "Eleven Planets." In this poem, he also takes on the voice of a Native American (of the Miskawakis), citing a long passage from it: "We do not write history/ . . . / in the evening in the autumn they will leave" (79).

2. Hammad, *Breaking Poems*. The section on Hammad appeared in a briefer and slightly modified version in "Translation and the Passage to Politics in Palestinian Art," *Intermédialités*, no. 20 (Fall 2012), a special online issue edited by Philippe Despoix, who has, along with *Intermédialités*, kindly given permission to reprint.

3. Hammad received many awards, including a Tony Award for the Special Theatrical Event for the *Russell Simmons Presents Def Poetry* (original cast member and writer), the American Book Award, The Audre Lorde Writing Award, the Emerging Artist Award at New York University, the Morris Center Award, and a Van Lier Fellowship. Her works include *Born Palestinian, Born Black* (New York: Harlem River Press, 1996); *Drops of This Story* (New York: Harlem River Press, 1996); and *Zaatar Diva* (New York: Cypher Books, 2005). Although all books trace a personal trajectory that has been overshadowed by a larger historical predicament shared with a collectivity, *Drops of This Story* does so in a more narrative (memoir) form. In it, she writes: "After all this time, I'm still writing. So that our stories be told. . . . So that we don't forget. So we always remember. I is we" ("Author's Note," n.p.). Her other works are poetic and lyrical.

4. The word "Qalā'id" (stars, necklaces) in pre-Islamic poetry also referred to poems. See Rahman, *Literary Disinheritance*.

5. Mahmoud Darwish, *Diwan*, vol. 2 (Beirut: Dar al-'awda, 1994), 135–36.

6. Hammad, "Break (Me)," in *Breaking Poems*, 51.

7. In a poem titled "Belonging," Mohamad Lafi, a Palestinian poet, writes about this ambivalence toward the sentiment of belonging when one is away and the feeling

is nonetheless all too overpowering: "How the threads reached toward me/ . . . /and my heart connected me to you." Mohamad Lafi, *Muqaffaʻbi al-rīmah* (Ramallah: Beit al-Shʻir, 2007), 78.

8. Muhawi, *Journal of an Ordinary Grief*, 154.

9. Ibid., 44.

10. As poetry, spoken word often expresses political commentary. Spoken-word poets include Gil Scott Heron, Spalding Grya, Hedwig Gorski, and Henry Rollins. It originated from the poetry of the Harlem Renaissance and blues music and proliferated among the African American community of the 1960s. Spoken-word poetry has been particularly inclusive of minority and women voices.

11. Definitions from *Le Petit Robert* (2014) and *Oxford English Dictionary* (2015).

12. Hammad, *Drops of This Story*, 11, 33.

13. "Break," *Merriam-Webster Unabridged Online Dictionary*.

14. Darwish, *Diwan*, 2: 135.

15. Carolyn Forché, back cover of Hammad, *Breaking Poems*.

16. Maurice Blanchot, *The Space of Literature*, trans. Ann Smock (Lincoln: Univ. of Nebraska Press, 1989).

17. Apter, *Translation Zone*, 9.

18. Ibid., 7.

19. This reading of Benjamin's conception of translation follows Paul de Man's reading in *Resistance to Theory* (Minneapolis: Univ. of Minnesota Press, 1986).

20. Hammad, *Breaking Poems*, 45.

21. Darwish, "Crypts, Andalusia, Desert," in *Diwan*, 2: 90–94

22. Hammad, "Break (Bayou)," *Breaking Poems*, 35, 25.

23. References to Isis and Osiris abound in literature and emphasize aspects of the myth that Hammad evokes in her poetry. Isis is evoked as the Egyptian goddess who mourns her lover/brother Osiris, killed and dismembered by Set. Isis sets out to look for him; she gathers his severed parts and so brings him to life. The most celebrated version is Plutarch's *De Iside et Osiride*. See, for instance, *Of Isis and Osiris: Or of the Ancient Religion and Philosophy of Egypt*, trans. William Baxter (n.p.: CreateSpace Independent Publishing Platform, 2011). Isis is featured in Ahdaf Souefi, *The Map of Love* (New York: Anchor, 1999).

24. Chris Abani, back cover of Hammad, *Breaking Poems*.

25. Wail Hassan, Preface, in Abdelfattah Kilito, *Thou Shalt Not Speak My Language* (Syracuse, NY: Syracuse Univ. Press, 2008).

26. Hammad, "Break (Clear)," in *Breaking Poems*, 44. Subsequent page numbers are cited parenthetically in the text.

27. Butler, "What Shall We Do without Exile?" See also Butler, *Parting Ways*; and Glenn Bowman, "A Country of Words: Conceiving the Palestinian Nation from the

Position of Exile," in *The Making of Political Identities*, ed. Ernesto Laclau (New York: Verso, 1994).

28. The term "minor" is in explicit reference to Deleuze and Guattari's notion of "minor literature." See Gilles Deleuze and Felix Guattari, *Franz Kafka: Toward a Minor Literature*, trans. Dana Polan (Minneapolis: Univ. of Minnesota Press, 1986).

29. Hall, "Cultural Identity and Diaspora," 235.

30. Rogoff, *Terra Infirma*, 37.

31. Rancière, *Dissensus*, 37, 152.

32. Ibid., 15, 151.

33. Apter, *Translation Zone*, 10.

34. Ibid., 245, 244.

35. Ibid., 6.

36. Rancière, *Dissensus*, 145.

37. Alain Badiou, cited by Apter, *Translation Zone*, 87.

38. Darwish, *Diwan*, 2: 117–18.

39. Jacques Derrida, *Monolingualism of the Other: Or the Prosthesis of Origin*, trans. Patrick Mensah (Stanford, CA: Stanford Univ. Press, 1998), 72.

40. Liana Badr, *Zanābiq al-daw'* (Cairo: Dār Sharqīyyāt, 1998).

41. Liana Badr e-mail to author, December 3, 2014. Instructed in the traditions of Arabic poetry since the age of ten by her father, her language, seeped in that tradition, emerges light and unique. She shared her other poetry collection, *Zaman al-Layl*, with Darwish before his death; the collection was published by Dār al-Sāqī in Beirut in 2008. Unfortunately, I was unable to address those poems in this book but hope to do so in subsequent publications.

42. Ahmad is a name and *za'tar* means thyme but refers also to Tel al-Za'tar, a refugee camp in Lebanon. The words literally mean "the hill of thyme."

43. These films include *Fadwa: A Tale of a Palestinian Poetess*, 1999; *The Gates are Open: Sometimes!*, 2006; and *Al-Quds-My City*, 2010, all produced in Ramallah, through the support of the Palestinian Ministry of Culture.

44. Badr, "A Voyage in the Mediterranean," in *Zanābiq al- daw'*, 121–22.

45. Badr, "Salālim alsamā" (Scaling the sky), in *Zanābiq al daw'*, 132.

46. Badr, "The Horoscopes of Man and Woman," in *Zanābiq al- daw'*, 61.

47. Badr, "Anāshīd" (Epic songs), 89n.

48. Ghassan Zaqtan also wrote the novel *Describing the Past* (1995) and the play *The Narrow Sea*, which obtained an honorable mention at the 1994 Cairo Festival. He edited the literary magazine *Bayāder*, the poetry journal *Al-Shu'arā'*, and the literary page of the Ramallah newspaper *Al-Ayyām*. A founding director of the House of Poetry in the West Bank city of Ramallah, Zaqtan also served as director general of the Palestinian Ministry of Culture's Literature and Publishing Department.

49. Fady Joudah, "Translator's Preface," in Ghassan Zaqtan, *Like a Straw Bird It Follows Me, and Other Poems*, trans. Fady Joudah (New Haven, CT: Yale Univ. Press, 2012), xi. Hereafter cited parenthetically in the text by page number.

50. Ghassan Zaqtan in an interview with PBS's Jeffrey Brown, March 22, 2007.

51. Zaqtan, "Wolves," in *Like a Straw Bird It Follows Me*, 31. Hereafter cited parenthetically in the text by page number.

52. Zaqtan, "The One You Accidentally Found in the Mirror," in *Like a Straw Bird It Follows Me*, 97.

53. Sacks, *Why Did You Leave the Horse Alone?*, 101.

54. Darwish's verse comes from the long poem *Ma'sāt al-narjis malhāt al-fiḍḍa*, in *Diwan*, 2: 435. The verse reads: "because the house is more beautiful than the path to the house" (435).

55. Zaqtan, "Alone and the River before Me," in *Like a Straw Bird It Follows Me*, 81. Hereafter cited parenthetically in the text by page number.

56. Joudah, translator's notes to "A Gambler's Hymn," in *Like a Straw Bird It Follows Me*, 119.

57. Zaqtan, "A Gambler's Hymn," in *Like a Straw Bird It Follows Me*, 15.

58. Zaqtan, "Wolves, Also," in *Like a Straw Bird It Follows Me*, 33–34.

59. Darwish, "A Soldier Dreams of White Lilies," in *Diwan*, 1: 311–22.

60. Zaqtan, "An Enemy Comes Down the Hill," in *Like a Straw Bird It Follows Me*, 35.

61. Zaqtan, "A Picture of the House at Beit Jala," in *Like a Straw Bird It Follows Me*, 98.

2. "A Coming to Language"

1. This observation is by an anonymous reader of the manuscript, to whom I am grateful.

2. Henri Bergson, *Laughter: An Essay on the Meaning of the Comic*, trans. Clousdesley Brereton and Fred Rotwell (New York: Macmillan, 1912), 135.

A version of this chapter appeared as "'Laughter That Encounters a Void?': Humor, Loss, and the Possibility for Politics in Palestinian Cinema," in *A Companion to Film Comedy*, ed. Andrew Horton and Joanna Rapf (New York: Wiley-Blackwell, 2012). Permission to reprint has been granted by Wiley. I wish to thank Andrew Horton for his thoughtful comments and for his inspiration, which led me to work on humor in Middle Eastern cultural production. I also would like to thank Livia Monnet for our engaging and insightful discussions of aesthetics and politics.

3. Dabashi, *Dreams of a Nation*, 144. On the question of cinema's liberatory possibilities, see David Barsamian's interview with Edward Said, in Said, *Culture et résistance*, 221. To the question whether cinema can be a means to advance a political cause, Said

thinks it absolutely can and gives the example of Elia Suleiman's film *Divine Intervention*, which he believes was successful through humor. He emphasizes that the film was entered under the category "foreign films" in the Motion Picture Academy and that it was refused since no country with the name "Palestine" exists. I follow Hamid Dabashi and others in considering Palestinian cinema to be one made by Palestinian filmmakers (*Dreams of a Nation*, 144).

4. Jacques Rancière, in *Dissensus*, conceives of politics as dissensus or the manifestation of "two worlds in one"; according to him we are in consensus, which establishes hierarchies and separation between the social and the political, art and culture, proper and improper activity or speech.

5. Edward Said, "Preface," in Dabashi, *Dreams of a Nation*, 3.

6. Félicia Chan, "What Dreams May Come: (Palestinian) Cinema/Nation/History," *Variant* 30 (Winter 2007): 8–9.

7. Ibid., 9.

8. This recognition is most notable in the Cannes Jury Prize for *Divine Intervention* in 2002, in the Golden Globe Award for Best Foreign Language Film, and the Oscar nomination for Hany Abu-Assad's *Paradise Now*, 2005.

9. Hamid Naficy, "Palestinian Exilic Cinema and Film Letters," in Dabashi, *Dreams of a Nation*, 91. See also Naficy, *An Accented Cinema: Exilic and Diasporic Filmmaking* (Princeton, NJ: Princeton Univ. Press, 2001); and Naficy, *Home, Exile, Homeland: Film, Media, and the Politics of Place* (New York: Routledge, 1998).

10. Chan, "What Dreams May Come," 9.

11. Dabashi, *Dreams of a Nation*, 10.

12. Naficy, "Palestinian Exilic Cinema," 91.

13. Bergson, *Laughter*, 135. Hereafter cited parenthetically in the text by page number.

14. Bergson defines gestures as "the attitudes, the movements and even the language by which a mental state expresses itself outwardly without any aim or profit, from no other cause than a kind of inner itching" (*Laughter*, 143).

15. For Bergson the comic is *human*, both in the sense of not being shared by other species and as a mark of our humanity and its limits (*Laughter*, 3).

16. See Howard Feinstein, "Laila's Birthday," *Screen International*, September 7, 2008; Ella Taylor, "Laila's Birthday Is Masharawi's Day in the Life of Ramallah," *Village Voice*, May 27, 2009; and Stephen Holden, "Navigating Ramallah, an Eye Out for the Absurd," *New York Times*, May 27, 2009.

17. DVD back cover. Rashid Masharawi, *Laila's Birthday* (Ramallah: Cinema Production Center, 2008). The DVD is a joint production of Palestine, Tunisia, and the Netherlands, and involves several production companies.

18. Rancière, *Dissensus*, 58.

19. Butler, "What Shall We Do without Exile?"

20. Butler, *Precarious Life*, 144, emphasis added.

21. Horton and Rapf, *A Companion to Film Comedy*, 10.

22. Rancière, *Dissensus*, 37.

23. Corcoran, "Editor's Introduction," 6.

24. Rancière, *Dissensus*, 139, emphasis mine.

25. Corcoran, "Editor's Introduction," 7.

26. Rancière, *Dissensus*, 38.

27. Butler, *Precarious Life*, 21, xviii.

28. Ibid., 22–23.

29. Rancière, *Dissensus*, 16, 133.

30. For Tzvetan Todorov's treatment of the fantastic, see *The Fantastic: A Structural Approach to a Literary Genre*, trans. Richard Howard (Cleveland, OH: Case Western Univ. Press, 1973), 33. According to Todorov, the fantastic needs three conditions: hesitation on the part of the reader as to whether what is taking place is natural or supernatural, identification of the reader with the character who elicits such hésitation, and refusal by the reader of a poetic or allegorical interpretation of what is taking place.

31. Gönül Dönmez-Colin, *The Cinema of North Africa and the Middle East* (London: Wallflower Press, 2007), 177.

32. Butler, "What Shall We Do without Exile?"

33. Richard Porton, "Notes from the Palestinian Diaspora: An Interview with Elia Suleiman," *Cineaste* 28, no. 3 (2003): 24–27.

34. Various reviewers of the film saw the fantastic as wish fulfillment, not for change but for vengeance. One critic asks if this use of the fantastic is an "acquiescence or violent desire for revenge? . . . Is Suleiman sidestepping serious questions about the tactics of the Palestinian intifada . . . by portraying anti-Israeli violence as harmless fantasy?" Elbert Ventura, "Ghost World," *Pop Matters*, February 20, 2003, http://popmatters.com/film/reviews/d/divine-intervention.shtml (accessed February 1, 2008).

35. The question of representation has preoccupied the work of Suleiman from the beginning. See, for instance, the film *Introduction to the End of An Argument* (1990), with Jayce Salloum, which takes up the depiction of Arabs in Western media. Suleiman's most notable films include *Sijl Ikhtifā'* (Chronicle of disappearance), which received the Venice Film Festival Award in 1996 for Best First Film, and *The Time That Remains* (2009).

36. Darwish, *Fī ḥaḍrat*, 35.

37. Ibid., 151.

38. Ibid., 19.

39. Najat Rahman, meeting with Darwish in 1996, in *Literary Disinheritance*.

40. Darwish, *Fī ḥaḍrat*, 143.

41. Gertz and Khleifi, *Palestinian Cinema*, 181.

42. Horton and Rapf, *A Companion to Film Comedy*, 10.

43. Ibid.

44. Gertz and Khleifi, *Palestinian Cinema*, 180–81.

45. Sobhi al-Zobaidi, "Tora Bora Cinema," *Jump Cut: A Review of Contemporary Media* 50 (Spring 2008), www.ejumpcut.org/archive/jc50.2008/PalestineFilm/index.html (accessed May 15, 2008).

46. Gertz and Khleifi, *Palestinian Cinema*, 178.

47. Zobaidi, "Tora Bora Cinema."

48. Naficy, *An Accented Cinema*, 18.

49. Like the other two films and many Palestinian films, this is a joint production (Palestine/France/Germany/the Netherlands/Israel). Conditions around filming were harrowing and included the kidnapping of a group member by a Palestinian faction and shelling by Israelis near the filming location; as a consequence, German members of the crew left work and the location of filming was changed from Nablus to Nazareth. Note also that the words "martyr" and "witness" are linked in Arabic (*Shahīd* and *Shāhed*, respectively). Other films by Hany Abu-Assad include *Omar* (2013), *Rana's Wedding* (2002), *Ford Transit* (2002), *Nazareth 2000* (2001), and *Sanctuary* (2002).

50. Corcoran, "Editor's Introduction," 21.

51. Rancière, *Dissensus*, 152.

3. A Memory for Disappearing Archives

1. Several studies on Palestinian art have appeared in the last years, most notably Boullata, *Palestinian Art: From 1850 to 2005*; and Ankori, *Palestinian Art*.

2. Ankori, *Palestinian Art*, 83, emphasis added.

3. See Said, "Art of Displacement," 7–17.

4. In an exchange with Livia Monnet.

5. Ilan Pappé, *The Modern Middle East* (New York: Routledge, 2005), 216.

6. See Boullata, *Palestinian Art*, 30, 28.

7. Ankori, *Palestinian Art*, 20.

8. In a conversation with Livia Monnet on contemporary international art.

9. Ankori, *Palestinian Art*, 83.

10. Rogoff, *Terra Infirma*, 15.

11. Stuart Hall, "Cultural Identity and Diaspora," cited in Fran Lloyd, *Contemporary Arab Women's Art: Dialogues of the Present* (London: Women's Art Library, 1999), 34.

12. Ankori, *Palestinian Art*, 125.

13. Boullata, *Palestinian Art*, 30.

14. Ankori, *Palestinian Art*, 15.

15. Ibid.

16. Ibid., 21.

17. Boullata, *Palestinian Art*, 27.

18. Ankori, *Palestinian Art*, 218.

19. Said, *After the Last Sky*, 34, cited in Ankori, *Palestinian Art*, 8.

20. Ankori, *Palestinian Art*, 15.

21. See also Boullata, *Palestinian Art*; and Ankori, *Palestinian Art*, 8, 217.

22. Hall, "Cultural Identity," 402, cited in Lloyd, *Contemporary Arab Women's Art*, 28.

23. See Boullata, *Palestinian Art*, 176; and Said, "Art of Displacement," 7–17.

24. See Ankori, *Palestinian Art*, 21, 18. Narratives about Palestinian art tend to locate its beginning in 1948, although many acknowledge that a vibrant art movement existed before the Nakba and is now difficult to trace.

25. See Said, "Art of Displacement," 7–17, cited in Boullata, *Palestinian Art*, 176.

26. T. J. Demos, "Emily Jacir: Poetry's Beyond," in *Guggenheim Museum Hugo Boss Prize* [Catalogue] (New York: Guggenheim Museum, 2008), 59.

27. Shafik, *Arab Cinema*, 209.

28. Ibid., 4.

29. Jacir's piece is also compiled in Christian Kravagna et al., *Emily Jacir, Belongings: Arbeiten/Works 1998–2003* (Vienna: Verlag, 2004), and Haram's photos are available at the Saatchi Gallery. Segments of this discussion on the work of Emily Jacir and Eman Haram appeared in "Against Erasures: Memory and Loss in the Art of Emily Jacir and Eman Haram," *The State of the Arts in the Middle East, Middle East Institute Viewpoints*, no. 4 (March 2009): 106–9. Permission has been kindly granted by John Calabrese and the *Middle East Institute Viewpoints*. Segments of my discussion of Mona Hatoum and a version of the section on Till Roeskens appeared electronically in "Translation and the Passage to Politics in Contemporary Palestinian Art," *Revue Intermédialités*, no. 20 (Fall 2012). I thank Philippe Despoix and *Revue Intermédialités* for permission to reprint.

30. Shabout, *Modern Arab Art*, xiii.

31. Boullata, *Palestinian Art*, 30.

32. Said, *After the Last Sky*; and Ankori, *Palestinian Art*, 84.

33. Rogoff, *Terra Infirma*, 90.

34. Jacir, interview with Stella Rollig, in Jacir, *Belongings*, 9. This section on Emily Jacir's *Where We Come From* and the introductory section on Eman Haram's artwork appeared in an earlier version as "Against Erasures: Memory and Loss in the Art of Emily Jacir and Eman Haram."

35. Jacir, *Belongings*, 8.

36. Demos, "Emily Jacir," 62 (my emphasis), and 61.

37. Jacir speaking to Rollig, in Jacir, *Belongings*, 9.

38. Demos, "Emily Jacir," 59.

39. See Jacir, *Belongings*, n.p.

40. Cited in Demos, "Emily Jacir," 59.

41. Baur and Wäspe, *Emily Jacir, Installation Shots at the Kunstmuseum St. Gallen*, 9–10.

42. Said writes: "Tout ce que ressemble à des archives et qui témoigne concrète-ment de l'existence d'une histoire est perçue comme étant à détruire. C'est l'obsession de n'importe quel conquérant impérialiste. . . . Face aux tentatives de répression, il y aura toujours une réaction ingénieuse et une volonté populaire qui résisteront." See Edward Said, interview with David Barsamian, 187. Said, *Culture et résistance*, 187.

43. Jacir speaking to Rollig, in Jacir, *Belongings*, 10.

44. Demos, "Emily Jacir," 61, 62.

45. Ibid., 61.

46. Baur and Wäspe, *Emily Jacir, Installation Shots at the Kunstmuseum St. Gallen*, 10.

47. Martin Strum, in Jacir, *Belongings*, 3.

48. John Menick, in Jacir, *Belongings*, 28.

49. Demos, "Emily Jacir," 60.

50. Michael Z. Wise, "Border Crossings between Art and Life," e-mail interview with Jacir, *New York Times*, February 1, 2009, AR28.

51. Ibid.

52. Ibid.

53. Demos, "Emily Jacir," 59, 60.

54. Wise, "Border Crossings."

55. Emily Jacir, cited in Demos, "Emily Jacir," 60.

56. Demos, "Emily Jacir," 60.

57. Suheir Hammad, *Drops of This Story* (New York: Harlem River Press, 1997), 33.

58. Osama Abu Sitta, "Topography of the Soul," *Home magazine*, February 2013, http://arabartex.wordpress.com/2013/03/06/topography-of-the-soul-eman-haram-at-nabad/. Eman Haram was born in Damascus in 1958 to Palestinian parents. She grew up in Beirut and moved to the United States to study and work. Haram holds a BS in archi-tecture and an MA in art history. Since 2001 she has been living in Montreal, Canada, intermittently visiting and working in Amman. Her photography is inspired with the tradi-tion of painting and is preoccupied with memory, exile, and belonging. For images of the exhibit at Nabad Gallery in Amman, see http://www.nabadartgallery.com/Public_Arti est/Exhibition_details.aspx?Rec_Idx=1&Exh_ID=74&Status=Current; and http://www .nabadartgallery.com/Public_Artiest/Artists_page.aspx?Artist_Id=46&Rec_Idx=40&t=l.

59. Abou Sitta, "Topography of the Soul."

60. From Eman Haram's exhibit catalogue for *Iconographies*, an exhibit at Nabad Gallery in Amman, March 22, 2013–May 8, 2013.

61. Osama Abou Sitta, "Topography of the Soul."

62. Phone conversation with Eman Haram, October 6, 2014.

63. Haram refers to a practice in some Palestinian villages: an olive tree is planted whenever a child is born, and in a manner becomes the child's double. Haram e-mail to author, March 3, 2015.

64. Shabout, *Modern Arab Art*, 122.

65. Ibid.

66. Rancière, *Dissensus*, 152, emphasis mine.

67. Corcoran, "Editor's Introduction," 6.

68. Cited by Ankori, *Palestinian Art*, 130. This early section on Hatoum's *The Negotiating Table* and *Present Tense*, as well as the section on Till Roeskens, appeared in "Translation and the Passage to Politics in Contemporary Palestinian Art."

69. Hammad, *Breaking Poems*, 25.

70. Rancière, *Dissensus*, 38, emphasis mine.

71. Hammad, *Breaking Poems*, 19. Hereafter cited parenthetically in the text by page number.

72. Cited in Ankori, *Palestinian Art*, 130.

73. Rancière, *Dissensus*, 37.

74. Ibid.

75. Cited in Ankori, *Palestinian Art*, 152.

76. Ibid., 151–52.

77. Ibid., 154.

78. On the question of order and Hatoum, see Martina Millà, *Mona Hatoum Projecció* (Barcelona: Fundació Joan Miró, 2011).

79. I first came across this image circulating in postcards just as I was entering college. I didn't know who the artist was or her background, but it spoke so powerfully to me as a woman's statement, above all against all efforts to oppress, which are often sanctioned by the police and the military whether they involve military occupation or not.

80. Catherine de Zegher, "Mona Hatoum: Beyond the Violence Vortex into the Beauty Vortex," in Millà, *Mona Hatoum Projecció*, 119.

81. Jaime Lanaspa, "English Texts," in Millà, *Mona Hatoum Projecció*, 115.

82. Said, "Art of Displacement," cited in Zegher, "Mona Hatoum," 117, original emphasis. "Said's 'exile' is an empowering idea that allows intellectuals to transform their pain to border crossing, homelessness, and marginal identity into the paradoxical pleasure of achieving intellectual freedom through a deeper and broader understanding of culture, identity and home." Michael Archer, Guy Brett, and Catherine de Zegher, *Mona Hatoum* (London: Phaidon Press, 1998), 119.

83. Zegher, "Mona Hatoum," 117–18.

84. Ibid., 117.

85. Ibid., 120.

86. Ibid.

87. See Till Roeskens's and Nicolas Féodoroff's introduction to the video work on the artist's website: http://documentsdartistes.org/artistes/roeskens/repro3-8.html (accessed December 20, 2012).

88. Rancière, *Dissensus*, 139, emphasis mine.

89. Corcoran, "Editor's Introduction," 7.

90. Yara al-Ghadban, "The Ghost in the Art Work," posted by Johannesburg Workshop in Theory and Criticism blog, September 10, 2009, http://jhbwtc.blogspot.com.

91. Shabout, *Modern Arab Art*, 134.

92. For a discussion on the co-option of Palestinian art, see Yara al-Ghadban, "Ghost in the Art Work."

93. See Said, "Art of Displacement," 7–17, cited in Boullata, *Palestinian Art*, 176, and in Ankori, *Palestinian Art*, 154.

94. Cited in Lloyd, *Contemporary Arab Women's Art*, 21.

95. Her work has been shown in Canada and internationally in both group and solo exhibitions and screenings, including the Montreal, Toronto, and Madrid Palestine film festivals, the One World Film Festival, the Contact Photography Film Festival, the Karsh-Masson Art Gallery, the Khalil Sakakini Cultural Centre, Gallery 101, the Art Gallery of Mississauga, the Ottawa X-photography Festival, A Space Gallery, the San Francisco Museum of Modern Art, and in various universities galleries in Canada. She has received a number of awards from the University of Ottawa, Ryerson University, and Western University. She is a recipient of grants, including from the Canada Council for the Arts, the Ontario Art Council, and the City of Ottawa. See also: *At Home*, Video Installation, May 2–26, IMA Gallery, Toronto, http://2012.scotiabankcontactphoto.com/featured-exhibitions/878.

96. Rehab Nazzal, cited in David Paterson, "Provocative Works Dominate AGM's Spring Show," March 13, 2013, http://www.mississauga.com/whatson-story/3133218-provocative-works-dominate-agm-s-spring-show/.

97. Nazzal comments on the reality of living under occupation: "witnessing the countless times of house search, arrest of my father and siblings, the killing of my brother, expelling my other brother and sister-in-law to the borders of Jordan, the demolishing of my grandfather's house, the arrest of tens of relatives, the killing of my 21-year-old cousin just last year on a checkpoint on the same day I arrived to my mother's house and countless images of humiliation and injustice." In Paterson, "Provocative Works."

98. Rehab Nazzal, "An Ongoing Struggle: A Paper in Support of the Multi-Channel Video Installation" (unpublished paper by the artist accompanying the exhibit *At Home*.

99. Ibid.

100. Ibid.

101. Paterson, "Provocative Works."

102. Nazzal, "An Ongoing Struggle."

103. Ibid.

104. David Paterson, "Provocative Works."

105. Martha Samar, "Palestinian Video Art," *This Week in Palestine*, February 1, 2010. http://archive.thisweekinpalestine.com/details.php?id=2965&ed=177. Samar points

to art that has had an impact on Palestinian video art production: "pop art, body art, Arte Povera, Fluxus, minimalist art, conceptual art, guerrilla art."

106. Samar, "Palestinian Video Art." See Chris Meigh-Andrews, *A History of Video Art* (London: Bloomsbury Academic Publishing, 2006), 2; and Doug Hall and Sally Jo Fifer, *Illuminating Video: An Essential Guide to Video Art* (San Francisco, CA: Aperture/ Bay Area Video Coalition, 1990), 32.

107. Samar, "Palestinian Video Art."

108. Ibid.

109. Ibid. See the website artpalestine.org for more Waked images.

110. On humor and Palestinian art, see *Humor and Palestinian Art*, http://www .youtube.com/watch?v=GSLr2D_eiX0. Sharif Waked, *To Be Continued*, can be partially seen at: http://vimeo.com/60501418. For Sharif Waked's *Beace Brocess*, see http://vimeo .com/22948064.

111. Sharif Waked, "Sharif Waked: Chic Point," *Nafas Art Magazine*, March 2005, http://universes-in-universe.org/eng/nafas/articles/2005/waked.

112. Ariella Azoulay and Sherene Seikaly, "Chic Point: Fashion for Israeli Check Points," *ArteEast* (Spring 2007): http://www.arteeast.org/2012/02/27/chic-point-fashion -for-israeli-checkpoints/.

113. Ibid.

114. Ibid.

115. Ilana Hammerman, "Seeing and Unseeing: After Laughter Has Loosened the Fetters of Fear and Hostility, Look at the Men Here and Think Not Only about Their Humanity and Vulnerability, but Also Your Own," *Haaretz*, December 20, 2007, http:// www.haaretz.com/misc/article-print-page/seeing-and-unseeing-1.235578?trailingPath=2 .169%2C2.203%2C2.205%2C.

116. Ibid., my emphasis.

117. Gil Z. Hochberg, "Check Me Out: Queer Encounters in Sharif Waked's *Chic Point: Fashion for Israeli Checkpoints*," *GLQ: A Journal of Lesbian and Gay Studies* 16, no. 4 (2010), emphasis added. Hochberg provides a fine analysis of Waked's video. However, I disagree with some of her conclusions, and the quote cited from her abstract articulates most clearly these conclusions.

4. "All We Have Is the Song"

1. Mahmoud Abu Hashhash, interview by Thorsén, in *Palestinian Music and Song: Expression and Resistance since 1900*, ed. Moslih Kanaaneh, et al. (Bloomington: Indiana Univ. Press, 2013), 167.

2. Chuen-Fung Wong, "Conflicts, Occupation, and Music-Making in Palestine," *Macalester International* 23 (2009): 270.

3. Ibid., 286.

4. "We Are Defending Our Culture: An Interview with Samir Joubran," *The Electronic Intifada*, March 29, 2010, http://electronicintifada.net/content/we-are-defending-our-culture-interview-samir joubran/8753.

5. Reem Talhami, interviewed by Heather Bursheh, "Realities for a Singer in Palestine," in Kanaaneh, *Palestinian Music and Song*, 115–16.

6. Wong, "Conflicts, Occupation," 279–80.

7. Ibid., 279.

8. McDonald, *My Voice Is My Weapon*, 131.

9. Wong, "Conflicts, Occupation," 279.

10. Ibid., 281.

11. Hashhash, interview by Thorsén, in Kanaaneh, *Palestinian Music and Song*, 158.

12. Cohen and Katz, *Palestinian Arab Music*, 235.

13. Ibid., 250.

14. Wong, "Conflicts, Occupation," 269.

15. Cohen and Katz, *Palestinian Arab Music*, 15.

16. Rima Tarazi, "The Palestinian National Song: A Personal Testimony" *This Week in Palestine*, April 2007. See also "Journey in the Palestinian Political Song." *This Week in Palestine*, April 2007, http://archive.thisweekinpalestine.com/details.php?id=2109&ed=139&edid=139.

17. Tarazi, "Palestinian National Song."

18. Wong, "Conflicts, Occupation," 277.

19. Cohen and Katz, *Palestinian Arab Music*, 15. See also Joseph Massad's essay, "Liberating Songs: Palestine Put to Music," *Palestine Studies.org* 32, no. 2 (2002–3), http://www.palestine-studies.org/jps/fulltext/41338.

20. Cohen and Katz, *Palestinian Arab Music*, 16.

21. Ibid., 32.

22. Benjamin Elon Brinner, *Playing across a Divide: Israeli-Palestinian Musical Encounters* (Oxford: Oxford Univ. Press, 2009), 264.

23. Cohen and Katz, *Palestinian Arab Music*, 325.

24. Ibid., 34, 251.

25. McDonald, *My Voice Is My Weapon*, 107.

26. Ibid., 104.

27. Wong, "Conflicts, Occupation," 269–71.

28. Ibid., 274, 272.

29. Souri-Tawil, "Where Is the Political in Cultural Studies?" 475-76. See also Souri-Tawil, "Coming into Being and Flowing into Exile: History and Trends in Palestinian Film-Making," *Nebula* 2, no. 2 (2005): 113–40.

30. Maira, "'We Ain't Missing,'" 14. See also Sunaina Maira, *Jil Oslo: Palestinian Hip Hop: Youth Culture and the Youth Movement* (Washington, DC: Tadween, 2013).

31. Ela Greenberg, "'The King of the Streets': Hip Hop and the Reclaiming of Masculinity in Jerusalem's Shu'afat Refugee Camp," *Middle East Journal of Culture and Communication* 2, no. 2 (2009): 231.

32. Maira, *Jil Oslo*, 72.

33. McDonald, *My Voice Is My Weapon*, 231.

34. Maira, *Jil Oslo*, 73.

35. Ibid., 24.

36. Ibid., 73–74.

37. Randa Safieh, "Identity, Diaspora, and Resistance in Palestinian Hip-Hop," in Kanaaneh, *Palestinian Music and Song*, 71.

38. Hira Nabi, "'We Will Continue to Sing': DAM's Suhell Nafar Interviewed," *The Electronic Intifada*, December 17, 2010,

http://electronicintifada.net/content/we-will-continue-sing-dams-suhell-nafar-interviewed/9787.

39. Ibid.

40. Tawfiq Zayyad, in Kanaaneh, *Palestinian Music and Song*, 8.

41. Ibid., 21, 31.

42. McDonald, *My Voice Is My Weapon*, 28, 32, 33, emphasis mine.

43. Ibid., 20.

44. Ibid., 24.

45. Sylvia Alajaji, "Performing Self: Between Tradition and Modernity in the West Bank," in Kanaaneh, *Palestinian Music and Song*, 98.

46. Sunaina Maira and Magid Shihade, "Hip Hop from '48 Palestine: Youth, Music, and the Present/Absent," *Social Text* 30, no. 3 (2012): 1–2.

47. Maira, *Jil Oslo*, 14, 115.

48. Ibid., 55, 11, 25.

49. McDonald, *My Voice Is My Weapon*, 21.

50. Ibid., 4.

51. Amany Jamal, "Inside and Outside the Box: The Politics of Arab American Identity and Artistic Representations," in *Art in the Lives of Immigrant Communities in the United States*, ed. Paul DiMaggio and Patricia Fernandez-Kelly (New Brunswick, NJ: Rutgers Univ. Press, 2010).

52. McDonald, *My Voice is My Weapon*, 237.

53. Maira, *Jil Oslo*, 193, 75.

54. Maira and Shihade, "Hip Hop from '48 Palestine," 1–26.

55. Maira, *Jil Oslo*, 77.

56. Ibid., 37.

57. Darwish, *Ḥālat Ḥiṣār* [*State of Siege*] (Beirut: Riad al-Rayyes, 2002), 204.

58. Darwish, interview with Rahman, in Nassar and Rahman, *Mahmoud Darwish, Exile's Poet*.

59. McDonald, *My Voice Is My Weapon*, 234.

60. Ibid., 237.

61. Evert-Jan Grit, "Where There's the Ghetto, There's Hip Hop," *The Electronic Intifada*, July 5, 2005, Electronicintifada.net/content/where-theres-ghetto-theres-hip-hop/5656.

62. Ibid.

63. Safieh, "Identity, Diaspora," 74.

64. Safa Hathoot, cited in Maira, *Jil Oslo*, 56.

65. Maira, *Jil Oslo*, 55.

66. Wong, "Conflicts, Occupation," 273.

67. McDonald, *My Voice Is My Weapon*, 255.

68. Ibid., 257.

69. Ibid., 260.

70. Ibid., 262.

71. Maira, *Jil Oslo*, 59–60.

72. Wong, "Conflicts, Occupation," 275.

Afterword

1. Darwish, *Ḥīrat al-ʻāʼid*, 157.

2. Ibid., 149.

3. Ibid.

4. Rebecca Dyer, "Poetry of Politics and Mourning: Mahmoud Darwish's Genre-Transforming Tribute to Edward W. Said," *PMLA: Publications of the Modern Language Association of America* 122, no. 5 (2007): 1459.

5. Salma Khadra Jayyusi, "Foreword," in Nassar and Rahman, *Mahmoud Darwish, Exile's Poet*, ix, emphasis mine.

6. Said, interviewed by Barsamian, in *Culture et résistance*, 191.

7. Darwish, interview with Randa Abou-Bakr, in Randa Abou-Bakr, *The Conflict of Voices in the Poetry of Dennis Butrus and Mahmoud Darwish* (Berlin: Reichert, 2004), 206, emphasis added.

8. Darwish, interview with Rahman, in Nassar and Rahman, *Mahmoud Darwish, Exile's Poet*.

9. Darwish, *Diwan*, 1: 162–63.

10. Darwish, *Fī ḥaḍrat al-ghiyāb*, 114.

11. Darwish, *Ḥīrat al ʻāʼid*, 151.

12. Ibid., 130.

13. Darwish, *Fī ḥaḍrat al-ghiyāb*, 143. See also Darwish, *Ḥīrat al ʻāʼid*, 156.

14. Darwish, *Fī ḥaḍrat al-ghiyāb*, 156.

15. Darwish, *Ḥirat al-ʻāʼid*, 61.

16. Ibid., 48.

17. Butler, *Precarious Life*, 22.

18. Dyer, "Poetry of Politics and Mourning," 1457.

19. Sacks writes that place "merely names *here*, this place at which 'we' occur and from which there is no exit or escape. It is the place at which 'we' take place." Jeffrey Sacks, "Language Places," in Nassar and Rahman, *Mahmoud Darwish, Exile's Poet*, 266.

20. Rogoff, *Terra Infirma*, 15.

21. Baur and Wäspe, *Emily Jacir, Installation Shots*, 9–10.

22. Darwish, "Lā'eb al-nard," translated by Fady Joudah, *The Nation*, October 2, 2006, 39. The translation is slightly revised. The Arabic original "Lā'eb al-nard" was first published in the daily *Al-Quds al-Arabion*, July 1, 2008. The poem has also been translated as "A River Dies of Thirst." See also Darwish, *Athar al-farāsha*, 35.

23. Darwish, interview with Rahman, in Nassar and Rahman, Mahmoud Darwish, *Exile's Poet*, 322.

24. Darwish, "Lā'eb al-nard," in *Athar al-farāsha*, 25–26.

25. Faisal Darraj's reading of Darwish's *State of Siege*, in Nassar and Rahman, *Mahmoud Darwish, Exile's Poet*, translated by Hala Nassar, 9.

26. Ibid., 74.

27. Darwish, *Ḥālat Ḥiṣār*, 265. Translation by Jeffrey Sacks.

Bibliography

Abboushi, Tarif, et al. *Made in Palestine*. Houston, TX: Ineri Publications, 2003.

Abou-Bakr, Randa. *The Conflict of Voices in the Poetry of Dennis Butrus [sic] and Mahmoud Darwish: A Comparative Study*. Berlin: Reichert, 2004.

Abu-Assad, Hany. *Al-Jana al-'ān (Paradise Now)*. Burbank, CA: Warner Home Videos, 2005.

———. *Al-Quds fī Yawm Ākhar* (Rana's wedding). Ramallah and East Jerusalem: Palestinian Film Foundation, 2002.

———. *Ford Transit*. Hilversum, Netherlands: VPRO & Augustus Films, 2002.

Abu Hashhash, Mahmoud. *Istibāha*. Beirut: Al-Mu'assassah al-'Arabiyyah lil-Dirāsāt wa al-Nashr, 2006.

Abu Sitta, Osama. "Topography of the Soul." *Home Magazine*, February 2013. http://arabartex.wordpress.com/2013/03/06/topography-of-the-soul-eman -haram-at-nabad/.

Adonis, Mahmoud Darwish, and Samih al-Qasim. *Victims of a Map: A Bilingual Anthology of Arabic Poetry*. Translated by Abdallah al-Udhari. London: Saqi Books, 1984.

Agamben, Giorgio. *The Coming Community*. Translated by Michael Hardt. Minneapolis: Univ. of Minnesota Press, 1993.

Ahmed, Sara, et al. *Uprootings/Regroundings: Questions of Home and Migration*. New York: Berg, 2003.

Akash, Munir, and Daniel Moore, eds. *The Adam of Two Edens*. Syracuse, NY: Syracuse Univ. Press and Jusoor, 2000.

Akash, Munir, Carolyn Forche, Amira al-Zein, and Sinan Antoon, eds. and trans. *The Raven's Ink*. Santa Fe, NM: Lannan Foundation, 2001.

Akash, Munir, and Carolyn Forché, with Sinan Antoon and Amira el-Zein, eds. and trans. *Unfortunately It Was Paradise*. Berkeley: Univ. of California Press, 2003.

Alajaji, Sylvia. "Performing Self: Between Tradition and Modernity in the West Bank." In Kanaaneh, *Palestinian Music and Song*, 97–113.

Alshaer, Atef. *Poetry and Politics in the Modern Arab World*. London: Hurst; New York: Columbia Univ. Press, forthcoming 2015.

Anastas, Ayreen. *Pasolini Pa*Palestine* [Video]. Jerusalem: Al Ma'mal: Foundation for Contemporary Art; Lebanon: Ashkāl Alwān, 2004.

Anderson, Benedict. *Imagined Communities: Reflections on the Origin and Spread of Nationalism*. London: Verso, 1991.

Anglesey, Zoë. *Listen Up!: Spoken Word Poetry*. New York: One World, 1999.

Ankori, Gannit. *Palestinian Art*. London: Reaktion Books, 2006.

Annani, Nabil. *Lost Horizon* [Sculptures]. Jerusalem: Al-Ma'mal: Foundation for Contemporary Art, 2011.

Antoon, Sinan. "Returning to the Wind: On Darwish's *Lā Ta'tadhir 'Ammā Fa'alta*." In Nassar and Rahman, *Mahmoud Darwish, Exile's Poet*, 215–38.

Appadurai, Arjun, ed. *Globalization*. Durham, NC: Duke Univ. Press, 2000.

Apter, Emily. *The Translation Zone: A New Comparative Literature*. Princeton, NJ: Princeton Univ. Press, 2005.

Aptowicz, Cristin O'Keefe. *Words in Your Face: A Guided Tour through Twenty Years of the New York City Poetry Slam*. New York: Soft Skull Press, 2007.

Araeen, Rasheed, et al. *The Third Text Reader: On Art, Culture, and Theory*. NY: Continuum, 2002.

Araj, Rumzi. *Slingshot Hip Hop*. New York: Fresh Booza Production, 2009.

Archer, Michael, Guy Brett, and Catherine de Zegher. *Mona Hatoum*. London: Phaidon Press, 1998.

Armburst, Walter, ed. *Mass Mediations: New Approaches to Popular Culture in the Middle East and Beyond*. Berkeley: Univ. of California Press, 2006.

Armes, Roy. *Arab Filmmakers of the Middle East: A Dictionary*. Bloomington: Indiana Univ. Press, 2010.

———. *Postcolonial Images: Studies in North African Film*. Indiana Univ. Press, 2005.

Azoulay, Ariella. "Cartography of Resistance." *Afterimage* 34, nos. 1–2 (July–October 2006): 80–81.

Azoulay, Ariella, and Sherene Seikaly. "Chic Point: Fashion for Israeli Check Points." *ArteEast* (Spring 2007): http://www.arteeast.org/2012/02/27/chic-point-fashion-for-israeli-checkpoints/.

Badr, Liana. *'Ayn al-mir'ā*. Amman: Dār al-Shurūq, 2009. Translated by Samira Kawar as *The Eye of the Mirror*. London: Garnett, 2008.

———. *Būṣala min ajl 'abbād al-shams*. Beirut: Dār al-Adāb, 1979. Translated by Catherine Cobham as *A Compass for the Sunflower*. London: Women's Press, 1990.

———. *Nujūm Arīḥa* (The stars of Jericho). Beirut: Dār al-Adāb, 2002.

———. *Samā' waḥida* (One sky). Beirut: Dar al-Saqi, 2007.

———. *Shurfa 'alā al-Fakihānī* (A balcony over the Fakihani). Amman: Dār al-Shurūq, 2007.

———. *Taghrīdat al-shā'ir: Athār al-makān 'alā al-hawiyya fī a'māl Mahmūd Darwīsh* (The song of the poet: The trace of place on identity in the work of Mahmoud Darwish). Amman: Dār al-Nāsher, 2013.

———. *Zanābiq al-daw'* (Lilies of light). Cairo: Dar Sharqiyāt, 1998.

Ball, Anna. "Between a Postcolonial Nation and Fantasies of the Feminine: The Contested Visions of Palestinian Cinema." *Camera Obscura* 23, no. 3 (2008): 1–33.

Barghouti, Houssein. *Al-daw' al-azraq* (The blue light). Ramallah: Bayt al-Shi'r, 2003.

Barghouti, Mourid. *Midnight*. Translated by Radwa Ashour. London: Arc Publications, 2008.

Barsamian, David. *Culture and Resistance: Conversations with Edward Said*. London: Pluto, 2003.

Bar-Yosef, Amatzia. "Traditional Rural Style under a Process of Change: The Singing Style of the 'Haddây,' Palestinian Folk Poet-Singers." *Asian Music* 29, no. 2 (1998): 57–82.

Baubock, Rainer, and Faist, Thomas. *Diaspora and Transnationalism: Concepts, Theories, and Methods*. Amsterdam: Amsterdam Univ. Press, 2010.

Baur, Andreas, and Roland Wäspe. *Emily Jacir, Installation Shots at the Kunstmuseum St. Gallen*. St. Gallen: Kunstmuseum St. Gallen, Galerie der Stadt Esslingen, Verlag für Moderne Kunst, 2008.

Bell, Vikki, ed. *Special Issue on Performativity and Belonging*. London: Sage, 1999.

Ben-Ze'ev, Efrat. "Transmission and Transformation: The Palestinian Second Generation and the Commemoration of the Homeland." In *Homelands and Diasporas*, edited by Efrat Ben-Ze'ev, 123–39. Stanford, CA: Stanford Univ. Press, 2005.

Benjamin, Walter. "The Task of the Translator." Translated by Harry Zohn. In Benjamin, *Illuminations*, 69–82. New York: Schocken, 2007.

Berger, John. *And Our Faces, My Heart, Brief as Photos*. London: Bloomsbury, 2005.

Bergson, Henri. *Laughter: An Essay on the Meaning of the Comic*. Translated by Clousdesley Brereton and Fred Rotwell. New York: Macmillan, 1912.

Blanchot, Maurice. *The Space of Literature*. Translated by Ann Smock. Lincoln, NE: Univ. of Nebraska Press, 1989.

Boullata, Kamal. *Istiḥḍār al-makān: Dirāsah fī al-fann al-tashkīlī al-Filasṭīnī al-muʿāṣir* (Presencing Place: A Study of Palestinian Contemporary Art). Tunis: Al-Munaẓẓamah al-ʿArabīyah lil-Tarbiyah wa-al-Thaqāfah wa-al-ʿUlūm, 2000.

———. *Palestinian Art: From 1850 to 2005*. London: Saqi, 2008.

Bourlond, Ann. "A Cinema of Nowhere: An Interview with Elia Suleiman." *Journal of Palestine Studies* 29, no. 2 (2000): 95–101.

Bowman, Glenn. "A Country of Words: Conceiving the Palestinian Nation from the Position of Exile." In *The Making of Political Identities*, edited by Ernesto Laclau, 138–70. New York: Verso, 1994.

Brammer, Angelika. *Displacements: Cultural Identities in Question*. Madison: Univ. of Wisconsin Press, 1994.

Braziel, Jana Evans, and Anita Mannur, eds. *Theorizing Diaspora: A Reader*. Malden, MA: Blackwell, 2003.

Brenner, Rachel Feldhay. *Inextricably Bonded: Israeli Arab and Jewish Writers Re-visioning Culture*. Madison: Univ. of Wisconsin Press, 2003.

Bresheeth, Haim, and Haifa Hammami, eds. "Special Issue: The Conflict and Contemporary Visual Culture in Palestine and Israel." *Third Text* 20, nos. 3–4 (2006).

Brinner, Benjamin Elon. *Playing across a Divide: Israeli-Palestinian Musical Encounters*. Oxford: Oxford Univ. Press, 2009.

Bronstein, Phoebe. "Paradise Now." *Jump Cut* (Summer 2010). http://www.ejumpcut.org/archive/jc52.2010/bronsteinParadiseNow/text.html.

Bubus, Ahmad. *Filasṭīn fi al-Ughniyah al-ʿArabiyah*. Damascus: Wizārat al-Thaqāfah, 2011.

Büchel, Christop, et al. *The Hugo Boss Prize 2008*. New York: The Guggenheim Museum, 2008.

Butler, Judith. *Parting Ways: Jewishness and the Critique of Zionism*. New York: Columbia Univ. Press, 2012.

————. *Precarious Life: The Powers of Mourning and Violence*. New York: Verso, 2006.

————. "What Shall We Do without Exile?" Sixth Annual Edward Said Memorial Lecture. November 7, 2010. The American University in Cairo. http://www.youtube.com/watch?v =MLgIXtaF6OA. Accessed November 30, 2010.

Butler, Judith, and Athena Athanasiou. *Dispossession: The Performative in the Political*. Malden, MA: Polity Press, 2013.

Chan, Felicia. "What Dreams May Come: (Palestinian) Cinema/Nation/History." *Variant* 30 (Winter 2007): 8–9.

Chang, Jeff. *Total Chaos: The Art and Aesthetics of Hip-Hop*. New York: Basic Civitas Books, 2006.

Chatterjee, Partha. *Nationalist Thought and the Colonial World: An Autonomous Discourse?* London: Zed Books, 1986.

Cheah, Pheng. *Spectral Nationality: Passages of Freedom from Kant to Postcolonial Literatures of Liberation*. New York: Columbia Univ. Press, 2003.

Cobham, Catherine, trans. *A River Dies of Thirst*. Brooklyn, NY: Archipelago Press, 2009.

Cohen, Dalia, and Ruth Katz. *Palestinian Arab Music: A Maqam Tradition in Practice*. Chicago: Univ. of Chicago Press, 2006.

Corcoran, Steven. "Editor's Introduction." In Rancière, *Dissensus*, 1–26.

Corwin, Will. "Emily Jacir." *Art Papers* 34, no. 1 (2010): 63–64.

Dabashi, Hamid, ed. *Dreams of a Nation: On Palestinian Cinema*. New York: Verso, 2006.

Dam. *Dedication*. n.p.: Red Circle Music, 2006.

————. *Dabke on the Moon*. CD. Unofficial release. 2012.

————. "Meen Irhabi." Single lyric. Unofficial release. 2002.

Darwiche, Mahmoud. *La Palestine comme métaphore*. Translated from Arabic by Elias Sanbar and from Hebrew by Simone Bitton. Paris: Actes Sud, 1997.

Darwish, Mahmoud. *Aḥada ʿashara kawkaban ʿalā ākhir al-mashhad al-Andalusī* (Eleven planets at the end of the Andalusian scene). Beirut: Dār al-Jadīd, 1992.

————. Al ʿAmāl al-Jadīdah (New works). Beirut: Riad al-Rayyes 2004.

————. "Al-beytu qatīlan" (A house fallen). In Darwish, *Athar al-farāsha*, 35–37.

————. *Athar al-farāsha: Yawmiyyat* (The butterfly's effect: A journal). Beirut: Riad al-Rayyes, 2008.

————. *Dhākira lil-Nisyān: Al-makān āb 1982, al-zamān Beyrūt*. Beirut: al-Muʾassah al-ʿArabiyya lil-Nashr, 1987. Translated by Ibrahim Muhawi as

Memory for Forgetfulness: August, Beirut, 1982. Berkeley: University of California Press, 1995.

———. *Diwan*. vols. 1 and 2. Beirut: Riyad al-Rayyes, 1989, 1994.

———. *Fī ḥaḍrat al-ghiyāb* (In the presence of absence: A text). Beirut: Riad al-Rayyes, 2006. Translated by Sinan Antoon as *In the Presence of Absence*. Brooklyn, NY: Archipelago Press, 2011.

———. *Ḥālat Ḥiṣār* (*State of Siege*). Beirut: Riad al-Rayyes, 2002.

———. *Ḥīrat al-ʿāʾid* (The hesitation of the returned: Selected essays). Beirut: Riad al-Rayyes, 2009.

———. *Jidāriyya* (Mural). Beirut: Riad al-Rayyes, 2000.

———. *Ka-zahr al-lawz aw abʿad* (*Almond Blossoms and Beyond*). Beirut: Riad al-Rayyes, 2005.

———. *Lā taʿtadhir ʿammā faʿalta* (Do not apologize for what you have done). Beirut: Riad al-Rayyes, 2004.

———. "A Player of Dice." In *Lā urīdu li-hadhī al-qaṣīda an tantahī* (I do not want this poem to end). Beirut: Riad al-Rayyes, 2009.

———. *Limāthā tarakta al-hiṣān waḥīdan?* (*Why Did You Leave the Horse Alone?*) Beirut: Riad al-Rayyes, 1995.

———. "Madīḥ al-Dhill al-ʿĀlī" (In praise of the high shadow). In Darwish, *Diwan*, 2: 7–77.

———. "On Translating Poetry: The Place of the Universal." *Banipal* (Summer 2000): 25–27.

———. *Yawmīyat al-ḥuzn al-ʿādī*. Beirut: Dār al-ʿAwda, 1973; Beirut: Riad al-Rayyes, 2007.

Deleuze, Gilles, and Félix Guattari. *Kafka: Toward a Minor Literature*. Translated by Dana Polan. Foreword by Réda Bensmaia. Minneapolis: Univ. of Minnesota Press, 1986.

DeMan, Paul. *Resistance to Theory*. Univ. of Minnesota Press, 1986.

Demos, T. J. "Desire in Diaspora: Emily Jacir." In *Contemporary Art in the Middle East*, edited by Paul Sloman, 42–49. London: Black Dog, 2009.

———. "Emily Jacir: Poetry's Beyond." *Guggenheim Museum Hugo Boss Prize* (Catalogue). New York: Guggenheim Museum, 2008.

Derrida, Jacques. *Mémoires: Pour Paul de Man*. Paris: Éditions Galilée, 1988.

———. *Monolingualism of the Other: Or, the Prosthesis of Origin*. Translated by Patrick Mensah. Stanford, CA: Stanford Univ. Press, 1998.

Devi, Gayatri, and Najat Rahman. *Humor in Middle Eastern Cinema*. Detroit, MI: Wayne State Univ. Press, 2014.

De Zegher, Catherine. "Mona Hatoum: Beyond the Violence Vortex into the Beauty Vortex." In Millà, *Mona Hatoum Projecció*, 11–28.

Dickinson, Peter. *World Stages, Local Audiences: Essays on Performance, Place, and Politics*. New York: Manchester Univ. Press, 2010.

Dönmez-Colin, Gönül. *The Cinema of North Africa and the Middle East*. London: Wallflower Press, 2007.

Dyer, Rebecca. "Poetry of Politics and Mourning: Mahmoud Darwish's Genre-Transforming Tribute to Edward W. Said." *PMLA: Publications of the Modern Language Association of America* 122, no. 5 (2007): 1447–62.

Elad-Bouskila, Ami. *Modern Palestinian Literature and Culture*. Portland, OR: Frank Crass, 1999.

Featherstone, Mike, ed. *Global Culture: Nationalism, Globalization, and Modernity*. London: Sage, 1990.

Feinstein, Howard. "Laila's Birthday." *Screen International*, September 7, 2008.

Free the P. Philistines (Musical Group) and N.O.M.A.D.S. (Musical Group). n.p.: N. Wattad, 2005.

Gertz, Nurith, and George Khleifi. "A Chronicle of Palestinian Cinema." In Gugler, *Film in the Middle East and North Africa*, 187–97.

———. *Palestinian Cinema: Landscape, Trauma, and Memory*. Bloomington: Indiana Univ. Press, 2008.

Ghadban al-, Yara. "The Ghost in the Art Work." Johannesburg Workshop in Theory and Criticism blog, September 10, 2009. http://jhbwtc.blogspot .com.

Ghassoub, Mai, and Emma Sinclair-Webb. *Imagined Masculinities: Male Identity and Culture in the Modern Middle East*. London: Saqi, 2000.

Ginsberg, Terri, and Chris Lippard. *Historical Dictionary of Middle Eastern Cinema*. Lanham, MD: The Scarecrow Press, 2010.

Golley, Nawar. *Arab Women's Lives Retold: Exploring Identity through Writing*. Syracuse, NY: Syracuse Univ. Press, 2008.

Greenberg, Ela. "'The King of the Streets': Hip Hop and the Reclaiming of Masculinity in Jerusalem's Shu'afat Refugee Camp." *Middle East Journal of Culture and Communication* 2, no. 2 (2009): 231–50.

Grit, Evert-Jan. "Where There's the Ghetto, There's Hip Hop." *The Electronic Intifada*, July 5, 2005. Electronicintifada.net/content/where-theres-ghetto -theres-hip-hop/5656.

Gugler, Josef, ed. *Film in the Middle East and North Africa: Creative Dissidence*. Austin: Univ. of Texas Press, 2011.

Hall, Doug, and Sally Jo Fifer. *Illuminating Video: An Essential Guide to Video Art*. (San Francisco: Aperture/Bay Area Video Coalition, 1990.

Hall, Stuart. "Cultural Identity and Diaspora." In *Identity: Community, Culture, Difference*, edited by Jonathan Rutherford, 222–37. London: Lawrence and Wishart, 1990.

Habiby, Emil. *Al-Waqā'ia' al-gharība fī ikhtifā' Sa'īd Abī Naḥs al-mutashā'il qiṣṣah*. Beirut: Dar Ibn Khaldun, 1989 [1974]. Translated by Salma Khadra Jayyusi and Trevor LeGassick as *The Secret Life of Saeed the Pessoptimist*. London: Zed, 1985.

Hammad, Suheir. *Born Palestinian, Born Black*. New York: Harlem River Press, 1996.

———. *Breaking Poems*. New York: Cypher Books, 2008.

———. "Directing My Pen Inwards." In *Scheherazade's Legacy: Arab and Arab American Women on Writing*, edited by Faisal al-Darraj, Susan Muaddi, Aziz, and Barbara Nimri, 79–83. Westport, CT: Praeger, 2004.

———. *Drops of This Story*. New York: Harlem River Press, 1996.

———. *Zaatar Diva*. New York: Cypher Books, 2005.

Hammerman, Ilana. "Seeing and Unseeing: After Laughter Has Loosened the Fetters of Fear and Hostility, Look at the Men Here and Think Not Only about Their Humanity and Vulnerability, but Also Your Own." *Haaretz*, December 20, 2007. http://www.haaretz.com/misc/article-print-page/seeing-and-unseeing-1.235578?trailingPath=2.169%2C2.203%2C2.205%2C.

Handal, Nathalie. *The Lives of Rain*. Northampton, MA: Interlink Books, 2005.

———. *The Neverfield*. Northampton, MA: Interlink Books, 2005.

Haram, Eman. "Family Photos: The Aesthetic of Time." MFA, University of South Florida, Tampa, Florida, 1992.

———. *Iconographies*. Exhibition at Nabad Gallery in Amman. March 22, 2013–May 8 2013.

———. *Involuntary Memory*. Photo exhibit. 2004. https:www.saatchi-gallery.co.uk/yourgallery/artistprofileEman+Haram/102099.html.

Harlow, Barbara. *The Resistance in Prison: Palestinian Prison Writing*. Audiobook on cassette, February 8, 1988. Ithaca, NY: Cornell University.

Hatoum, Mona. *Home*. Art installation. 1999.

———. *Measures of Distance*. Video. Vancouver: The Western Front, 1988.

———. *Nablus Soap*. Sculpture. 1996.

———. *Over My Dead Body*. Billboard. 1988.

———. *Present Tense*. Installation. Jerusalem: Al Ma'mal: Foundation for Contemporary Art, 1996.

———. *The Negotiating Table*. Performance. Vancouver: The Western Front, 1983.

———. *Turbulence*. Transparent glass marbles installation. 2012.

Hochberg, Gil Z. "Check Me Out: Queer Encounters in Sharif Waked's *Chic Point: Fashion for Israeli Checkpoints*." *GLQ: A Journal of Lesbian and Gay Studies* 16, no. 4 (2010): 577–98.

Horton, Andrew, and Joanna Rapf, eds. *A Companion to Film Comedy*. New York: Wiley-Blackwell, 2012.

Hourani, Khalid. *Allāh Maḥabba*. Jerusalem: Al Ma'mal: Foundation for Contemporary Art, 2007.

Iordanova, Dina, et al., *Cinema at the Periphery*. Detroit, MI: Wayne State Univ. Press, 2010.

Jacir, Annmarie. *Like Twenty Impossibles*. Brooklyn, NY: Philistine Films, 2003.

———. *Milḥ hatha al-baḥr* (Salt of the sea). Ennetbaden: Trigon Films, 2009.

Jacir, Emily, and T. J. Demos. "Desire in Diaspora." *Art Journal-New York* 62, no. 4 (2003): 68–79.

———. *Untitled*. Jerusalem: Al Ma'mal: Foundation for Contemporary Art, 2011.

Jacob, Wilson Chacko. *Working Out Egypt: Effendi Masculinity and Subject Formation in Colonial Modernity, 1870–1940*. Durham, NC: Duke Univ. Press, 2011.

Jamal, Amany. "Inside and Outside the Box: The Politics of Arab American Identity and Artistic Representations." In *Art in the Lives of Immigrant Communities in the United States*, edited by Paul DiMaggio and Patricia Fernandez-Kelly. New Brunswick, NJ: Rutgers Univ. Press, 2010.

Jayyusi, Salma Khadra. *Anthology of Modern Palestinian Literature*. New York: Columbia Univ. Press, 1992.

Joudah, Fady, trans. *The Butterfly's Burden*. Townsend, WA: Copper Canyon Press, 2006.

———. "Translator's Preface." In Zaqtan, *Like a Straw Bird It Follows Me*, ix–xx.

"Journey in the Palestinian Political Song." *This Week in Palestine* 108 (April 2007). http://archive.thisweekinpalestine.com/details.php?id=2109&ed=139 &edid=139 .

Kanaaneh, Moslih, et al., eds. *Palestinian Music and Song: Expression and Resistance since 1900*. Bloomington: Indiana Univ. Press, 2013.

Kanafani, Ghassan. *Al-Adab al-filastīnī al-muqāwim tahta al-ihtilāl, 1948–1968.* Beirut: Mu'assasat al-Abhāth al-'Arabiyya, 1987 [1968].

———. *Al-Athār al-Kāmila: Al-Riwayāt.* Beirut: Dar al-Talī'a, 1972.

Kanazi, Remi. *Poets for Palestine.* New York: Al Jisser Group, 2008.

Khalidi, Rashid. *Palestinian Identity: The Construction of Modern National Consciousness.* New York: Columbia Univ. Press, 1997.

Khatib, Lina. *Filming the Modern Middle East: Politics in the Cinemas of Hollywood and the Arab World.* New York: I. B. Tauris, 2006.

Khoury, Elias. *Abwāb al-madīna.* Beirut: Dār al-Adāb, 1981. Translated by Paula Haydar as *Gates of the City.* Minneapolis: Univ. of Minnesota Press, 1993.

———. *Bāb al-shams.* Beirut: Dār al-Adāb, 1998. Translated by Humphrey Davies as *Gate of the Sun.* New York: Archipelago, 2006.

———. *Al-Dhākira al-mafquda.* Beirut: Dār al-Adāb, 1990.

———. *Dirāsāt fī naqd al-shi'r.* Beirut: Mu'assasat al-Abhath al-'Arabiyya, 1979.

———. *Rihlat Ghāndi al-saghīr.* Beirut: Dār al-Adāb, 1989.

———. *Yalu.* Beirut: Dār al-Adāb, 2002.

———. *Zaman al-ihtilāl.* Beirut: Mu'assasat al-Abhāth al-'Arabiyya, 1985.

Kilito, Abdelfattah. "Dog Words." Translated by Ziad Elmarasfy. In *Displacements: Cultural Identities in Question,* edited by Angelika Brammer. Bloomington: Indiana Univ. Press, 1994.

———. *Thou Shalt Not Speak My Language.* Preface by Wail Hassan. Syracuse, NY: Syracuse Univ. Press, 2008.

King, A. D. *Culture, Globalization, and the World System.* Minneapolis: Univ. of Minnesota Press, 1997.

Kravagna, Christian, et al. *Emily Jacir, Belongings: Arbeiten/Works 1998–2003.* Vienna: Folio Verlag, 2004.

Lafi, Mohamed. *Muqaffa' bi al-rimah.* Ramallah: Beit al-Sh'ir, 2007.

Lanaspa, Jaime. "English Texts." In Millà, *Mona Hatoum Projecció,* 6–7.

Layoun, Mary N. *Travels of a Genre: The Modern Novel and Ideology.* Princeton, NJ: Princeton Univ. Press, 1990.

———. *Wedded to the Land?: Gender, Boundaries, and Nationalism in Crisis.* Durham, NC: Duke Univ. Press, 2001.

Lionnet, Françoise, and Shu-mei Shih, eds. *Minor Transnationalism.* Durham, NC: Duke Univ. Press, 2005.

Lloyd, Fran. *Contemporary Arab Women's Art: Dialogues of the Present.* London: Women's Art Library, 1999.

Maira, Sunaina. *Jil Oslo: Palestinian Hip Hop: Youth Culture and the Youth Movement*. Washington, DC: Tadween, 2013.

———. "'We Ain't Missing': Palestinian Hip Hop, a Transnational Movement." *CR-East Lansing* 8, no. 2 (2008): 161–92.

Maira, Sunaina, and Magid Shihade. "Hip Hop from '48 Palestine: Youth, Music, and the Present/Absent." *Social Text* 30, no. 3 (2012): 1–26.

Mansour, Sliman. *Introducing the Other*. Jerusalem: Al Ma'mal: Foundation for Contemporary Art, 2007.

Månsson, Anette. *Passage to a New Wor(L)D: Exile and Restoration in Mahmoud Darwish's Writings, 1960–1995*. Uppsala, Sweden: Uppsala Universitet, 2003.

Masharawi, Rashid. *'Eid mīlād Layla* (Laila's birthday). Ramallah: Cinema Production Center and Fortissimo Films, 2008.

Massad, Joseph. "Liberating Songs: Palestine Put to Music." *Journal of Palestine Studies* 32, no. 3 (2003): 21–38.

Mattawa, Khalid. *Mahmoud Darwish: The Poet's Art and His Nation*. Syracuse, NY: Syracuse Univ. Press, 2014.

McDonald, David A. *My Voice Is My Weapon: Music, Nationalism, and the Poetics of Palestinian Resistance*. Durham, NC: Duke Univ. Press, 2013.

McLuhan, Marshal. *Pour comprendre les médias: Les prolongements technologiques de l'homme*. Translated by Jean Paré. Paris: Seuil, 2001 [1966].

Méchoulan, Éric. "Intermedialités: Le temps des illusions perdues." *Intermédialités: Histoire et théorie des arts, des lettres et des techniques* 1 (Spring 2003): 9–27.

Meigh-Andrews, Chris. *A History of Video Art*. London: Bloomsbury Academic Publishing, 2006.

Melis, Wim. *Nazar: Photographs from the Arab World*. New York: Aperture Foundation, 2004.

Mercer, Kobena, ed. *Exiles, Diasporas, and Strangers*. London: Institute of International Visual Arts; Cambridge, MA: MIT Press, 2008.

Millà, Martina, ed. *Mona Hatoum Projecció*. Barcelona: Fundació Joan Miró, 2012.

Moberg, Thomas Ulf. *Palestinian Art*. Stockholm: Cinclus, 1998.

Morgan, Andy, and Mu'tasem Adileh. "The Sounds of Struggle." In *World Music: Africa, Europe, and the Middle East*, ed. Simon Broughton and Mark Ellingham, with James McConnachie and Orla Duane, 1: 385–90. New York: Penguin Books, 2000.

Muhawi, Ibrahim, trans. *Memory for Forgetfulness: August, Beirut, 1982* [*Dhākira lil-Nisyan*, 1987]. Berkeley: Univ. of California Press, 1995.

————, trans. *Journal of an Ordinary Grief* [*Yawmiyyāt al-ḥuzn al-ʿādi*, 1973]. Brooklyn, NY: Archipelago Books, 2010.

Naficy, Hamid. *An Accented Cinema: Exilic and Diasporic Filmmaking.* Princeton, NJ: Princeton Univ. Press, 2001.

————. *Home, Exile, Homeland: Film, Media, and the Politics of Place.* New York: Routledge, 1998.

————. "Palestinian Exilic Cinema and Film Letters." In Dabashi, *Dreams of a Nation*, 90–104.

Nahas al-, Hashim, ed. *Al-insān al miṣrī ʿalā al-shāsha* (The Egyptian on the screen). Cairo: General Egyptian Book Organization, 1986.

Nassar, Hala, and Najat Rahman, eds. *Mahmoud Darwish, Exile's Poet: Critical Essays.* Northampton, MA: Interlink Books, 2008.

Nasser, Amjad, and Youssef Rakha. "Mahmoud Darwish between the Political and the Aesthetic." *Banipal: Magazine of Modern Arab Literature* 33 (Autumn-Winter 2008): 32–33.

Nazzal, Rehab. *At Home.* Multivideo installation. Markham, Ontario. 2012.

————. *A Night at Home.* Video documentary, part of *At Home.* 2009.

————. *An Ongoing Struggle: A Paper in Support of the Multi-Channel Video Installation.* Toronto: I.M.A. Gallery, 2012.

————. *Bil'in.* Video, part of *At Home.* 2010.

————. *Target.* Video still, part of *At Home.* 2012.

————. *Mourning,* Video still, part of *At Home.* 2012.

————. *One Thousand Palestinian Political Prisoners.* Photos, part of *At Home,* 2012.

Nye Shihab, Noemie. *You & Yours: Poems.* n.p.: Boa Editions, 2005.

Oliver, Anne Marie, and Paul Steinberg. "Popular Music of the *Intifada.*" In *Garland Encyclopedia of World Music* (2002), 6: 635–40.

Olson, Alix. *Word Warriors: 35 Women Leaders in the Spoken Word Revolution.* Emeryville, CA: Seal Press, 2007.

Oosterling, Henk. "Sens(a)ble Intermediality and Interesse: Towards an Ontology of the In-Between." *Intermédialités* 29, no. 1 (2003): 29– 46.

Pandolfo, Stefania. "'Nibtidi mnin il-hikaya (Where are we to start the tale?)': Violence, Intimacy, and Recollection." *Social Science Information* 45, no. 3 (2006): 349–71.

Pappé, Ilan. *The Modern Middle East.* New York: Routledge, 2005.

Parmenter, Barbara McKean. *Giving Voice to Stone: Place and Identity in Palestinian Literature.* Austin: Univ. of Texas Press, 1994.

Poché, Christian. "Palestinian Music." In *Grove Music Online, Oxford Music Online.* http://www.oxfordmusiconline.com/subscriber/article/grove/music/47332. Accessed September 22, 2008.

Porton, Richard. "Notes from the Palestinian Diaspora: An Interview with Elia Suleiman." *Cineaste* 28, no. 3 (2003): 24–27.

Pyott, Lauren. "Emerging from an 'Age of Defeat': Interview with Poet Ghassan Zaqtan." *Electronic Intifada,* December 7, 2012. http://electronicintifada.net/content/emerging-age-defeat-interview-poet-ghassan-zaqtan/11978.

Qasim, Samih. *Al ʿAmāl al-Nājizah (The Complete Works).* vol. 6. Cairo: Dār Suʿād al-Ṣabāḥ, 1993.

Rabinowitz, Dan. "Postnational Palestine/Israel?: Globalization, Diaspora, Transnationalism, and the Israeli-Palestinian Conflict." *Critical Inquiry* 26, no. 4 (2000): 757–72.

Radhakrishnan, R. *Diasporic Mediations: Between Home and Location.* Minneapolis: Univ. of Minnesota Press, 1996.

Rahman, Najat. *Literary Disinheritance: The Writing of Home in the Works of Mahmoud Darwish and Assia Djebar.* Lanham, MD: Lexington Books, 2008.

Rancière, Jacques. *Dissensus: On Politics and Aesthetics.* Edited and translated by Steven Corcoran. London: Continuum, 2010.

Roeskens, Till. *Videomapping: Aida Camp, Palestine.* 2009.

Rogoff, Irit. *Terra Infirma: Geography's Visual Culture.* New York: Routledge, 2000.

Saadeh, Raeda. *Conquering Space.* Installation. 2002.

———. *Untitled Photographs.* Jerusalem: Al Maʿmal: Foundation for Contemporary Art, 2003.

Sabella, Steve. "The Colonization of the Imagination." *Contemporary Practices* 10 (2012): 28–33. http://stevesabella.com/published-essays.html. Accessed January 5, 2013.

———. *Exit.* Installation shots. 2006.

———. *In Exile.* Installation shots. 2008.

———. *Metamorphosis.* Photographs. 2011.

———. *Search.* Photographs. 1997.

———. *Till the End, Spirit of the Place.* Photograph. 2004.

Sabra, Samah. "Re-Imagining Home and Belonging: Feminism, Nostalgia, and Critical Memory." *Resources for Feminist Research* 33, nos. 1–2 (2008): 79–102.

Sacks, Jeffrey. *Iterations of Loss*. New York: Fordham Univ. Press, 2014.

———. "Language Places." In Nassar and Rahman, *Mahmoud Darwish, Exile's Poet*, 239–72.

———, trans. *Why Did You Leave the Horse Alone?* Brooklyn, NY: Archipelago Books, 2006.

Sadoul, George, ed. *The Cinema in the Arab Countries*. Paris: UNESCO, 1966.

Safieh, Randa. "Identity, Diaspora, and Resistance in Palestinian Hip-Hop." In Kanaaneh, *Palestinian Music and Song*, 69–81.

Said, Edward. *After the Last Sky*. Photographs by Jean Mohr. New York: Columbia Univ. Press, 1999.

———. "The Art of Displacement: Mona Hatoum's Logic of Irreconcilables." In Said, *Mona Hatoum: The Entire World as a Foreign Land*, 1–44. London: Tate Gallery, 2000.

———. *Culture and Imperialism*. New York: Alfred A. Knopf, 1993.

———. *Culture et résistance: Entretiens avec David Barsamian*. Translated by Christian Calliyannis. Paris: Fayard, 2004.

———. *On Late Style: Music and Literature against the Grain*. New York: Vintage Books, 2007.

———. "On Mahmoud Darwish." *Grand Street* 48 (Winter 1994): 112–15.

———. *Orientalism*. New York: Pantheon Books, 1978.

———. "Orientalism Reconsidered." *Cultural Critique* 1 (1985): 89– 107.

———. "Preface." In Dabashi, *Dreams of a Nation*, 1–5.

———. *Reflections on Exile and Other Essays*. Cambridge, MA: Harvard Univ. Press, 2000.

Salloum, Jacqueline. *Slingshot Hip Hop: The Palestinian Lyrical Front*. New York: Fresh Booza Productions, 2006.

Saloul, Ihab, and Aniko Imre. "'Performative Narrativity': Palestinian Identity and the Performance of Catastrophe." *Cultural Analysis* 7 (2008): 5–39.

Samar, Martha. "Palestinian Video Art." *This Week in Palestine*, February 1, 2010. http://archive.thisweekinpalestine.com/details.php?id=2965&ed=177.

Samarkani, Mohamad Habib, ed., "Créations palestiniennes: Roman, nouvelle, poésie, récit, art contemporain." *Horizons Maghrébins: Le droit à la mémoire* 57 (2007): 1–200.

Sanbar, Elias. *Figures du Palestinien: Identité des origines, identité de devenir*. Paris: Gallimard, 2004.

Sansour, Larissa. *Land Confiscation Order*. Video installation. Jerusalem: Al-Ma'mal: Foundation for Contemporary Art, 2011.

Sassen, Saskia, ed. *Deciphering the Global: Its Scales, Spaces, and Subjects*. New York: Routledge, 2007.

Schechner, Richard. *Performance Theory*. New York: Routledge, 1988.

Schulz, Helena Lindholm, with Juliane Hammer. *The Palestinian Diaspora: Formation of Identities and Politics of Homeland*. London: Routledge, 2003.

Shabout, Nada. *Modern Arab Art: Formation of Arab Aesthetics*. Gainesville: Univ. of Florida Press, 2007.

Shafik, Viola. *Arab Cinema: History and Cultural Identity*. Cairo: The American Univ. of Cairo Press, 1998.

Shaheen, Mohammad, trans. *Almond Blossoms and Beyond*. Northhampton, MA: Interlink Books, 2009.

Shammout, Ismail. *Art in Palestine*. Kuwait: n.p., 1989.

Shehadeh, Raja. "Mahmoud Darwish." *Bomb* 81 (Fall 2002): 57–58.

Sheehi, Stephen. *Foundations of Modern Arab Identity*. Gainesville: Univ. Press of Florida, 2004.

Shibli, Adania, and Murtaza Vali. *Emily Jacir*. Nuremberg: Verlag Fur Moderne Kunst Nurnberg, 2008.

Spivak, Gayatri Chakravorty. *An Aesthetic Education in the Era of Globalization*. Cambridge, MA: Harvard Univ. Press, 2012.

Stein, Rebecca L., and Ted Swedenburg. *Palestine, Israel, and the Politics of Popular Culture*. Durham, NC: Duke Univ. Press, 2005.

Strehle, Susan. *Transnational Women's Fiction: Unsettling Home and Homeland*. New York: Palgrave Macmillan, 2008.

Suleiman, Elia. "Illusions nécessaires." Translated by Hélène Frappat. *Cahiers du Cinéma* 560 (September 2001): 54–56.

———. *Sijl Ikhtifā'* (Chronicle of disappearance). New York: Kino on Video, 2005 [1996].

———. *The Time That Remains (Al-Zaman al-bāqi)*. Palestine: Elia Suleiman, 2009.

———. *Yadun Ilāhīya* [Divine intervention]. Paris: Vidéo France Télévision, 2003.

Suleiman, Elia, and Jayce Salloum. *Introduction to the End of An Argument*. Canada: n.p., 1990.

Swedenburg, Ted. "Popular Culture in the Middle East and North Africa." In *Popular Culture in the Middle East and North Africa: A Postcolonial Outlook*, edited by Mounira Soliman and Walid El Hamamsy. Durham, NC: Duke Univ. Press, 2012.

Tarazi, Rima. "The Palestinian National Song: A Personal Testimony." *This Week in Palestine,* April 2007.

Tawil-Souri, Helga. "Coming into Being and Flowing into Exile: History and Trends in Palestinian Film-Making." *Nebula* 2, no. 2 (2005): 113–40.

———. "Where Is the Political in Cultural Studies?" *International Journal of Cultural Studies* 14, no. 5 (2011): 467–82.

Todorov, Tzvetan. *The Fantastic: A Structural Approach to a Literary Genre.* Translated by Richard Howard. Cleveland, OH: Case Western Univ. Press, 1973.

Vali, Murtaza. "Archiving Palestine: Notes on Emily Jacir's 'Accumulations.'" In Baur and Waspe, *Emily Jacir, Installation Shots,* April 1, 2008.

Waked, Sharif. *Beace Brocess.* Video. Sharif Waked Collection, Haifa, 2010.

———. *Chic Point: Fashion for Israeli Checkpoints.* Toronto: Vtape, 2003.

———. *Jericho First.* Acrylic on canvas. Sharif Waked Collection, Jerusalem, 2002.

———. *Melancholia.* Photography. n.p.: Andalus Publishing, 1998.

———. "Sharif Waked: Chic Point." *Nafas Art Magazine,* March 2005. http://universes-in-universe.org/eng/nafas /articles/ 2005/waked.

———. *To Be Continued.* Video installation. Sharif Waked Collection, Haifa, 2009.

White, Rob. "Sad Times: An Interview with Elia Suleiman." *Film Quarterly* 64, no. 1 (2010): 38–45.

Wilson, Rachel Beckles. *Orientalism and Musical Mission: Palestine and the West.* Cambridge, UK: Cambridge Univ. Press, 2013.

Wise, Michael Z. "Border Crossings between Art and Life." E-mail interview with Jacir. *New York Times,* February 1, 2009, AR28.

Wong, Chuen-Fung. "Conflicts, Occupation, and Music-Making in Palestine." *Macalester International* 23 (2009): 267–84.

Yaqub, Nadia. "Paradise Now: Narrating a Failed Politics." In Gugler, *Film in the Middle East and North Africa,* 219–27.

Yehudai, Nir. "Creating a Poetics in Exile: The Development of an Ethnic Palestinian-American Culture." In *Creativity in Exile,* edited by Michael Hanne, 193–203. Amsterdam: Rodopi, 2004.

Zaqtan, Ghassan. *Ashtar* (Ishtār). Ramallah: Ashtar, 2005.

———. *Istidrāj al-jabal* (*Luring the Mountain*). Beirut: Al-Mu'assassah al-'Arabiyah lil Dirāsāt wa-al-Nashr, 1998.

————. *Ka-ṭayr min al-qashsh ya-tbaʿunī* (*Like a Straw Bird It Follows Me*). Beirut: Dār al-Rayyes, 2008.

————. *Like a Straw Bird It Follows Me, and Other Poems*. Translated by Fady Joudeh. New Haven, CT: Yale Univ. Press, 2012.

————. *Ṣabāḥ mubakkir: Shiʿr* (*Early Morning*). Beirut: Dār Ibn Kahldūn, 1980.

————. *Tartīb al-Waṣf* (Orderding descriptions). Jerusalem: Ittihād al-Kuttāb al-falasṭiniyyīn, 1998.

————. *Waṣf al-māḍi* (Describing the past). Amman: Azminah, 2005.

Zobaidi al-, Sobhi. "Tora Bora Cinema." *Jump Cut: A Review of Contemporary Media* 50 (Spring 2008). http://www.ejumpcut.org/archive/jc50.2008/PalestineFilm/index.html. Accessed May 15, 2008.

————. *Ubūr Qalandia* (Crossing Qalandia). Palestine: Sobhi al-Zobaidi: 2002.

Zubaidi al-, Kais. *Palestine in Cinema*. Beirut: Institute for Palestine Studies, 2006.

Zuhur, Sharifa, ed. *Images of Enchantment: Visual and Performing Arts of the Middle East*. Cairo: American Univ. in Cairo Press, 1998.

Index

NAJAT RAHMAN is Professor of Comparative Literature at the Université de Montréal. She is the author of *Literary Disinheritance: The Writing of Home in the Work of Mahmoud Darwish and Assia Djebar* (Lexington Books, 2008). She is coeditor of *Mahmoud Darwish, Exile's Poet: Critical Essays* (Interlink Books, 2008) and *Humor in Middle Eastern Cinema* (Wayne State Univ. Press, 2014). She is presently a EURIAS Senior Fellow at the European Institutes for Advanced Study and a resident at IMéRA, the Institute for Advanced Study at Aix-Marseille Université in France.